ENTREPRENEURSHIP

THROUGH

ACQUISITION

HOW TO BUY A BUSINESS

RICHARD A. JOSEPH

ANNA M. NEKORANEC

CARL H. STEFFENS

KAPLAN PUBLISHING

Dedication

This book is dedicated to our parents, to Professor Ed Moldt and to anyone who has the courage to be an entrepreneur.

Vice President and Publisher: Cynthia A. Zigmund
Acquisitions Editor: Mary B. Good
Senior Managing Editor: Jack Kiburz
Interior Design: Lucy Jenkins
Cover Design: Design Alliance
Typesetting: Elizabeth Pitts

© 1993 by Richard A. Joseph, Anna M. Nekoranec, Carl H. Steffens

Published by Kaplan Publishing,
a division of Kaplan, Inc.

Printed in the United States of America

06   20   19   18   17

Library of Congress Cataloging-in-Publication Data

Joseph, Richard A. 1963–
     How to buy a business : entrepreneurship through acquisition / by Richard A. Joseph, Anna M. Nekoranec, Carl H. Steffens.
          p. cm.
     Includes index.
     ISBN 0-7931-0450-5 (pbk) : $19.95
     1. Small business—Publishing. 2. Small business—Management. 3. Small business—United States—Purchasing. I. Nekoranec, Anna M. II. Steffens, Carl H. III. Title.
     HD62.7.J67   1992   92-31303
     658.1'141—dc20   CIP

Kaplan Publishing books are available at special quantity discounts to use for sales promotions, employee premiums, or educational purposes. Please call our Special Sales Department to order or for more information at 800-621-9621, ext. 4444, e-mail kaplanpubsales@kaplan.com, or write to Kaplan Publishing, 30 South Wacker Drive, Suite 2500, Chicago, IL 60606-7481.

Acknowledgments

Size :
- up to $\cancel{\pm}$ 200-~~500~~k EBITDA
- EV $<$ $\pm$ 1 mm
  $\Rightarrow$ Equity (20%) : $\pm$ 100,000

OR : - Majority stake (70%) of a EV = $\pm$ 2 mm

We would like to thank Jeremy Solomon, Patrick Hogan, Jeff Babin, Ivan Bailey, Lynne Scalapino, Trish Malbon, Doug Wilbourne, Leslie Benoliel, Alex Hamilton, the Sol C. Snider Entrepreneurial Department and all of the entrepreneurs who shared their stories with us so that we could incorporate them into this book.

Ideas
- Specialty food retailers
- Sharp cash flow
- Waste Management companies
- Renewable resources
- Specialty manufacturing
- Fragmented industry
- Turnaround?
- Healthcare business

Contents

Foreword

The subject of buying a business has been an exciting concept for individuals as long as businesses have existed. But the process for accomplishing an acquisition has been shrouded in complexity and confusion. The thought of using brokers, merger and acquisition specialists, investment bankers, equipment appraisers and other such professionals makes the acquisition goal appear too costly and unattainable.

It is true that mega-acquisitions headlined in the media require legions of professionals to accomplish. But the thousands of manufacturers, retailers, service companies and hospitality businesses bought and sold every year undergo a much simpler acquisition process for both buyer and seller.

This book meets the needs of those individuals who want to understand the process so they can begin their search for a business to purchase. It comes at a particularly opportune time because of the massive changes occurring in American society and the role that acquisitions will play in those changes.

First, the graying of America, and therefore the graying of the American business owner, will accelerate the sale of businesses to allow those owners to retire. The types of businesses will be as diverse as American industry and will provide a wide array of choices for potential buyers.

Second, the downsizing, rightsizing and general restructuring of America's largest businesses will continue unabated through the balance of the 20th century. The result will be the layoff of hundreds of thousands of individuals, who will find self-employment in a new start-up or acquired business a viable alternative to finding another job. Many of these individuals may be of an age where self-employment is their only alternative.

Third, those individuals who choose early retirement may do so with the idea of creating a second career. They have probably accumulated sufficient capital to allow them to finance the acquisition of the business they have always dreamed of. With as many productive years ahead of them as they have already devoted to their first career, they find the idea of business ownership a fascinating opportunity to do just what they want to do. Transferring their previous experience to a successful, operating business is a more appropriate use of their talent than developing the completely new skills needed to start a business.

Fourth, the thousands of graduating college students who have studied entrepreneurship and small business in some 700 colleges and universities are interested in owning their own businesses. They have learned the fundamental business skills and studied the success and failure of those folk heroes we call entrepreneurs. They want to explore new ideas, new niches and new opportunities. Some will find their skills, talents and risk quotient better suited to maintaining the momentum of an existing business than starting a new business.

The first personal acquisitions class at the Wharton School of the University of Pennsylvania was introduced in 1990 on an experimental basis at the request of students interested in acquiring businesses. Case studies of acquisitions in other entrepreneurship classes had whetted their appetites. Each of the subsequent personal acquisition experimental classes attracted greater numbers of students, and actual acquisitions became the badge of success among the students. In the fall of 1992, two sections of the class were offered to accommodate the demand.

I applaud the efforts of the authors, my former students, for their fine work in capturing the essence of the class in this book. In this way, they can expose many others to the process involved in locating, evaluating, valuing, financing and negotiating for a business to purchase.

This book will demonstrate to its readers that the acquisition process is one that they are capable of pursuing. It will remove much of the mystique behind acquisitions and show the value of thorough investigation, common sense and vision. Our students have followed these guidelines and found out how well they work.

It is my hope that potential entrepreneurs will recognize as a result of this book that acquisitions are a reasonable alternative to start-ups. The perpetuation of existing businesses and the millions of jobs they support must be a vital element in the economic strength of our country.

—Edward M. Moldt
  Managing Director
  Snider Entrepreneurial Center
  The Wharton School

Preface

It is happening all around us—corporations are downsizing, people are retiring earlier and college graduates are increasingly disenchanted with the career opportunities available to them. Our country and our economy have made fundamental shifts from the stable military-industrial complex that flourished following World War II. No longer will young college graduates join a company expecting to remain in its employ for the rest of their lives, and no longer is a job with a company considered more secure than striking out on one's own. People are beginning to realize that they must create a place for themselves in the more competitive global economy that has emerged with the 1990s. Pursuing entrepreneurship by buying a small business is just one of the manifestations of that shift in focus. People who buy businesses come from all walks of life; they are doctors, teachers, students, businessmen/women and recent retirees or corporate refugees. One of them might be you.

If you are interested in pursuing an entrepreneurial career by acquiring a business, this book will help you achieve your goal. It will help you decide if pursuing an acquisition is the right choice for you and whether you are ready for the commitment required to turn this dream into reality. It will provide example of how others have purchased businesses at various stages in the process. It will tell you how to plan your search, how to evaluate candidates, how to eventually make an offer and how to consummate the transaction and take over as the new owner. But all of these topics *should* be covered in a book on business acquisitions.

What else does this book tell you? It tells you about paradigms, which can affect your search in ways that you might not consider. It tells you about nonstandard sources of businesses—those beyond the newspapers and business brokers. It tells you about possible sources of financing and about the various options for structuring your business. These sections are what makes this book different from others.

Most important, this book will help you realize that you can buy a business if you so desire, and it will show you, step by step, how to do it. While it covers all of the technical topics that are necessary for business acquisitions, it also will stimulate thought about why you are searching for a business and what type of business is most appropriate for you.

The book is written for the business person who has rudimentary knowledge of at least one area of business, such as finance, marketing, operations or sales. It is designed to help you apply that knowledge to your search. Seasoned business professionals will find the book a helpful refresher on the acquisition process. Less experienced entrepreneurs will find it a valuable guide on a process that can be at the same time frustrating and challenging, overwhelming and refreshing.

We have learned a great deal from our own searches for businesses and from our work with others interested in acquiring businesses. We hope that, through this book, these experiences will help you as you begin this phase of your entrepreneurial career.

■ CHAPTER ONE ■

Why Buy a
Small Business?

So you'd like to buy a business! You're not alone. The cover of the February 1991 issue of *Inc.* magazine headlined "Why You Should Buy a Business Now" and featured the glowing face of an entrepreneur who decided to acquire a company rather than start one. The article noted, "As the 1990s get a little older, we're likely to witness the biggest, brassiest, fastest-moving bazaar of businesses you'll ever want to see."

Why is there a sudden interest in buying small businesses? Who are the purchasers? Why do they choose to buy rather than start a business? And how does one go about buying a business? These questions are just a few of the ones you may be asking yourself right now. By reading this book, you will take the first step toward answering them.

Most people have some idea of what a small business is; when asked to describe one, they'll often name the local shoe-repair shop, ice cream store or corner market. Their perception is correct; these are all small businesses. What most people don't realize is that for every business they know of, there are a dozen more of which they are not aware. Commercial printers, electrical supply companies and wholesale food distributors are all examples of businesses that are essential to daily life, but people don't often think about the owners and managers of these less visible businesses.

Taken in the aggregate, small, privately held businesses make up a major portion of our economy. D. Bruce Merrifield, former Assistant U.S. Secretary of Commerce, recently noted: "There are

15 million companies in the United States and only 5 percent are publicly traded." And this figure does not include partnerships or sole proprietorships—two of the most common forms of business entities. Since 1982, the United States has been creating new businesses at the rate of 600,000 to 700,000 per year.

These businesses are bought and sold like other assets, such as houses and cars. Some estimate the yearly market for small businesses at over $200 billion.

WHY ARE PEOPLE BUYING
SMALL BUSINESSES?

As the 1980s drew to a close, Americans were forced to look back and consider the consequences of what many referred to as the "greed" decade. Many people felt that the country was like a child who had eaten too much and would now need to sit and digest for a while. People felt that, after a decade of growth fueled by debt and what some called greed, it was now time to return to a life-style of more traditional values. Small business ownership is one route to this life-style. While small business owners do not necessarily work less, their time is more flexible and self-controlled. Those adopting this attitude range from baby boomers to "baby busters" (those in their early to mid-20s) to those over 50.

The spate of recent articles in the popular press is evidence of the wide appeal of owning one's own business. *Fortune* felt this topic to be of such significance that its December 17, 1990, cover story, titled "Breaking Away," discussed the mass exodus (voluntary and involuntary) of baby boomers and older managers from corporate America to small business.

The generation following the baby boomers (the "busters") is also increasingly interested in small business ownership. *Fortune* also published a cover piece about this group, titled "The Twenty-Five-Year-Olds." The article discussed the motivations of the younger generation and how they are leaning toward more traditional values, which favor self-employment. This is evidenced by the growing interest in purchasing a small business among graduates of business schools across the country. In response to this interest, leading business schools are currently offering courses in the subject.

Regardless of the different characteristics of these groups—baby boomers, baby busters and older managers—they all have one thing in common: they seek to pursue entrepreneurship by buying an existing business rather than starting one. The reason is simple. Buying an ongoing business is much less risky than starting one; it also takes significantly more work to start a business, as the founder of any company will quickly confirm. Baby boomers and older managers often do not wish to devote the time and energy necessary to start a business, or they may not have an idea in which they are confident enough to risk their entire life savings.

The emergence of a new model of entrepreneurship is being fostered by shifts in cultural attitudes and values. This new model emphasizes acquisition as a viable alternative to venture initiation.

THE DEMAND FOR SMALL BUSINESSES

Traditionally, there have been two types of small business buyers: those who seek *income substitution* and those who seek to *create wealth*. Income-substitution buyers are content to purchase a business in which they can earn the same amount of money as they would working for someone else, while gaining the freedom and independence of being their own boss. Their goal is to improve their life-style without sacrificing their earning potential.

Those buyers who seek to create wealth plan to either purchase a business that they can build or purchase a number of businesses that they will own and manage. Their goal will be to earn more money than they could as an employee working within a larger company, while enjoying the nonmonetary benefits of being an entrepreneur.

Exactly who are the people buying small businesses? Retiring executives; people displaced by corporate "downsizing"; graduating students; and people working full-time who want to pursue other career options on the side. Many different types of people have decided that owning a business represents a viable career option.

- In 1990, Russell Palmer retired as dean of the Wharton School of Business, one of the country's most prestigious business schools. Formerly the managing director of Touche Ross, a major accounting firm, Mr. Palmer was well-known in the business community and could easily have secured a position as the CEO of a major corporation. Instead, he decided to pursue entrepreneurship by setting up an investment group to take equity positions in small companies. His first acquisition was a small trophy-manufacturing company—hardly high-technology, and certainly not large. But the purchase of this company led to the purchase of others. According to reports, he is enjoying the small business acquisition process immensely.

- A highly paid executive at the investment bank Goldman Sachs resigned his position to purchase a small restaurant in Connecticut. Although the yearly net profits of the business were less than half of his previous annual salary, he pursued the acquisition against the advice of his peers and associates. While he has been operating the restaurant for only a short time, he is very excited by the improvement he sees in its operation every day. He has no regrets about leaving his lucrative position to be in business for himself.

- An accountant of 12 years who was a partner in a large New England regional firm left his job to purchase an equity stake in a cable distribution company in Vermont. He had never considered going into business for himself, but the opportunity to acquire an interest in an ongoing company was too attractive for him to turn down. Today he owns 100 percent of the company and is actively pursuing several other entrepreneurial ventures.

- Two recent graduates of an MBA program shunned the traditional jobs being offered to many of their peers and instead decided to search for a business to purchase. Encouraged by both their classmates and their professors, they searched for approximately 12 months before finding a candidate that was attractive and affordable. They purchased the company—a computer retail and service firm—and are extremely happy that they pursued entrepreneurship through acquisition rather than taking more traditional jobs.

- Another graduate of a business school program also decided not to pursue a traditional job, but instead searched for acquisitions. He eventually found a chocolate and ice-cream retail store for $135,000 that he purchased almost entirely with borrowed money. Almost immediately he was able to identify areas in which the operation could be improved, and by making changes he has dramatically increased the operating profits of the business.

These are just a few examples of the many people who buy businesses each year. No prerequisites are needed; however, you must have the desire and perseverance to succeed. The process can be difficult and frustrating. You must overcome many obstacles and continue your search with conviction despite what those around you may say.

Many of the country's (and the world's) most prominent companies are the result of someone buying an existing company and applying either fresh ideas or energy. It has often been said that companies aren't successful, people are. This is one of the major reasons that buying a company is an attractive alternative to a more traditional career. With the right mix of enthusiasm, judgment and hard work, the company can be the vehicle for your success.

In the early 1960s Wayne Huizenga, a young man from Florida, dropped out of college after a year and a half to buy a beat-up garbage truck and a garbage route for $500, which he borrowed. Now, 30 years later, he is the chairman of Waste Management, one of the country's largest waste-disposal companies. His experience with his first corporation led him to start another company in 1984—Blockbuster Entertainment. All this grew from the purchase of what was essentially a trash-pickup company.

THE SUPPLY OF SMALL COMPANIES

During the industrial expansion that followed World War II, millions of businesses were created. Since many of these businesses were founded during the 1950s and 1960s, aging owners are now preparing for retirement. In many cases one obstacle confronts them: the owner is solely responsible for running the business. Without willing offspring to whom they can simply give the business, these owners are often forced to sell. In addition to those businesses offered by retiring owners, many more appear on the market due to an owner's death or declining health. In other cases, the owner's decision to sell is based on a desire to pursue other opportunities, or to realize a financial return on his or her investment of time and money in the business.

One business owner who was nearing retirement sought a successor. Although his son-in-law worked in the business, the owner did not feel that he was capable of running the company. Consequently, he started searching outside the family. His search led him to a willing and able entrepreneur. For $25,000, the entrepreneur purchased an 18 percent interest in the company, which earned $1 million on gross sales of $6 million. Over time, the owner relinquished his entire interest in the business to his successor—the entrepreneur.

The owner of an advertising company in the Caribbean wanted to sell his company so that he could spend more time sailing with his children. He and his wife had started three different companies, each of which was successful. They had earned and accumulated substantial wealth, and they decided that it was time to relax and enjoy life for a while. Their search for a buyer led them to an able businessperson who today runs the company.

In another case, a couple had started a gourmet food company out of their garage. One of their original distribution outlets was a small store near their hometown. As the company grew, managing production and selling to major customers began taking more and more of their time. Eventually, they decided it would be best to sell the original store so that they could concentrate on other aspects of the business. This created an excellent opportunity for an entrepreneur to purchase an established business.

As these examples demonstrate, the reasons owners have for selling their businesses are as diverse as the businesses themselves. And, while current demographics indicate that the number of sales motivated wholly or in part by the owner's age will continue to increase at an accelerated rate in the 1990s, the supply of businesses being sold for other reasons will always exist.

EXTERNAL FACTORS AFFECTING SMALL BUSINESS ACQUISITIONS

In addition to a growing number of businesses for sale and more people interested in acquiring a business, external factors that affect the ability of a purchaser to buy a business are changing the marketplace for small businesses as well.

The most critical issue in buying a business is access to capital. Businesses have traditionally been purchased using personal savings, seller financing and third-party sources. The deregulation of America's financial institutions during the Reagan era from 1980–88 has resulted in a "credit crunch" whereby conventional third-party financing has become difficult to secure. The result is that sellers have to be more willing to provide financing than they were in the past.

As conventional sources of financing are drying up, alternative sources of third-party capital are becoming more prevalent. For example, traditional financiers of entrepreneurial start-up ventures have turned their attention to financing the purchase of ongoing businesses. The June 20, 1991, issue of *The Wall Street Journal* featured an article (p. 2B) about the renewed interest on the part of venture capitalists to participate in purchases of existing entities rather than financing new ventures. As attractive investment opportunities offering large but risky returns have decreased in number, ongoing businesses with smaller but more certain returns are becoming more attractive to venture capitalists, investment funds and private investors.

Thus, while cultural and social attitudes are changing to make small business ownership an increasingly attractive alternative at both personal and professional levels, those who desire to pursue entrepreneurship through acquisition will continue to have access to capital through seller financing, venture capitalists, banking institutions and finance companies.

THE MARKET: WHERE BUYERS AND SELLERS MEET

There is a large and healthy market of small businesses for sale. Knowledge of the small business acquisition process has traditionally resided with those directly involved in the field. However, this has been changing as the marketplace has become more visible through magazine and newspaper articles, books and other media. The marketplace consists of buyers, sellers, investors, brokers, consultants and other professionals, all of whom play a unique role in the transfer of businesses.

Buyers can now meet sellers in an increasing number of ways. Nearly every metropolitan and most local newspapers have a separate classified section for businesses for sale; national papers such as *The Wall Street Journal* and the national Sunday edition of *The New York Times* feature extensive listings of businesses for sale in all areas of the country. As with real estate, there is also a large group of brokers who sell businesses. In the past ten years, the Multiple Listing Service concept has found its way into the small business marketplace, facilitating the transfer of information between buyers and sellers. Many national magazines, such as *Entrepreneur* and *Inc.*, have classified sections for businesses. *Inc.* also devotes an editorial page in the magazine to a section it calls "American Dream," which features a particular business for sale with comments from the editors. These are just a few of the means through which you might learn about businesses for sale and meet owners interested in selling. The market for businesses is large, diverse and open to anyone interested in participating.

WHAT DOES ALL THIS MEAN TO BUYERS?

In the 1990s, buying a business will be a much more prevalent form of entrepreneurship than it has been in the past. The traditional view of the entrepreneur only as someone who starts businesses will no longer be applicable. Buyers of small businesses will gain the freedom of being their own boss, coupled with the potential financial rewards associated with ownership. The current trend is that more individuals will turn to acquisition as a form of entrepreneurship. If you are one of these people, you are to be commended. By owning a small business, you can help improve the economy, your community and your own well-being!

In the chapters that follow, we will discuss the acquisition process from the early stages of self-assessment and creating "deal flow" to the final stages of closing the deal and managing the acquisition. Whether you eventually purchase a business or not, participating in this dynamic and growing marketplace will certainly be a valuable experience.

■ CHAPTER TWO ■

Considerations When Buying a Small Business

Making the decision to pursue the acquisition of a business is no small matter for most of us. It generally means giving up something else—like a job or a future career—and possibly risking much of what we have in terms of savings and contacts in the business community. Is it worth it? Only you can answer that question. To be sure, of the many people interviewed during the writing of this book, only a few expressed even the slightest regret at having risked careers, homes and futures to pursue ownership of their own business. There are, however, many people who have purchased businesses and failed miserably—for any number of reasons. Do these people regret their decision? Not necessarily. The bottom line is that you are the only person who can decide if you are prepared to take the risks associated with buying your own business. Many have succeeded before you and many have failed; there is no guarantee of either. What is guaranteed is that if you do decide to pursue the acquisition of a business, you will be engaging in a process that is challenging, educational, rewarding and sometimes frustrating—a process we feel is highly enriching regardless of whether you actually end up owning the business of your dreams.

In this chapter we discuss many of the personal considerations you will have as a prospective business buyer. There are a number of personal issues you should think about before you begin your search. These range from the more "psychological" considerations to practical issues, such as how you will support yourself during your search. In this chapter we address the former, while some of the more practical considerations are discussed in Chapter 3, "Planning Your Search."

BROADENING YOUR SCOPE

If you ask people what they consider a small business, people first think of the businesses with which they are familiar. For some this may be retail shops, while for others manufacturing or distribution businesses may immediately come to mind. The way that you define "small business" will depend to a large degree on your employment history, your educational and family background, and the amount of interaction you have had with the small business community.

When most people think about purchasing a small business, they have some idea of what they consider "small" and what they consider a "business." They often envision themselves as the owner of a business that they consider small. To some people, "small" means a business with less than $100,000 in sales per year, while to others, up to $5 million would be considered small. People may also define size in nonmonetary terms, such as the number of employees or the size of the facility in which the business operates. No matter what your definition, you should start to think more in terms of finding a business that meets your criteria for industry, revenue, cash flow and future opportunities. Don't limit yourself to what you consider to be "small businesses." There are many attractive acquisition candidates that most of us would never think about or that seem beyond our reach, but that offer benefits beyond just monetary.

One entrepreneur was evaluating an advertising agency in the U.S. Virgin Islands. When she first received the information on the business, it seemed too large to fit her acquisition criteria. It had gross revenues of almost $5 million, and she was interested in a business more in the neighborhood of $1 million in revenue. However, upon examining the financial statements and talking with the owner, she was able to determine that some advertising agencies have a unique way of recording revenue: they book ad space for their clients, then bill the clients directly. This results in a low gross margin as a percentage of revenues, since revenue to the advertising vehicle is passed through the agency, but the agency incurs few overhead costs in generating this revenue; therefore, the net profit margin is still fairly high. Once she had learned this, the entrepreneur focused on the fees that the agency generated, which were more reflective of the revenue that it produced. The agency then seemed a much more likely acquisition candidate, and she was able to proceed.

In making the decision to search for a business, you will want to be as open-minded as possible. Businesses in the United States are so varied that if you restrict your search to only those with which you are familiar, you may not see some excellent businesses that would allow you to accomplish your personal and professional objectives. As you start to consider pursuing entrepreneurship through acquisition, remember that there is an incredible range of businesses available. Being a small business owner does not necessarily mean running your own shop or supervising employees. As you begin your search, you will learn about many business types that you never even knew existed.

PARADIGMS

The term *paradigm* has been used, often incorrectly, to describe many things. But what exactly is a paradigm? The following example may help to illustrate.

An entrepreneur was searching for a business. He was very well educated, having attended a major east coast university, and had received his graduate business degree from a well-known Ivy League school. Between his undergraduate and graduate studies, he had worked on Wall Street as an investment analyst. During his final year of business school, he decided to acquire a small business rather than take a job at a corporation. While searching the classified ads in *The Wall Street Journal,* he saw an ad for a sponge manufacturing company that was for sale for $250,000. Although the price was within his reach, he investigated no further, because he could not envision someone with his education or family background working in the sponge industry.

This entrepreneur's experience demonstrates a personal paradigm affecting his search for a business. A paradigm, according to Webster's dictionary is "a pattern or model." Paradigms were examined in great depth in Thomas Kuhn's book, *The Structure of Scientific Revolutions,* in which Kuhn, a theoretical physicist, discusses the influence of paradigms in the context of scientific research. Kuhn explains that paradigms, while providing a model of past progress, activity and norms, often limit the thinking of scientists faced with new problems. Many of the most revolutionary scientific discoveries came about because people were willing to depart from traditional thinking.

One excellent example of this is An Wang, the well-known entrepreneur and founder of Wang Computer Company who, as a postdoctoral fellow at Harvard University, was trying to develop a method to read magnetic-core computer memories. Wang had to depart completely from conventional wisdom to solve the problem he was facing: "...But then one day when I was walking through the Harvard Yard, an idea came to me in a flash. Like everybody else, I had been so preoccupied [with the traditional formation of the problem] that I had lost sight of the objective." Dr. Wang subsequently developed a method for reading data in computer memories that fundamentally changed the way computers operate. Had he not looked beyond conventional wisdom (the paradigm), he might never have solved this complex problem.

Another interesting example of a personal paradigm is that of Alexander Hamilton, one of the New York delegates to the Constitutional Convention at Philadelphia in 1788. Hamilton proposed, despite rising popular sentiment against such a structure, that the supreme power in the United States be a monarch elected for life by the people, thus mixing democratic and autocratic ideals. Why did Hamilton propose such a structure? Because his paradigm, or model, for government was shaped by the structure of the government in his native England. Hamilton said, "...the British government forms the best model the world ever produced." While this may have been true at the time, the other delegates knew that a different system was necessary if they were to truly escape the oppression they had felt in Britain. They therefore looked outside of the traditional model to the separation of powers that forms the backbone of the government of the United States.

Although paradigms were originally described by Kuhn in the context of the scientific world, they apply to our business and personal lives as well. Paradigms basically help to guide us through life and, to some extent, define the arena in which we are comfortable living our lives.

Why is it important to understand paradigms, and how do they apply to the small business acquisition process? First of all, paradigms may affect you as you decide whether or not you will seriously pursue acquiring a business. For instance, although many more graduates of top business schools these days are pursuing acquisition through entrepreneurship rather than starting businesses or accepting jobs, they are still largely looked upon as cavaliers. It seems that the popular paradigm for a business student's career does not include purchasing a business directly out of school. For people in career-oriented jobs, the paradigm is often that if you stay in your company or industry long enough, you will advance as far as you desire. Therefore, there is no reason to leave the industry. Thus, those people who decide to leave their company or industry are often not understood.

Second, once you have decided to pursue the acquisition of a business, you need to be aware of the personal paradigms you have developed and how these will affect your search. In the case of the above entrepreneur, he had developed a paradigm based on his education and family history that limited the types of businesses he would consider. For him, conventional wisdom held that a well-educated person with a distinguished family background should not consider purchasing a business as "unglamorous" as a sponge manufacturer. However, had he evaluated the business further, he may have found that the sponges manufactured by the firm were the best bath sponges available and had brand recognition with buyers at the most exclusive department stores. Had he been aware of the paradigm affecting his search, he might at least have requested information on the business and realized that it was something he should investigate further.

Our personal paradigms can affect the flow of information during the search for a business, and this is when they are perhaps the most harmful. If you discard or overlook a potential acquisition candidate because of a personal paradigm, you could be missing out on an attractive opportunity. As you start to see some flow of acquisition candidates, you will need to decide which you will pursue further and which you will not. Make sure you understand how your own personal paradigms will affect this portion of the search. If you make a decision not to pursue a business further after receiving information, then you have made an informed decision. However, if you reject the business out-of-hand because your paradigm precludes you from considering it, you may be cheating yourself. For instance, if you have the preconceived notion that you should not acquire a retail business, you may not consider a business that might really be exciting.

One of the authors encountered just such a situation. He was searching for a business and had decided that small retail shops, for various reasons, were not of interest. However, he learned about a specialty foods retailer in the geographical area where he wanted to relocate. In addition to the low purchase price, a special arrangement with the manufacturer of the principal good carried by the store would allow the new owner to obtain product at very favorable prices. Upon investigating further, the author found that the store represented an opportunity to expand to retail in other geographical areas; because of its unique purchasing relationship, the business would have a significant advantage over other shops. Additionally, the current store was located in a heavily traveled tourist area on a main highway that provided a constant stream of customers. These people became "ambassadors" for the business: by visiting the store while traveling, they would become familiar with the products and provide a ready market for expansion locations. Had the author let his paradigm regarding the type of business he should pursue affect his search process, he probably would have skipped over this business altogether. However, he realized that other aspects of the business might be very attractive despite its retail nature.

As you begin to consider searching for a small business to acquire, think about the paradigms that will affect you: your own models for your life; people in similar positions; and the models of those around you, such as friends and family. Paradigms are not necessarily harmful. After all, we all need guidelines—they help us make more rapid decisions and enable us to focus on only those opportunities that might be attractive to us. However, be aware of how your paradigms will affect you so that you can recognize a valuable opportunity that might not necessarily fit into your model but should not be rejected solely on that basis.

THE CORRIDOR PRINCIPLE

Originally described in a paper by Robert Ronstadt of Babson College, the corridor principle likens the entrepreneurial process to walking down a long, narrow hallway that has many doors and other hallways leading off in other directions. Ronstadt's study found that the majority of entrepreneurs do not limit themselves to a single venture, but rather pursue multiple ventures—or alternative directions. Moreover, most entrepreneurs entered into their second venture early on in their entrepreneurial careers—or early on in their journey down the hallway. While the study was based on entrepreneurs who started, rather than purchased, companies, the concept of the corridor principle can be extended to the purchase of companies as well.

Envision the corridor, or hallway, that might result from the purchase of a first business. Looking down the hallway before you enter, it is difficult to see the doorways and connected hallways. However, once you are in the hallway, it becomes possible to see some of the other directions available. Thus, if your objective is to make a career of purchasing companies, it is important to take the first step into "the corridor." Ronstadt suggests that, for entrepreneurs interested in multiple ventures, the first venture should be viewed as a stepping-stone rather than the final destination. And, in fact, the ability to avoid career failure (as opposed to venture failure) is enhanced by participating in multiple ventures rather than just a single venture.

The extension to small business acquisitions is fairly straightforward. Purchasing the first business is often the most difficult step to take. A great deal of uncertainty looms. Aside from financial pressures, you will probably put pressure on yourself to succeed, feel pressure (real or imagined) from your family and friends, and stake a great deal of your future on the venture. However, if you think in terms of the corridor principle, some of the initial anxiety may be mitigated.

Imagine the opportunities that might present themselves after you take the first step. You might find other businesses in the same industry that are ripe for acquisition. If the company you purchase manufactures a product, you might find a component of your product that could be improved drastically and consider "backward integrating." If the company you buy provides a service, you may learn of an unmet need of your customer base that could be served by your company or by a newly formed venture. Consider the following example.

A young woman had worked for a number of years for a large financial firm in the mergers and acquisitions department. One day, one of her clients mentioned that he might be interested in selling his company. He asked if she knew anyone who might be interested. Although she had not considered buying her own business and did not think that this was necessarily the optimum business, the young woman decided to place a bid nevertheless. Her offer was accepted; she was able to secure the financing necessary to complete the transaction and was the new owner of the business shortly thereafter. After managing the business for approximately a year, she realized that she was not needed full-time and began to search for other businesses to acquire. She soon was able to identify a number of attractive candidates that were suppliers to her first business. In this example, the entrepreneur would never have identified the subsequent acquisition candidates had she not taken the first step in acquiring the initial business.

As you consider pursuing the acquisition of a business, remember that it may be important to acquire one business in order to learn about other opportunities. If you adopt this attitude, you may not put as much pressure on yourself to hit a "home run" with the first acquisition. Instead, concentrate on getting on base; then work your way around the other bases with other acquisitions and ventures.

OTHER CONSIDERATIONS

While paradigms and the corridor principle are two of the most important personal considerations you will have as you contemplate pursuing a business acquisition, there are certainly others. They may not be as pervasive or universal, and how they affect you and your decision to pursue entrepreneurship through acquisition is largely dependent on your personal situation.

Family

Before you jump head-first into the world of acquisition, think about how your family might react and whether this matters to you. Will they support you (either emotionally or financially) if your acquisition does not work out? Can they identify with your entrepreneurial interests? If they are dependent on you, are you confident that you can support them, or do you have contingency plans in case things don't work out? These are important questions to ask yourself. If you find a business quickly, purchase it and succeed beyond your wildest dreams, then perhaps these issues won't be important. However, in the worst case, having thought about these things beforehand will help you in the future.

Friends/Business Associates

Many of the same issues that arise regarding family should be considered when thinking about friends and business associates. The search for a business can be a lonely and frustrating endeavor—just ask anyone who has left a "normal" job to search for a company. Having an infrastructure of friends and associates can help immensely. If you've left a job, perhaps talking with former co-workers will remind you of why you decided to strike out on your own. By talking to friends, you will be reminded of all the other aspects of your life, taking the spotlight away from your search for a business. How all these people feel about your decision may be important to you. If so, consider these issues beforehand. Informing people who are close to you of your intentions will certainly help later on as you seek support in making an acquisition decision.

Yourself

Don't forget the most important person—you! As mentioned earlier, the search for a company can be challenging. If you are leaving a job, you will be leaving behind much of the infrastructure to which you are accustomed. You may not have an office any more; perhaps most of your work will be done from your home. You may have financial concerns that will affect your decision and search. While a multitude of issues might arise before, during and after your decision to acquire a business, no one can address them all beforehand. Rather, you should focus on preparing yourself psychologically for the search. Understand that the search will be challenging, that many of those challenges will be new to you and that often only you will be able to resolve them. By adopting this attitude, you might spare yourself a great deal of concern and worry over things that you have not encountered before.

Regardless of whether you actually decide to acquire a business or not, understanding concepts like the corridor principle, paradigms and other personal considerations will help you make an informed decision and approach the process with the correct mind-set. Not all of these concepts and considerations will apply to you; however, they should not be ignored or glossed over just because you don't immediately recognize them in your past behavior or past business endeavors. Experience shows that they are part of the process in pursuing entrepreneurship through acquisition, so having knowledge of them can only help you!

■ CHAPTER THREE ■

Planning Your Search

If you want to buy a business, you need to create a search plan that helps determine your needs. An effective search plan will allow you to focus on the issues of greatest concern to you so that you proceed with your search in an efficient manner. To create your plan, you must first identify your key criteria, such as the type and size of business, cash-flow requirements and geographic considerations. Then prioritize them. Many of the issues are interrelated; consequently, you should consider them together rather than individually.

Planning is an important part of the search process. Without it you may expend unnecessary time, energy and money pursuing opportunities that you are not really interested in; careful planning will pay off.

This chapter describes a typical search plan that presents a general outline of the issues to consider in the construction of your own plan (see Figure 3.1). However, your plan should be designed to accommodate your own needs and specific desires. Your plan should also be updated throughout your search.

WHAT YOU BRING TO THE TABLE

Creating a thorough search plan requires a good understanding of yourself and what you want in a business. Knowing what you want will allow you to react promptly. Many acquisition opportunities

FIGURE 3.1   Search Plan

A. **Your Skills**
- What experience do I have?
- What are my greatest strengths?
- What are my greatest weaknesses?

B. **Industry**
- What industry experience do I have?
- Do I have a well-developed network?
- Do I enjoy a particular industry? → *D. Building products • Food retaic*

C. **Geographic Preference**
- Where do I want to live? *London*
- Can I commute? *Yes*
- Where can I look for companies? *UK*

D. **Business Type**
- Do I want to manufacture a product? *Yes*
- Do I want to provide a service? *No*
- Do I want to run a retail establishment? *Yes*
- Do I want to run a franchise? *No*

E. **Size**
- How large of a company do I want to run? *≠ 5MM in sales*

F. **Current Situation**
- Do I want a cash cow, star or turnaround? *Cash cow / Star*

G. **Cash Flow**
- What do I want in year one? two? three?

H. **Absentee Owner or Manager**
- Do I want to manage the business? *No*
- Do I want to be an investor? *✓*

I. **Time**
- How much time do I want to spend searching?
- How much time can I spend searching?

---

have only a small *window of opportunity*—the amount of time that a business is available before another purchaser recognizes the opportunity and capitalizes on it—so you'll have to be prepared to act fast. If you don't make a decision within this time period, the window may shut and leave you out in the cold.

Begin your search by identifying what you bring to the table. What are your strengths and weaknesses? What special skills do you have that will benefit a company? Do you have industry-specific experience? Do you have specific resources, such as a well-developed industry network?

As you proceed with your search, you should seek companies that are a good "fit" for you. Such companies will have resources that complement rather than duplicate your skills.

INDUSTRY

Before you decide on what type of business you would like to buy, you should decide if you would prefer to buy a business in a particular industry. Some prospective buyers have years of experience in a particular industry and prefer pursuing acquisition opportunities within that field. They intend to manage the company and feel that their industry-specific knowledge will benefit them. They have also spent years building an industry-related network and want to utilize it. Based upon their knowledge and their connections, they may recognize opportunities that outsiders simply won't see. As the following vignette demonstrates, this knowledge can be extremely useful when evaluating a candidate.

One entrepreneur had over ten years of experience in the oil industry. Consequently, he decided to acquire an industry-related business in Texas. After a short search, he located a company that acted as a personnel agency for oil industry workers and also sold industry supplies. As part of the purchase price, the owners wanted $100,000 for the inventory. The entrepreneur inspected the inventory and noticed that much of it was obsolete; if he purchased it, he might only recover a small portion of his investment. His knowledge of the industry enabled him to convince the owners to substantially reduce their price.

Other prospective buyers want to purchase businesses in a particular industry because of the actual or expected growth potential. Purchasing a business provides easy access to such an industry. Alternatively, some pay more attention to other characteristics of the business, such as cash flow and current management. These buyers may seek to buy a business solely for investment purposes. Since they do not intend to run the business, industry knowledge will not necessarily benefit them.

A student began her search for a business during her second year of business school, because she was disillusioned with the more traditional career paths open to her and felt that an entrepreneurial venture held the most promising prospects for the future. Since she did not have an original concept for a start-up business, she decided to purchase an ongoing concern. Initially, she focused her search on service or light manufacturing businesses in the northeast with sales of under $1 million. During a nine-month period, she reviewed an electrical contracting business, a jewelry manufacturer, an ad agency and a furniture upholsterer. Although the industries differed, all of the businesses had one thing in common—a strong cash flow.

Answering the following questions can help you decide whether or not you want to be in a particular industry:

- Do you have industry knowledge that would be beneficial to the operation of a business within that industry? No
- Do you intend to manage the business? No
- Would you like to be in a particular industry? Why? Retail /No
- Can you gain access to the industry another way? Could you purchase a company in another industry that serves companies within the primary industry?
- Do you have contacts in a particular industry that might be beneficial during the search? No

GEOGRAPHIC PREFERENCE

Deciding on a geographic region is another critical aspect of creating your search plan. If you have resided in the same area for a number of years, you may want to limit your search to the surrounding region. Personal responsibilities may make it impractical to look beyond your area. If you own a home and have children, you may have difficulty moving. Additionally, it may be in your best interest to stay. By merely living in an area, you build up a network of business relationships, bankers, lawyers and others who could be helpful to you, both in your search and after you have purchased a business.

One purchaser was able to utilize such a network in his search. He discovered an appealing acquisition prospect through a source very close at hand. He was looking for a business in his local community and had discussed his search with a number of business acquaintances and friends of his family. Several had brought him leads; however, the best came from his father.

A friend of the family owned a catalog company that specialized in selling dental laboratory supplies. This friend was semiretired and wanted to sell the business. Although the owner had children, none of them wanted to participate in the business. On sales of $5.5 million, it generated cash flow of almost $500,000—more than enough to pay him a salary and help cover the debt that he had to incur to finance the purchase. In addition, it would allow him to use his expertise in the direct-marketing field. The business was a good fit for the purchaser and it was in his "own backyard"!

Owning a small business does not necessarily mean that you have to live in the same geographic area, particularly if you're interested in an "absentee owner" arrangement. If you're not committed to a specific region, then consider broadening your search to include an area where you would like to live or the area that you feel has the most opportunities. Also, by broadening your search area you will be able to build up a larger network of people who want to buy a business. This can be invaluable, both in terms of finding a business and arranging financing.

BUSINESS TYPE

You need to identify the type of business that you want to buy. Too broad a search will result in an inefficient use of time. When one entrepreneur began her search, she was certain of only one thing: she wanted to buy a business. She didn't care what type of business it was and she didn't care about location; she could move anywhere.

She gathered together all of her resources and tackled the search with full force. She answered ads in the major newspapers and contacted brokers on both coasts. She reviewed the offering packages of 40 different businesses over a three-month period. After spending hundreds of hours and dollars, she realized that she really wanted to buy a light manufacturing business on the east coast.

Had she analyzed what she wanted more carefully before she started her search, she might not have wasted so much time looking for her acquisition.

In order to identify what type of business is right for you, you should ask yourself four questions:

1. Do I want to manufacture a product? *Yes / Maybe*
2. Do I want to provide a service? *No*
3. Do I want to sell something that someone else has made? or ✓
4. Do I want to act as an intermediary between the manufacturer and the retailer? ✓

There are basically four types of businesses: manufacturing, service, retail and distribution. *Manufacturers* make products to sell to retailers or distributors. Many types of manufacturers exist. For example, heavy manufacturers produce such products as industrial machinery and equipment, cars, trucks, or tractors. The manufacturing process is usually intricate, and the cost of the finished products can be substantial. In comparison, light manufacturers produce such products as cups, combs, jewelry, toys, or sunglasses. Some manufacturers start with raw materials and create the end product all within the company. Other companies may function as assemblers and subcontract others to manufacture the necessary components of the finished product.

[· Light manufacturing
· Outsourcing / assembly]

Service businesses provide services to customers. They differentiate their services from others based upon price, quality and reputation. Dry cleaners, temporary healthcare agencies and travel agencies are examples of service businesses.

Retail stores sell the products produced by manufacturers. Examples of retail stores are candy shops, card stores, office equipment outlets, bakeries and sporting goods stores. Retail stores are generally very dependent on the location of the business, because most require their customers to enter the store before they purchase anything. If there is insufficient parking for customers or if the store is located in an area that is not physically appealing, business may suffer.

Finally, *distributors* act as intermediaries between manufacturers and retailers. They purchase products from manufacturers, mark up the prices and then sell and deliver the products to retailers. They are essentially the marketing arm for manufacturers; they must locate the retail stores that want to sell the manufactured product.

As you review information on businesses and visit companies, what you want will become clearer to you. Read the classified section of *The Wall Street Journal, The New York Times* and *Inc.* magazine. This will help you determine what types of businesses are for sale and get you thinking about businesses you might want to purchase and those you definitely don't want to consider.

RISK

You should also consider the amount of risk you are willing to assume when you buy a business. Some businesses are inherently riskier than others. For example, oil exploration is much more speculative than a pizza restaurant. While the potential profits in an oil exploration business are huge, so are the potential losses! For this reason, you should know how much risk you can bear. You may seek a high-risk, high-return business. However, if you have a family to support and a mortgage to pay, you may favor something more secure—i.e., an established business with a steady cash flow.

You should also consider how much of your assets you can risk and how large of an investment you are prepared to make.

SIZE

To a certain degree, the size of a business that you target will depend upon your experience level, the amount of cash you have access to and whether or not you want to manage the business yourself. The size of a company can refer to its gross annual sales volume, its profits, the number of employees, the number of customers or the purchase price. These are all factors to consider.

Identify the amount of money that you are willing to invest in a business. This will help determine how much you can afford to pay. Once you determine a price range you are comfortable with, consider the other factors. For example, if you have never managed a large group of people, you may prefer to buy a business that doesn't require a lot of employees. There can be big differences in the number of employees who work for companies that sell for the same price.

The same holds true for the number of customers. Consider your marketing skills and your ability to service existing customers. These issues will be critical to the future success of any business.

CASH FLOW

Cash flow is a key element of any potential acquisition, particularly if you intend to leverage the purchase. If you plan to draw a salary from the business, you will need to focus your search on profitable businesses with enough cash flow to pay your salary and the debt service. Alternatively, if you seek a turnaround or a growth opportunity, then a strong, steady cash flow may not be critical to your search.

ABSENTEE OWNER OR MANAGER

Do you want to manage the business that you eventually purchase? This is one of the most important questions you will have to ask yourself. What you decide will affect almost every aspect of your search. It could impact the size of the company that you look for and its location. If you do not intend to manage the business, you can broaden your geographic search and you may not need specific industry experience. However, you will need to find a business with adequate cash flow to pay a manager a market salary plus earn a reasonable return on investment for you.

CURRENT POSITION IN GROWTH CYCLE

Are you looking for a cash cow, a growth company or a turnaround? A *cash cow* is a business that has a steady cash flow; it is a profitable company that is usually in a strong competitive position in a stable market. For example, a company that has a high profit margin and earnings that have remained nearly the same for the past five years would be a cash cow. If you seek a cash cow, then you might target businesses being sold by older retiring owners.

A *growth company* is one that has had, or is expected to have, increasing revenues and net profits. When you purchase a growth company, expect to pay a premium; the seller usually demands compensation for the upside potential of the business. If you seek a growth company, then you might obtain results by targeting entrepreneurial forums, trade magazines or venture capital firms.

Finally, a *turnaround* company is a business that is going through difficult financial times; often the company is either entering into, in or just emerging from bankruptcy. Most troubled companies are either: overleveraged—they have the wrong capital structure and fixed-debt payments are stripping the business of working capital needed for daily operations; poorly marketed—the company has not reached the critical level of sales revenues needed to be profitable; or poorly managed—employees are not properly trained and directed, which results in an inefficiently run company.

There are different ways to succeed with a turnaround; however, realize that the momentum is not in your favor. You can: restructure the debt and thereby reduce fixed-loan payments to a level that the company can withstand; hire a new management team to operate the business more efficiently; or develop a new marketing strategy that will increase sales to the level necessary to prosper. If you seek a turnaround, bankruptcy lawyers, lending institutions and venture capitalists can be good sources of information.

TIME HORIZON

It is difficult to predict how long it will take to locate a company worth purchasing. The amount of time will depend on whether you intend to conduct a full-time or a part-time search. If you search part-time, it may take longer to find the right opportunity. However, part-time searches allow you to maintain another career and generate cash on which to live. In contrast, if you intend to conduct a full-time search, then your savings will limit the time horizon of your search.

An acquisition search can take a long time and cost a lot of money. Some people find businesses within months; others search for years. During the period of your search, you will incur living expenses and business search expenses. Search costs include phone calls, travel and entertainment expenses, audits, and fees for lawyers, brokers and accountants.

A budget detailing how much it will cost you to live during the search period and estimated search costs is helpful. An example of such a budget can be found in Figure 3.2. Once you have estimated your expenses, determine how much capital you will need on hand before you begin the search and how much, if any, you will need to earn during the search period. The availability of funds is a constraint; make sure you realize it upfront.

Some recommend that, if you have sufficient funds, you should search on a full-time basis. A full-time search will allow you to focus on acquiring a business. Your search will be more efficient and productive, and sellers are more likely to recognize you as a credible buyer.

FIGURE 3.2 Budget

	Monthly	*Annually*
Income		
Investments	_____	_____
Pension	_____	_____
Rent	_____	_____
Other	_____	_____
Expenses		
Housing (rent or mortgage)	_____	_____
House Maintenance	_____	_____
Insurance	_____	_____
Utilities (electric, gas, water)	_____	_____
Telephone	_____	_____
Car (payments)	_____	_____
Car Maintenance	_____	_____
Gas	_____	_____
Food	_____	_____
Life Insurance	_____	_____
Health Insurance	_____	_____
Medical Bills	_____	_____
Education	_____	_____
Clothing	_____	_____
Dry Cleaning	_____	_____
Entertainment	_____	_____
Travel	_____	_____
Debt Payments	_____	_____
Miscellaneous	_____	_____
TOTAL	$_____	$_____

FIGURE 3.3 Search Plan

A. **Industry**
1. Computer software
2. LANs

B. **Geographic Preference**
1. Virginia
2. Maryland
3. Washington, D.C.

C. **Business Type**
1. Retail
2. Service (consulting and installation)

D. **Size**
1. Under $2 million

E. **Current Situation**
1. Growth

F. **Cash Flow**
1. Minimum of $50,000

G. **Absentee Owner or Manager**
1. Want to manage

H. **Time Horizon**
1. One year

CREATION OF THE SEARCH PLAN

Once you have identified the most important issues and prioritized them, you will have the basis for your search plan. Figure 3.3 provides a good example of a checklist and search plan. As soon as you complete the search plan, consider how you will conduct the actual search, including where and when you will look and whom you will contact.

FIGURE 3.4   PERT Chart

Week	Task	Time Needed
1	Prepare search plan	2 days
	Prepare budget	
	Contact brokers	2 days
	Read newspapers	
2	Draft and send letters	3 days
	to lawyers and accountants	
3	Begin to look at companies	2 days
	Continue search efforts	3 days
	Contact acquaintances	
4	Continue search	5 days
	Visit companies	
	Send letters, etc.	
5	Continue search	5 days
	Contact area businesses	
6	Continue search	5 days
7	Continue search	5 days

PERT CHARTS

You can use a PERT chart to help you. A PERT chart consists of a chronological list of the tasks that need to be completed and estimates of the time required to complete them. Figure 3.4 contains an example of a search PERT chart.

Such a chart will help you monitor your search. For example, if you have allocated three months to finding a business, and after two and one-half months you realize that you will not accomplish this goal, you will need to reevaluate your position. If your search takes longer than estimated, you will need to recalculate your budget and closely analyze why your search has not been productive.

BUYING WHEN THE OPPORTUNITY IS NOT "PERFECT"

Many people, when embarking on a search for a business, look for the perfect opportunity—something in their price range, in the industry and geographical area of their choice, and in their preferred area of business (i.e., manufacturing, service, retail or distribution). While you should have an idea of your "optimal" business, often there are reasons to buy a business even though it may not meet this ideal. If you focus on finding the optimal business, you may not find anything at all.

STARTING SMALL

Regardless of the opportunities you find, it may be necessary for you to start with a smaller business than you would eventually like to own. You may lack the capital to make an acquisition that will provide the salary or prestige that you would like. For instance, if you can only afford to purchase a business that will provide $30,000 in income but you seek a salary of $50,000, you may need to purchase something in a lower price range and wait until the business grows to a level that can support your needs.

You may also need to "learn" to be a small business owner. People who decide to start or purchase a small business come from diverse backgrounds. Some have worked at large corporations, while others have either been between jobs or in school; all will need to adjust their work style as the owner/manager of a small business. Whatever your situation, you may be better off starting small. Making mistakes at something new will be a lot less painful if the stakes are smaller. Then, after you understand how to operate the business, you can work your way up either by building your existing business or by acquiring other businesses.

ACCESS TO A PRODUCT

Is there another market for the target company's product? Sometimes a business may not be attractive enough to buy based on the marketing of its current product line. However, repositioning a product may lead to increased sales. A new market or product application could have tremendous potential. The following example illustrates how this can happen.

In their book *Entrepreneurs*, Joseph and Suzy Fucini tell the story of Conrad Hubert, a restaurateur who bought an invention consisting of a tube with a battery and light inside. The tube was attached to the side of a flowerpot so the light would shine up the tube and illuminate the flowers. When it failed to sell as an "electric flowerpot," he decided to sell the light mechanism on its own, which he renamed the Eveready Flashlight. By repositioning his product, Mr. Hubert developed a successful business.

As you evaluate businesses, don't just think in terms of the current uses of products; think about other potential uses. An ability to see other opportunities is a valuable asset.

If you do see potential in an existing company, investigate it thoroughly and try to analyze the business as if changes had been made. However, you should determine what the business is worth in its *current* state and make an offer based on that. If you tell the owner how you would alter the business to increase sales or profits, he or she may use the idea or try to raise the price based on this "potential." Remember, never pay for potential that you will create!

ACCESS TO A MARKET

Does the business have a captive customer base that would purchase new products offered by the company? Just as companies often have products that might sell in other markets, companies also have access to markets through which they could sell other products or services. It may require your objectivity to realize this, and such potential should be factored into your valuation.

The specialty foods retailer example given in the last chapter demonstrated such an opportunity. Although the current product line was lucrative and provided a good base level of sales, this business also offered the new owner access to a group of people who enjoyed specialty foods. A new owner could have expanded the product line in many different ways to take advantage of the access to this market.

RECOGNIZING AN OPPORTUNITY AND ACTING ON IT

As we mentioned earlier, when you find a good business you may have to make a decision quickly. Often you are not the only person looking at the business. Consequently, there is always the risk that it might be sold out from under you.

One entrepreneur experienced such a situation when she was pursuing an acquisition in the south. The business seemed like the perfect target. It had strong cash flow, was the most reputable business of its type in the region, and the owner would take a minimal down payment and finance the bulk of the acquisition at a low interest rate.

She hadn't considered the acquisition well enough in advance and wanted to spend a few weeks thinking about it. Unfortunately, by the time she could make a commitment, the owner informed her that the business was about to be sold.

A window of opportunity exists for any given venture. If you are well-prepared before you begin your search, then you will be able to take advantage of it when it appears. One broker with over 20 years of experience in the market believes that aggressive people who know what they want will be those most likely to close a deal.

One purchaser decided to pursue an entrepreneurial venture after he looked at the small business market and saw that most companies were selling for three to six times earnings. He looked at the stock market and noted that public companies were selling for 20 times earnings. With such a disparity between the public and private markets, the entrepreneur decided that this was the perfect time to purchase a business, and he began to define what he wanted in a company: low risk, high margins, low-tech and a stable cash flow.

One of the first opportunities he encountered was a retail carpet store in the northeast. The business had about $1 million a year in sales and almost $200,000 in earnings. The sellers wanted $550,000 for the business. An offer was made, and eventually a deal was struck whereby the company was sold for significantly less than the original asking price. The purchaser knew what he wanted, recognized it when he saw it and closed the deal quickly.

REVISING YOUR SEARCH PLAN

Once you have constructed your plan and have begun your acquisition search, you may need to make revisions. As you look at different businesses, it may become clear that your initial criteria do not adequately address your needs or interests. You should then reevaluate your plan. For example, if you initially decide to look at businesses with sales of under $500,000 and then find that these do not generate enough cash flow, you should modify your search plan.

Also be wary of adhering too closely to your plan. Use it as a guide rather than a mandate. If you choose not to look at a business simply because it does not meet all of the criteria of your plan, then you may end up not looking at any deals at all. Try not to get caught up in the paradigm that you create with your search plan. If you do, it may constrain you to the point that you miss a great opportunity.

YOUR NEXT STEP

Once you have determined what you want, you will be ready to begin your search. The next chapter provides information on where to look.

■ CHAPTER FOUR ■

Your Advisers

Legal and tax advice is essential during any acquisition. Obtaining good advice requires retaining the services of seasoned professionals as advisers and knowing how and when to use them. This chapter describes how to find competent professionals who have experience in acquisitions and how to control the associated costs.

CHOOSING YOUR ADVISERS

After an acquisition candidate has been identified and the preliminary negotiations have commenced, you will want to consider hiring an accountant and an attorney. If you are going to use an acquisition vehicle, e.g., a corporation, you should have an attorney set it up. Depending on your level of experience and competence, you may want to seek this counsel earlier in the search process. In any case, allow yourself time so that your advisers are on board when you need them.

When determining which prospective advisers you will hire, consider four factors: their qualifications, your ability to work with them, what it will cost and whether you will want to keep using their services once you have acquired the business. Each component is critical. Your initial concerns should be the reputation and level of experience of the adviser.

Perhaps you already have an accountant and attorney that you use in other business matters. You might have an accountant who has prepared your tax returns for years, or an attorney who has also helped out from time to time. If so, carefully consider whether these people are qualified to be your advisers for the acquisition. Do not feel obligated to commission their services. These friends and past business associates may or may not be great advisers; you will have to accurately determine their capabilities.

Regardless of whether you have prior contacts or not, you should do some comparison shopping. One way to search for advisers is to ask friends and business associates. If you know someone who has purchased a business before, find out who his or her advisers were. Make sure that you get input about the quality and cost of the professionals who are being referred.

If you are not satisfied with the prospects who have been referred, start searching elsewhere. Look in the *Yellow Pages*. Lists of area lawyers can be found in the *Martindale-Hubbell Legal Directory*; lists of accountants can be found in *The National Society of Public Accountants Membership Directory*.

Once you have some names, your next step is to schedule interviews. Ask if there will be any charge when you schedule the appointment. Clearly state that you are searching for an adviser for your acquisition, and that this meeting is an informational interview to help you decide whose services to retain; you are not seeking immediate legal or tax advice. Potential advisers should not charge for the visit.

If the adviser is going to charge for an informational interview, then you are probably better off using someone else. It is probably an indication that you will be charged for every minute that you speak with him or her, either in person or over the phone. It is important to be able to call an adviser with simple questions without having the billing clock ticking away. You may give your attorney a call just to say hello and find out that your friendly 15-minute conversation cost you $50. The advisers that you choose will be paid thousands of dollars; don't settle for someone who will nickel-and-dime you by charging for every conversation regardless of its significance.

FIGURE 4.1   Recommended Questions for Advisers

Attorneys:
- What acquisition work have you done in the past?
- Were you responsible for all of the legal aspects of the acquisition?
- How large were the acquisitions that you worked on?
- Did all of the deals close? If not, what percentage did you close?
- How long have you been doing acquisition work?
- Have you ever been involved in a lawsuit as the result of one of these acquisitions?
- How much do you charge on an hourly basis? What constitutes hourly work?
- How much in total does an acquisition of _____ (indicate size) normally cost?
- In how many cases have you been retained as legal counsel after the acquisition?

Accountants:
- How many acquisitions have you worked on?
- What size were they?
- Were you retained as the accountant after the acquisition?
- Would you be willing to prepare monthly reports on the company detailing not only the financials, but what the numbers really mean?
- What are your fees?
- How much do fees for acquisitions work usually run?
- Can you provide me with a list of references?
- Have you ever been involved in a lawsuit regarding your work?

You should use the interview with your potential adviser as an information-gathering session. First and foremost, determine whether or not you would enjoy working with him or her. (If you are uncomfortable for any reason, you should move on to the next candidate.) Then gather information about experience, fees and references. Figure 4.1 contains a recommended list of questions that you should ask an accountant and an attorney. Prior to the interview, you should prepare your own list of questions based upon your specific transaction, such as the size of the deal; the type of business;

FIGURE 4.2 Criteria for Evaluation

1. Competence, experience
2. Compatibility
3. Willingness to do the best for clients
4. References
5. Fees

potential liabilities; outstanding sales contracts; and the type of deal structure.

Once you have found a candidate who has experience and a personality you can work with, consider his or her fees. Price alone should not be the most important factor in your decision. As with any purchase, the objective is to get the best value for your dollar. Avoid choosing someone merely because of low fees. There may be hidden costs—so what appears cheap may not be. In addition, mistakes are costly; avoid using someone who may make mistakes that you will pay for in the future. For example, a well-qualified adviser might cost more on a per-hour basis than a general practitioner; however, a general practitioner will need to spend more time learning about the necessary issues. Consequently, the general practitioner's bill may be larger. And since acquisitions are not his or her area of expertise, he or she may also make mistakes. Figure 4.2 summarizes selection criteria.

Once you have found an adviser who meets your preliminary criteria, check references to verify qualifications and on-the-job performance. Ideally, any problems should be identified and dealt with before an adviser is hired. Ask references if they were satisfied with the adviser's quality and responsiveness; was the cost in line with original estimates, and was it reasonable after considering the services that were provided?

Cost containment will be critical during the acquisition period. Attorney's fees can range from $60 per hour to $400 per hour. Attorneys in small rural towns will charge less than those in large cities. Typically, attorneys charge for every six minutes (one-tenth of an hour of service time). Additionally, they like to pass on all costs, including photocopying, phone calls, taxi rides and overnight mail. Fees are often negotiable. Total legal fees for an acquisition can range from $2,000 to $20,000—or more for large, complicated deals.

Accountants bill similarly to attorneys. Most bill on an hourly basis; however, some may work for a flat fee. Hourly rates vary widely depending on the location, level of expertise and the size of the firm. The "Big Six" accounting firms may charge $250 an hour or more, while regional firms may charge $150 an hour; local firms and independent accountants may charge between $50 and $150 an hour. Total accounting fees for an acquisition will usually not cost as much as legal fees. Expenses will probably range between $250 and $10,000 depending on the intricacy of the deal, whether the target will be audited, and the purchaser's knowledge of tax and accounting issues.

In order to reduce upfront cost, you can try offering your advisers an equity position in the business in lieu of all or a portion of their fees. Paying them with an equity stake has the advantage of aligning their interests with your own and lessening your immediate capital needs. Most advisers will want to be paid upfront, however, because most small businesses are not very liquid; it can be difficult for an adviser to sell his or her stake in exchange for money.

If an adviser is interested in participating in the acquisition, try to estimate what portion of the actual equity invested the adviser's fees would represent, and offer him or her that equivalent stake in the company as compensation for services. For example, if an attorney estimates charging $8,000 and the equity investment in the acquisition is $100,000, offer an 8 percent interest in the newly acquired business. The actual equity stake an adviser gets will likely be subject to negotiation.

Some advisers will work for a flat fee, which can be very advantageous. If you agree upon a predetermined price for legal and accounting services, then you limit the risk of incurring unexpected costs. Even if your advisers are not receptive to working for a flat fee, you may be able to get them to put a cap on the cost of their services. For example, if your accountant estimates that charges will be $3,000, you can try to get him or her to agree that the maximum bill will not exceed $4,000.

A final consideration is an adviser's contacts and reputation. If you need to raise capital in the future, an adviser with a network of bank or venture capital contacts may be a tremendous asset to you. Ask about a potential adviser's contacts and whether he or she is willing to make any introductions that will help you consummate your deal. A well-known and respected adviser, such as a Big Six accounting firm or reputable law firm, will help instill confidence in potential investors, financial institutions and the seller.

THE ROLE OF THE ADVISER

Your advisers are there to provide assistance on specific issues—legal and tax implications. Do not rely on them to make business decisions. And don't expect an adviser to tell you whether or not you should purchase a company. That is a decision that you must make. Advisers are not entrepreneurially minded and they do not want to be held accountable for the success or failure of your business. Professional advisers are a valuable and necessary resource; you must know how and when to use them.

The Role of the Lawyer

Your attorney will play an important role in the acquisition. He or she can help you in the due diligence process, create the acquisition vehicle, structure the deal, review your letter of intent, prepare the purchase agreement, draft employment agreements or noncompete clauses, review various legal documents such as lease or loan agreements, and prepare for and consummate the closing.

The purchaser's knowledge of legal issues and the specific complications of the deal will determine the degree that an attorney will be involved in an acquisition. Some purchasers may not feel confident pursuing an acquisition without having their attorney involved every step of the way. Others will draft their own letter of intent and review leases and sales contracts without any help. If you have experience with these issues, you may not need a lawyer until the purchase agreement and closing documents are to be drafted; you may want legal review of your letter of intent, but your attorney does not need to prepare it for you.

Your lawyer should be able to provide you with a legal due diligence checklist that can be tailored to meet the needs of your acquisition. The checklist can serve as an outline of the duties the lawyer can perform in the acquisition.

The Role of the Accountant

During the acquisition, the accountant can help you analyze the financial statements, value the business and perform due diligence. He or she can also advise you on how to structure the deal, taking into account the tax implications (see Chapter 11). The accountant will be essential to you during the deal and can continue to advise you once the company is purchased.

The role of your accountant will vary depending on your knowledge of valuation techniques and tax matters. When choosing an accountant, search for someone who will fit your needs. For example, if you are not certain how to value a company, hire an accountant who understands the different valuation techniques and how the deal structure will impact after-tax cash flow.

You should seek an accountant who has experience with other companies of the same size and in the same industry as your acquisition target. This may help you gain valuable insight into how the target compares with similar businesses. Additionally, your accountant may have certain contacts within the industry that can be used to help build the business.

Consult with your accountant before submitting a letter of intent. He or she can verify that your proposed deal structure accounts for tax considerations. Once a letter of intent is submitted, it is difficult to make major changes in the deal structure; make sure that your first offer is well-structured.

Your accountant can be helpful in guiding you through the due diligence process. If the acquisition is large enough, it may warrant having an audit performed to verify that the target company's finan-

cial statements are accurate. This will be costly—$10,000 to
$40,000—and therefore may not be cost-effective on smaller deals.

Even if your accountant does not perform an audit, he or she
should review the target company's financial statements. Accountants can help to identify potential and unrecorded liabilities. For
example, they can investigate whether the company has complied
with federal, state and local laws; that the payroll taxes have been
paid; that the pension has been properly funded; that the accrued
vacation time has been accurately accounted for in the financial
statements; and that the inventory has been properly valued.

One entrepreneur who purchased a business hired an accountant
who helped flush out two issues that affected the value of the
business. First, the accountant determined that the target company
had written down the value of its inventory to $28,000 when the
actual value was estimated at $250,000. This business had inflated
its costs of goods sold by increasing the value of the inventory sold.
It deferred its tax liability by reducing the value of the inventory
account. The purchaser—who was buying the stock of the company—would eventually be responsible for this liability. By being
aware of this liability, he was able to negotiate the purchase price
accordingly.

The company had also listed unexpired service contracts in the
equity section of the balance sheet. The purchaser had already
negotiated the purchase price and terms of the deal when the accountant pointed out that this item was a liability and not equity. The
money for the service contracts had been paid for upfront, but all of
that money already belonged to the seller. The cost of the unexpired
service contracts would be incurred by the purchaser, even though
he would not receive any money for the repairs. To compensate for
the unexpired service contracts, the seller agreed to reduce the
purchase price of the business by $20,000. The accountant more than
earned his fee.

While searching for an accountant, consider whether you want
to retain his or her services after the acquisition has been completed.
This could be the beginning of a long-term relationship. Consequently, it is important to determine whether the accountant will
meet your future needs.

A good accountant should be willing to prepare monthly reports on the company—reports detailing not just the numbers, but what the numbers indicate in layman's terms. Such reports will be invaluable to you and to the success of the business.

CONTROLLING YOUR ADVISERS

Although it is necessary to hire professional advisers, you should not rely on them blindly. It will be your responsibility to control and guide them as you see fit. To maximize the quality of their work at a minimum cost, you should be cognizant of certain issues: the accuracy of their log time; the quality of advice they are giving you; their level of efficiency; and the actual work you have commissioned.

If your advisers work on a per-hour basis, they will keep a log of the time they have allocated to your job and use this as a basis for your bill. Nevertheless, you should keep your own log to track the services you have authorized them to perform. Then you can determine your own billing estimates, which can be compared with your advisers' bills.

Substantiate your relationship by making notes about business conversations. Important conversations and verbal agreements should be confirmed with letters, preferably sent by certified mail. This includes drawing formal lines to clarify relationships. If you keep these records, then you will be prepared for any dispute. The importance of controlling your advisers is exemplified in the following story.

In 1986, an entrepreneur hired an attorney to undertake the legal work involved in forming a corporation to purchase a business venture in Texas. The entrepreneur raised money from 11 people, including the attorney. The attorney also sat on the board of directors. The venture turned out to be unsuccessful, and the investors filed suit against the entrepreneur for negligent management, false representation and noncompliance with federal and state securities laws. The entrepreneur lost the suit. Afterwards, the entrepreneur brought suit against the attorney for malpractice and corporate director liability. The entrepreneur argued that the primary claim in his lawsuit with the investors concerned nonregistration of securities, and he claimed that the attorney failed to advise him on the need to register. The issue in the subsequent suit was whether the attorney assumed any liability beyond incorporating the company. Unfortunately, the entrepreneur did not substantiate his dealings with the attorney; consequently, it was one person's word against the other's. The court deferred making a decision.

You can control the quality of your advisers' work by carefully reviewing all of the documents they prepare. Your advisers are only human, and they are capable of making mistakes. If you have questions about a certain issue, ask your adviser to explain it. Try not to blindly accept his or her advice. The more educated you are regarding legal and tax issues, the better able you will be to control your advisers.

Finally, make sure that your advisers are working efficiently. They are probably billing on an hourly basis, so you should be concerned about how they spend their time—and your money. If they are wasting time drafting unnecessary documents, or researching issues that they should be familiar with, make sure that you are not footing the bill. For example, your attorney should have some standard purchase agreements, consulting contracts and noncompete documents that can be modified to encompass the specifics of any deal. If your attorney has to "reinvent the wheel" and draft these documents from scratch, it could be costly.

■ CHAPTER FIVE ■

How To Find
Acquisition Candidates

Acquiring a business can be a difficult and frustrating process. Some people may be lucky enough to locate a viable target within a few months; for others it will take years. There is no right or wrong place to look, and the right business may appear when you least expect it.

Consider any lead that comes to your attention. Although it may not be the right opportunity, it might provide useful information. If you gather information about the current business market and make contact with people who can provide leads, you will increase your likelihood of finding a business.

There are many sources of information describing the types of companies for sale and how they can be contacted. The most common include brokers, mergers and acquisitions consultants, accountants, lawyers, commercial bankers, newspapers, industry journals, trade magazines, local chambers of commerce and personal contacts. The remainder of this chapter provides useful background information on each.

WHERE TO BEGIN

Begin your search by building a database of contacts that may be able to assist you and businesses currently offered on the market. Your database of contacts should be used to help generate leads.

Include contact names and addresses, their position, the deals to which they may have access and the date of your last contact with them. Keep in touch with your contacts; let them know that you are actively searching, and keep them posted on your progress. Have business cards and stationery printed with your name or the name of your acquisition vehicle. You will appear more credible, and your contacts will have something to remind them of you.

Your database of businesses will give you a feel for the opportunities that are currently on the market and what they are selling for. It provides a basis for comparing new deals that you evaluate. At a minimum, include the name of the company, its address, the market, its sales, the selling price, reason for sale and a description of the business.

These databases will be useful tools, in terms of both lead generation and information on available opportunities. Figure 5.1 gives an example of the information that you should keep on each contact and business.

Business Brokers

Business brokers are a useful way to find deals. They function much like real estate agents, acting as intermediaries between buyers and sellers of local businesses. A broker will work either on behalf of an owner interested in selling his company or on behalf of a buyer looking for an acquisition. Brokers keep lists of companies that are for sale, much like the lists of houses you would find at a real estate agent's office. Some also provide additional services, such as business plan preparation, financial consulting and valuation, and arranging financing.

Unlike real estate agents, business brokers do not need to meet any standard state or national qualifications; some states do require business brokers to be licensed. In either case, the prospective buyer should carefully scrutinize any broker that he or she uses. Some are honest and extremely competent; others are unsophisticated and less professional.

Keep in mind that a broker's incentive is to close deals, regardless of whether it makes good business sense or not. The broker also

FIGURE 5.1   Database Format

1. **Contacts**
   Name: _____
   Address:
   (work) _____   (home) _____
   _____   _____
   Phone:
   (work) _____   (home) _____
   (car) _____   (Fax) _____
   Occupation: _____
   Potential Business Leads: _____
   _____
   _____
   Contact Diary: _____
   _____
   _____

2. **Businesses on the Market**
   Name: _____
   Address: _____
   Primary Market: _____
   _____
   Annual Sales: _____
   Adjusted Cash Flow: _____
   Selling Price: _____
   Listed by Owner, Broker, Other: _____
   Seller's Name: _____
   Phone: _____
   Broker's Name: _____
   Address: _____
   _____
   Phone: _____   (work) _____
   (car) _____   (Fax) _____
   Reason for Sale: _____
   _____
   Description of Business: _____
   _____
   Date Listed: _____
   Date Sold: _____
   Seller's Attorney: _____

has an incentive to obtain the maximum sales price for a business, because the more you pay, the more commission he or she earns. Do not rely on a business broker's judgment. If you need business advice, you are better off paying an adviser whose fee is not contingent on closing the deal.

Depending on the broker, the commission can be paid by the buyer or the seller, although it is generally paid by the seller. Commission rates vary from broker to broker and often from business to business. While negotiable, they typically range from 6–10 percent of the sales price to a figure based on the Lehman scale (Figure 5.2), which was developed by Lehman Brothers and has become an industry standard.

Once you begin dealing with a broker, you lose some control of the search process. Your attempts to gain information about businesses may be frustrating if the broker insists on filtering information. It is the broker's duty to prevent undue concern on the part of the company's customers, and in his or her interest to keep you from meeting with or speaking directly to the owner of the business. Many brokers fear that if direct contact occurs in the early stages of the acquisition, they will be cut out of the deal and lose their commission.

Each broker will work differently. Some feel that they must be included in the negotiations, while others feel that by staying involved they will get in the way. If the broker is interfering, tell him or her that the introduction alone is enough to warrant the fee, and if the deal is worthwhile payment will be forthcoming. If the deal is tight—the business makes sense but the asking price is a little more than you want to pay—all three parties may have to make some compromises.

Two entrepreneurs found a broker who was willing to work for them as an agent. They told him what type of company they sought and he went out and searched for it. He located a business that they eventually bought. In return for his services, a phone call and a link to a seller, he received a substantial five-figure commission. The broker did no more than locate the opportunity and make the introduction.

In an effort to close the deal without wasting time and energy, a broker will try to "qualify" a buyer before revealing any information

FIGURE 5.2   The Lehman Scale

5 percent for the first $1 million of the sales price
4 percent for the second $1 million
3 percent for the third $1 million
2 percent for the fourth $1 million
1 percent for the fifth $1 million
½ percent for the excess over $5 million[1]

1. Lawrence W. Tuller, *Buying In: A Complete Guide to Acquiring a Business or Professional Practice* (Liberty Hall Press, 1990), 70.

about the company. He or she may want to review a purchaser's financial statements to verify that there is sufficient capital to close a deal. Some prospective buyers are unwilling to disclose this information for various reasons.

You may have to be creative in order to circumvent such questions. However, if you are not confident that you have the wherewithal to purchase a business, either with your own savings or by raising capital, don't waste the broker's time.

One entrepreneur did not have the financial strength to purchase a business on his own. However, he had family friends and relatives who expressed interest in backing him, contingent on the quality of the deal. The entrepreneur did not have firm commitments for the money, but he was confident that the financial backing was available.

When a broker tried to verify that the entrepreneur had the wherewithal to purchase a business that they were discussing, the entrepreneur explained that he would use family trust fund assets for the acquisition, believing that this was the easiest way to convince the broker that he was qualified. Although he could not send any information to the broker directly, he was willing to give the broker the name and phone number of the executrix of the trust, his mother. The entrepreneur immediately phoned his mother and described the situation. He asked her to play along when and if the broker called. His mother received the call within minutes. She acted as if the price of the business was a paltry sum and the broker shouldn't bother her with such trivial matters. The entrepreneur was immediately qualified.

We do not condone lying; however, we do believe that it is in your best interest to keep this information confidential. By stating that you are highly confident in your ability to provide a large equity contribution, or that you are purchasing the business for your family and will not disclose their financial situation until you have made the decision to buy, you may be able to avoid this problem altogether. Also be aware that some brokers will require additional information from you, such as how much cash you can use, your willingness to move quickly, how long you have searched for a business, how long you expect to search before you find one and your background.

Once the broker has qualified you, he or she will generally insist that you sign a confidentiality agreement before you obtain any identifiable information about the company. Confidentiality agreements require prospective buyers to keep all information they receive in complete confidence and to return it to the broker within a specified period of time. The purpose of this agreement is to keep competitors from discovering potentially dangerous information about a company and to keep customers from undue concern about a potential sale. Once you have executed this agreement, the broker will send you the information.

Brokers generally conduct some research and prepare information on the companies they are selling. This can range from a memorandum of sale to Schedule C Tax returns. A memorandum of sale is an in-depth report on the company's industry, market, management, customers, suppliers, operations and financials. Although this information will provide you with a good basis for your own analysis, be aware that brokers generally do not guarantee the accuracy of any information they provide and often place disclaimer statements in any documents they send out.

Listings of brokers in your area can be found in the *Yellow Pages*, the business section of the local newspaper, through the local chamber of commerce or from the International Business Brokers Association (IBBA). You can contact the IBBA by mail at P.O. Box 704, Concord, MA 01742, or by phone at (508) 369-2490.

Mergers and Acquisitions Consultants

Mergers and acquisitions consultants handle slightly larger businesses—generally those with over $2 million in sales—and cover a larger geographic area than do business brokers. Some consultants specialize in specific industries; others are generalists. The companies they deal with range from original-owner sales to corporate divestitures.

An M&A consultant does more than "broker" the deal; he or she offers consulting services to both buyers and sellers and advice on how to structure the purchase and get financing. Sometimes an M&A consultant will participate in the negotiations on behalf of the buyer or seller and will perform a valuation of the company. (We discuss this in Chapter 8.)

Most work on a contingency basis; however, some require retainer fees. These fees range from $2,000 to $15,000 per month. If the prospective buyer purchases the business, the consultant applies these fees to the purchase price. Most M&A consulting commissions are based upon the Lehman Scale.

You can locate M&A consultants in your area by contacting the International Association of Merger and Acquisition Consultants at 200 S. Frontage Rd., Suite 103, Burr Ridge, IL 60521, (708) 323-0233.

Accountants

As a result of their intimate relationship with businesses, accountants are often the first to know when an owner wants to sell. Consequently, they can be a good source of information for the prospective buyer. In addition to knowing about the sale, they usually have an in-depth knowledge of the financial position of the company.

Small accounting firms can help you locate acquisition targets; however, some may be hesitant if they fear losing a valued client and, consequently, jeopardizing their income stream. You can encourage these accountants to assist you by offering to retain their services post-acquisition, or you can offer them a finder's fee—a fee

FIGURE 5.3   Sample Search Letter

Harry Accountant/Lawyer
Firm
123 Maple Lane
Anytown, USA 12345
Date

Dear Harry:

Please allow this letter to serve as an introduction. I am a business executive seeking to purchase a small to medium-sized company. My interest in acquiring a business is one of a long-term owner and operator. I have financial resources sufficient to support such an acquisition.

As a professional in the field of _____, you may be aware of a client or acquaintance who wishes to sell a business. If you learn of such an opportunity I would appreciate your referral. Any referrals will be held in the strictest confidence so as not to alert either employees or competitors of your client's firm.

Thank you for your time and consideration.

Yours truly,

---

that you will pay them if they bring you a deal that you end up purchasing. Large firms can be helpful, too. Often these firms have their own M&A departments and/or accountants specializing in small business acquisitions.

If you intend to use accountants as a resource, send a letter, stating who you are and the type of business you seek, to accountants in your target area (see Figure 5.3). Follow up the letter with a telephone call, and consider scheduling an appointment with someone at the firm to discuss your search. An in-person interview demonstrates your level of interest and commitment to the search and will give you the opportunity to determine the types of businesses that the firm serves. Use the interview to gather information and determine if they might have any contacts who could help you.

You can obtain a list of area accountants from *Emerson's Directory of Leading U.S. Accounting Firms*.

Lawyers

Lawyers can provide another good source of information. They may know of estates that are divesting businesses, turnaround or bankruptcy situations, or businesses being sold as the result of a divorce. In particular, you should target firms specializing in small business acquisitions, bankruptcy, and estate planning and probate.

Again, sending a letter of introduction, phoning and scheduling a meeting with the lawyer you contact will provide you with the most valuable leads. A meeting will demonstrate your commitment to the search. If you use the meeting to communicate the type of business in which you are interested, then the lawyer won't waste your time with a lot of unsuitable companies.

The names and addresses of law firms in your area can be found in the *Martindale-Hubbell Legal Directory*. This directory also includes information regarding the attorneys in the firms and the types of legal work that they perform.

Banks

Trust departments of banks are another excellent source of acquisition candidates. These departments often manage the liquidation of estates upon the death of a client. When someone dies, some of their assets may be placed in a trust with a local bank or trust company. The person managing the trust is the trustee, and the person for whom the property is being held is the beneficiary.

When a small business owner dies, his or her interest in the business is often placed in trust. A business would go into trust because the beneficiary has neither the ability nor the interest to run it. In this case, you may be able to purchase the business from the trust. To do this, you would work with the trust officer at the bank or trust company. Trust officers do not usually participate in the business on a day-to-day basis but will have an understanding of its general operations. While this is not a pleasant way for a business to come onto the market, it does happen. And you could be doing both the trustee and the beneficiary a tremendous favor by buying the business.

When working with trust officers, you should remember that they have a fiduciary responsibility to the deceased's estate. Therefore, they will try to obtain the highest price possible for the business.

Newspapers

Often owners who hope to sell their business without the assistance of a broker advertise in the classified sections of local or national newspapers. Local newspapers are generally a good source of information for small businesses like hair salons and auto repair shops. National newspapers generally have listings of larger businesses. On Thursdays, *The Wall Street Journal* lists businesses for sale by owner or broker in the business opportunities section of the classified ads; *The New York Times* has a similar section on Sundays. If you want to focus on a particular region, obtain a copy of the regional edition of *The Wall Street Journal* for that area.

One entrepreneur who sought a company in Texas subscribed to the Sunday edition of several local newspapers, including the Houston, San Antonio, Corpus Christi and Dallas dailies. His diligence paid off. Within weeks he had found a business on which he eventually made an offer.

Generally it is sufficient to respond to these ads with a letter stating that you are interested in obtaining additional information. Whoever is selling the business will contact you either by phone or by mail. Be aware that the seller may require additional information about you before sending any information.

Placing an ad in a newspaper is another way to generate leads. Two buyers had been looking for their dream business for over six months. They contacted brokers, bankers, attorneys and accountants. Around the fifth month their leads began to dry up and disappointment started to set in. Then they came up with the idea of placing an ad in *The Wall Street Journal* stating that they were a young executive couple looking for a business to buy. The ad generated 15 leads, five of which were worth evaluating further. One lead led them to the company they eventually purchased.

Trade Journals

If you are looking at a particular industry, trade journals or industry magazines might contain useful information. Some actually list business opportunities.

A purchaser who located a business this way had worked for a Fortune 1000 direct-mail department before deciding to buy a business. Because of his expertise, he chose to focus on direct-mail companies. As part of his search, he ran an ad in the *DM News,* a direct-mail newspaper. He advertised as an executive looking for a direct-mail company and used a blind box for the responses. One of the companies that responded was a mail order orchid club that required only four hours a day of work and would supply the owner with a yearly cash flow of over $50,000. It was just what the purchaser wanted.

Some trade journals have advertisements for shows and conferences. A trade show or conference often presents a wonderful opportunity to network. By attending such shows, meeting people and circulating business cards, you can inform people in the industry that you are looking for a business. If they do not know of an opportunity, they may know of someone who could help you.

Chambers of Commerce

If you have a regional preference, the local chamber of commerce may be able to provide you with a list of contacts and possibly a list of area businesses for sale.

An entrepreneur was in contact with a northeastern chamber of commerce in her capacity as a consultant to a small business. She happened to mention to one of the officials that she was also looking for a small business to purchase. The official immediately suggested three area companies that were for sale.

Personal Contacts

As we discussed in earlier chapters, one of the most important aspects of your search will be forming a network of contacts and entering the "corridor." This will require telling friends, relatives and business acquaintances that you want to buy a business. Increasing the network of people who know that you are actively searching increases your likelihood of finding an attractive candidate.

A recent MBA graduate had been searching for a company for five months. Initially, his search was not well-defined; he randomly answered ads in *The Wall Street Journal*, studied general industry magazines and contacted a broker now and then. As the months passed, he concentrated his efforts on three cities, contacting brokers, lawyers and accountants. Within a few weeks, he no longer needed to actively search out deals; they started to come to him. His contacts knew that he was actively searching and was a "qualified" buyer, so they sent him information on businesses that met his criteria.

Becoming active in local civic organizations will also assist you in your search. Clubs like the Kiwanis and the Civitans have a wealth of powerful community members who are "in the know" when it comes to local business transactions. Consequently, they may be a good source of leads.

Attending local small business symposia and entrepreneurial forums (frequently sponsored by local entrepreneurial groups) may be another way of generating leads in your area. The people who attend these meetings may be interested in selling their own business or know of someone who is.

Other Sources

There are other sources for finding businesses. Several publications list businesses for sale throughout the United States. ADmax, a Ft. Lauderdale–based company, will give you a computerized listing of businesses for sale by owner based on specified criteria. A subscription runs three to twelve months and costs between $45 and $1,950. First List is another subscription service. For $350 you can receive an annual subscription, which lists companies for sale all over the United States. You can contact First List at (800) 999-0920. World Mergers and Acquisitions Network is yet another publication that compiles businesses for sale. These businesses generally have over $1 million in sales. After you pay a subscription fee, you can request specific leads. This service is provided by International Executive Reports in Washington, D.C., (202) 628-6900.

In addition to these subscriptions, brokers like Business Advertising Specialists in Austin, Texas, (512) 339-0276, also will send you lists of companies upon request. If you are interested in obtaining further information on any of the listed companies, Business Advertising Specialists will send you a videotape of the business for a nominal fee.

THINGS TO REMEMBER

1. *A structured search is always better than an unstructured search.* Identify who you want to contact: brokers, lawyers, accountants, etc. Then draft a letter of introduction and purpose and send it to them. Follow the letter with a call. Follow-up calls demonstrate dedication and are often more difficult to reject than a random letter.

2. *Read the classifieds.* Finding great opportunities takes dedication and stamina. A full day of searching is insufficient. A search will take place over a relatively long period of time. Most people search months, even years, before finding the right opportunity. So perseverance is required. A weekly mass mailing of responses to classifieds in *The Journal* or *The Times* will ensure that you have constant deal flow.

3. *If you find one opportunity that looks good, don't stop searching.* To hedge against the risk of placing all your hopes on one deal, it is best to keep a constant deal flow going.

4. *Keep an updated list of people and companies you have contacted.* First, this will allow you to monitor how much work you have done in the search. Second, it will allow you to easily reference the status of any one deal or contact.

5. *Unless your career situation demands otherwise, notify everyone you know that you are interested in buying a small business.* The more people who know you are looking, the greater your network.

6. *Don't rely on just one method of searching.* Diversifying the channels through which you pursue businesses will increase the likelihood that you find something attractive.

7. *When working with intermediaries such as brokers, remember that you are just as qualified as anyone else to evaluate an acquisition candidate.* The seller eventually will consider many more factors than just the ability to make the down payment.

YOUR NEXT STEP

The purpose of this chapter was to provide you with an understanding of how to locate businesses. Once you have found something you would like to pursue, you will need to evaluate it. The next two chapters provide you with the tools you will need to do so.

CHAPTER SIX

Financial Evaluation of an Acquisition Candidate

Now that we have discussed the reason to acquire a small business, how to plan your search and where to find the market for such businesses, we can discuss how to evaluate an acquisition candidate. Acquisition targets should be evaluated on a number of dimensions, both quantitative and qualitative. Factors that should be considered include the financial history and soundness of the business, your ability to manage it, its position in the competitive environment and its ability to help you meet both your short-term and long-term objectives.

The most important thing to keep in mind when looking at a business is your own objectivity. It will be very important to keep your perspective when you talk to owners and see businesses in person. Many businesses will look great and everything the owner/broker tells you may confirm your feeling that this is absolutely the right business for you. However, don't jump to any sudden conclusions. Keep in mind that the owner's/broker's incentives are not the same as your own. The following example demonstrates just how biased an owner's assessment can be.

An entrepreneur wanted to acquire a small manufacturing business in Southern California. During his search, he found a manufacturer of nylon traffic cones. The financial history appeared to be good, the owner stated that all the machinery was the newest and the most advanced, and the company had strong sales. Based on a series of telephone conversations with the owner, our friend thought that he had found an excellent opportunity and decided to visit the company. When he arrived and met the owner, he took a tour of the plant and discussed possible purchase terms. Then he left to phone one of his advisers. Unable to reach the adviser, our friend decided to visit one of the company's competitors to check on the information the owner had given him. Sensing that he was a "good guy" and not wanting to see him taken advantage of, the owner of the competing firm proceeded to tell our friend the real story—that the company had severely outdated equipment, that manufacturing techniques had rendered the company uncompetitive and that they had not produced anything in over 11 years! Startled but thankful, our friend notified the seller that he would not proceed with the deal.

When you evaluate a business on paper, you may feel favorably toward it; however, when you actually visit the company you may be disappointed for any number of reasons (the facility is old, the employees do not seem friendly, the location is bad—it simply is not what you imagined). No matter what the situation, step back and look at the business according to the dimensions discussed in this chapter and the next. Your own evaluation should guide you into a decision on whether to buy. Naturally, the advice of people you trust and the comments of the owner/sales agent will be valuable, but ultimately you will own the company. Therefore, it is crucial that the business is the right one for you!

This chapter and the next one discuss some of the formal methods of evaluating businesses; they are not exhaustive but rather are designed to give an overview of the factors you should consider. You may want to consult with an expert in each area if you do not feel confident with your knowledge.

FINANCIAL EVALUATION

The financial evaluation will help you learn about much more than the "money" side of the business; conduct it with diligence and use it as a tool to understand how the business operates. Your proposed purchase price also will depend to a large degree on the financial status of the business, so the more you understand this aspect, the more confidence you will have in your valuation (valuation is treated separately in Chapter 8).

A personal computer with a good spreadsheet program can assist you in this analysis. A spreadsheet program will allow you to enter past and projected numbers and analyze them much more easily than can be done by hand. If you do not have access to a computer, or are not knowledgeable in any particular spreadsheet program, many local colleges offer evening or extension courses in specific computer topics and may have facilities you can use. Additionally, Appendix B contains valuable information regarding the use of computers in your search.

This chapter is intended to be an overview of financial analysis. Those readers familiar with finance may want to skip certain sections, and those readers desiring additional information should refer to one of the reference texts listed in Appendix A.

Historical Financials

Historical financials are like the medical charts of a business: examining them can tell you where the business has been, its current state and the direction it is headed. The majority of small businesses will not have audited statements, but most should at least have statements prepared by the firm's accountant. (Some of the smaller firms will only provide you with copies of tax returns—Schedule Cs.) If these statements are not audited, they will either be compilations or reviews. The accountant's cover letter discloses the process used to compile the statements.

Be aware that each type of statement is prepared with a different level of diligence. For a compilation, the accountant merely uses the numbers provided by management and presents them in the proper format. He or she does not verify them. For a review, the accountant looks at the numbers and makes some attempt to verify their accuracy. Finally, for audited financials, the accountant verifies all numbers in the report. However, even audited financials do not guarantee that the numbers are not fraudulent.

Consequently, be aware of the source of preliminary financials! You should confirm financials later in the due diligence stage, but accuracy now will help you avoid wasting time. To help determine the efficacy of financials, ask the source (either the owner or the accountant) about a few of the key numbers and what is behind them. An uncertain or "hedged" answer may be a warning sign that the actual operations of the business do not substantiate the numbers.

Cash versus Accrual Accounting

The statements you receive will be prepared on either an accrual or a cash basis. The accrual basis is the most common method of preparing financial statements; federal tax returns are usually prepared using the cash method. Each method of accounting attempts to demonstrate the activity that took place in the business for a given period. For example, under the accrual method, if a business sends an order out to a client with an invoice in 1991 but does not receive actual payment until 1992, the company will record this transaction in the books as a sale in 1991. Under the alternative (cash) method, the business would not record this transaction on the books until 1992. The cash method attempts to show only the actual cash that has moved in and out of the business.

Financial Statements

There are four parts to the financial statements: the income statement, the balance sheet, the statement of cash flow and the notes. Each section is discussed below in detail.

The Income Statement The income statement reflects the activity that takes place in a business over a fiscal year. Figure 6.1 shows an income statement for the hypothetical business Metro Printing. The income statement can be divided into five parts: (1) sales or revenues, (2) cost of goods sold, (3) operating expenses, (4) financial expenses and (5) taxes and net income. The *sales* or *gross revenue* section states the dollar value of products or services sold during the year. For 1992, Metro Printing had sales of $225,000. (If the statement was constructed using the cash accounting method,

FIGURE 6.1   Metro Printing Income Statements

	1992
Revenue	$225,000
Costs of Goods Sold	98,500
Gross Margin	$126,500
Operating Expenses	
Supplies	$ 8,750
Advertising	5,250
Rent	18,000
Insurance	2,000
Salaries	55,000
SG&A	17,500
Depreciation	2,500
Total Expenses	$109,000
Earnings Before Interest and Tax	$ 17,500
Financial Expenses Interest	720
Tax	6,125
Net Income	$ 10,655

this number represents the amount of cash that the business received during the year.) The *cost of goods sold* section shows how much it cost the business to produce those goods or services. This number, $98,500, includes the cost of inventory sold or produced and/or any labor costs. Sales or revenues minus the cost of goods sold reflect the business's *gross margin*—or the amount of money left to cover the overhead costs of running the business. The *operating expenses* section of the income statement includes all administrative and sales expenses necessary to the day-to-day operations of the business. This section contains such figures as office salaries, travel and entertainment, sales commissions and often depreciation. Based on $109,000 in operating expenses; Metro Printing had $17,500 in earnings before interest and tax (often called EBIT). The *financial expenses* section contains interest expense and other financing costs incurred by the business. This should be minimal for most businesses. Finally, the *tax and net income* sections of the statement show the amount of tax owed to the government by the business and the amount of money that the business earned after all expenses were taken out of the revenue or sales number.

At a minimum, you should have three years of income statements. You will want to look for trends in all of these sections over time. You can use two exercises to assist you in this process. First, calculate all of the expense items, including cost of goods sold, as a percentage of sales (this is easily accomplished using a spreadsheet program). Comparing numbers on a percentage basis from year to year will help you gain insight to recent operational patterns. What you might see as a small or relatively insignificant dollar change in an expense category—say, an increase of $5,000—might reflect a large percentage increase from the previous year and signal a potential problem. Second, calculate the percentage change in each category from year to year. This will show you if expenses grow faster, slower or simultaneously with sales.

In the expense category, you should examine the following items:

- Rent
- Maintenance
- Expense for bad debt
- Employee wages
- Selling, general and administrative expenses (SG&A)

- Insurance
- Utilities
- Depreciation, amortization
- Executive compensation

You will also want to examine income before and after taxes using the same analysis. Naturally, an increase in net income in absolute terms is a healthy sign, but a decline as a percentage of sales could warn you of rising costs.

The Balance Sheet While the income statement reflects activity over the entire fiscal year, the balance sheet only shows the business's position at one point in time—the end of the fiscal year. This financial statement derives its name from the fact that total assets = total liabilities + shareholder's equity; the equation must always be in balance. The Metro Printing example is shown in Figure

FIGURE 6.2   Metro Printing Balance Sheet as of 12/31/92

Current Assets
Cash	$8,000	
Accounts receivable	7,400	
Inventory	7,800	
Prepaid lease	9,600	
Prepaid insurance	4,000	
Other current assets	1,500	
Total Current Assets	$38,300	

Long-Term Assets

Furn., fixtures & equip.	23,000	
Leasehold improvements	8,000	
Total Long-Term Assets	$31,000	
Total Assets		$69,300

Liabilities and Owner's Equity

Current Liabilities
Accounts payable	$6,500	
Payroll taxes due	2,800	
Total Current Liabilities	$9,300	

Long-Term Liabilities
Note payable	7,000	

Owner's Equity	$53,000	

Total Liabilities & Owner's Equity		$69,300

6.2. The balance sheet is divided into three sections: assets, liabilities and stockholder's equity. The asset section is separated into two components, current assets and long-term assets. Current assets are those assets that will be converted into cash within one year, such as accounts receivable, inventory, marketable securities and cash. Long-term assets are those assets that will not be converted into cash within the next fiscal year. They include property, plant and equipment. Total assets is the sum of current and long-term assets. For Metro Printing these total $69,300.

Like the asset section, the liability section is divided into two components, current and long-term liabilities. Current liabilities include all debts of the company that will be paid within the next fiscal year, such as accounts payable, taxes payable and loans that will mature within the year. Long-term liabilities, in contrast, include debt that has been used to finance the operations of the company, such as capital leases or long-term loans. Finally, the shareholder's equity section of the balance sheet includes the amount of money that the original investors put into the company plus any earnings that have been retained in the business over the years. Notice that for Metro Printing, total assets ($69,300) are equal to the sum of liabilities and equity ($16,300 + $53,000 = $69,300). This should always be true.

At a minimum, you should have a balance sheet for the last year, although it would be preferable to have one for the last three years. You should use a spreadsheet to analyze this section of the financial statements so that you can perform ratio analysis, which is discussed later in this chapter. The goal of your analysis will be to identify and understand year-to-year changes.

On the balance sheet, look for pronounced changes in both asset and liability accounts. Examine cash, accounts receivable, plant/equipment and inventory closely. Marked increases may be good in the case of cash or equipment, but you should note drastic increases in accounts receivable or inventory and bring them to the attention of the owner. Many times there will be valid reasons for an increase, such as an increased level of sales, but increases in either of these accounts can also indicate mismanagement of the firm's assets. If the accounts receivable or inventory figures show marked increases as a percentage of sales, it may signal that the customers do not pay their bills in a timely manner or that inventory has not been moving. On the liability side, note increases in trade payables, notes payable or long-term debt. Accrued payroll tax liabilities can cause long-term problems, especially if the company does not have enough money to pay them. State and federal tax authorities will put liens on the assets of a company that does not pay payroll taxes.

Cash Flow Analysis The most commonly used tool for understanding the cash flow of a business is the "Statement of Cash Flows" or, alternatively, "Sources and Uses of Cash." A sample statement can be found in Figure 6.3. The statement is basically like a checking account register; it has a beginning cash balance, a list of all of the "checks" (uses of cash) and "deposits" (sources of cash), and a final ending balance. The statement of cash flows reflects the movement of cash through the business over the fiscal year. If you buy a business, a monthly analysis of cash flow is an extremely valuable tool and should be produced by your financial controller or accountant on this basis.

A shortage of cash is the deciding factor in the failure of the majority of small businesses. Usually the entrepreneur has underestimated the amount of cash that will be necessary to perform certain tasks, such as launching a product line or ramping up production. A

FIGURE 6.3   Metro Printing Statement of Cash Flows

Cash Flows from Operating Activities	
Net income	$10,655
Adjustments:	
Depreciation expense	2,500
Increase in accounts receivable	(3,055)
Increase in accounts payable	1,200
Net Cash Provided by Operating Activities	$11,300
Cash Flows from Investing Activities	
Purchase of equipment	(4,500)
Net Cash Used by Investing Activities	$ 500
Net Increase in Cash	$6,800
Cash at End of Year	$8,000
Cash at Beginning of Year	$1,200

business may be doing well in other areas—its products are well received, the production process is working perfectly—but if it does not have enough cash to pay its operating expenses, success in other areas may be moot. A popular saying in small business circles is, "If you are starting a business, there are ten basic rules: (1) Don't run out of cash; (2) Don't run out of cash; (3) Don't run out of cash . . ." and so on.

If you are evaluating a business, you will want to analyze the cash flows to determine the timing of payments/receipts. This can give you a good indication of any seasonality that may exist with the business and expose periods in which additional working capital is necessary. If such periods do exist, you will want to discuss with the owner how he or she has addressed this shortage in the past. If the owner has used personal funds, you will need to either have such funds or arrange a working capital facility with a lending institution. If the owner has arranged such a facility, you will want to be sure that the lender is willing to transfer it to you when you buy the assets or stock of the business.

Notes to the Financial Statements In your review you should also pay particular attention to the notes to the financial statements. In these notes the accountant provides an explanation of how some of the numbers were derived. For example, the notes may give a breakdown of real estate owned by the company or what financing is owed to which institutions and under what terms. These notes will be critical to your financial analysis. If anything is hidden in the income statement and balance sheet, it can often be found in the notes.

In Your Review Remember that while the names of financial statement accounts may be the same across industries, the actual numbers will be markedly different. The financial statements of a manufacturing company look radically different from those of a service business, which in turn differ from those of a retailer.

One of the authors learned this lesson all too well while investigating an opportunity to acquire an advertising agency. The accounts receivable and accounts payable outsized revenues by a factor of four. Initially the author thought that the company might be insolvent. However, after investigation with people knowledgeable in the industry, the author discovered that this was typical for an advertising agency, since agencies generally accept bills for production costs in advance of payment from clients.

RATIO AND COMPARATIVE ANALYSIS

If historical financial statements are the medical charts of a business, ratios give you an "x-ray" of the inner workings. Much can be learned from financial ratios. By keeping an eye on critical ratios during the operation of a business, you may be able to detect problems before they start. This is why banks often use ratios when evaluating business loans. If you examine the operating ratios of a business during the evaluation stage, you will become familiar with them from the beginning. This will enable you to better manage the business if you do end up as the owner. There are a number of ratios you can calculate. We will discuss a few and refer you to a good finance text to obtain a more complete description of each and information on additional ratios. Examples of all the ratios we calculate and formulas to calculate them can be found in Figure 6.4.

Depending upon what information they provide, ratios fall into one of four categories: (1) Liquidity, (2) Leverage/Capital Structure, (3) Return on Investment and Profitability, and (4) Turnover. Liquidity ratios tell you how easily the company can convert its assets into cash. Common liquidity ratios include the current ratio, quick ratio, days sales receivable and average days payable. They give an indication of the liquidity of the business.

The current ratio is a measure of whether or not the company has enough assets in the near term to cover its liabilities. If the current ratio is less than 1, the company does not have enough current assets to meet its current obligations. A healthy company has a current ratio of 2 or more. The quick ratio provides similar information. The current and quick ratios for Metro Printing are 4.1 and 3.3, respectively. Based on these ratios, one could conclude that if the business failed for some reason, the sale of assets would more than cover the liabilities.

FIGURE 6.4 Ratios

I. Liquidity

$$\text{Current ratio} = \frac{\text{Current assets}}{\text{Current liabilities}}$$

$$\text{Quick ratio} = \frac{\text{Current assets} - \text{Inventory}}{\text{Current liabilities}}$$

$$\text{Days sales receivable} = \frac{\text{Accounts receivable}}{\text{Average credit sales per day}}$$

$$\text{Days payable} = \frac{\text{Accounts payable}}{\text{Average purchases per day}}$$

II. Capital Structure and Long-Term Solvency

$$\text{Total debt to capital} = \frac{\text{Current liabilities} + \text{Long-term liability}}{\text{Equity capital} + \text{Total liabilities}}$$

$$\text{Long-term debt to equity} = \frac{\text{Long-term liabilities}}{\text{Equity capital}}$$

$$\text{Interest coverage} = \frac{\text{EBIT} + \text{Depreciation}}{\text{Interest payments}}$$

III. Return on Investment and Profitability

$$\text{Return on assets} = \frac{\text{Net income} + \text{Interest expenses} (1 - \text{Taxes})}{\text{Average total assets}}$$

$$\text{Return on equity} = \frac{\text{Net income}}{\text{Average equity}}$$

$$\text{Gross margin} = \frac{\text{Gross profit}}{\text{Sales}}$$

$$\text{Net income to sales} = \frac{\text{Net income}}{\text{Sales}}$$

$$\text{Operating profits to sales} = \frac{\text{Operating profit}}{\text{Sales}}$$

IV. Turnover

$$\text{Inventory turns} = \frac{\text{Sales or cost of goods sold}}{\text{Inventory}}$$

Days sales receivables measures the average number of days it takes the company to collect from its customers. If days sales receivables is much above 45, it indicates that the company does not collect cash quickly enough from its customers. Average days payable indicates how quickly the company is paying its customers. If average days payable is significantly lower than days sales receivables, it is an indication that the company is experiencing cash flow problems.

Leverage and capital structure ratios measure the solvency of the company. They include total debt to total capital, long-term debt to equity, and interest coverage. Total debt to total capital and long-term debt to capital indicate whether the company is overleveraged, or has taken on too much debt relative to the amount that investors have contributed in the form of equity. This ratio should be significantly less than 1, preferably in the 25 percent range. The interest coverage ratio indicates the ability of the company to make fixed payments such as interest charges (a similar ratio is the fixed charge ratio, which also includes lease payments in both numerator and denominator). You would like to see an interest coverage ratio of at least 1.5 to 2, taking into consideration any debt for the purchase of the business or shortly thereafter.

Return on investment and profitability ratios indicate how efficiently the company is using the money invested in it and how much cash it is generating. They include return on assets, return on equity, gross margin, operating profits to sales and net income to sales. Generally speaking, the larger they are, the better.

Finally, turnover ratios indicate how often inventory moves through a company. The best measure is the inventory turnover ratio. The inventory turnover ratio is an indication of how long the company holds inventory or, conversely, how often the inventory "turns" or completely changes. Benchmarks for inventory turns depend on the business, but if the ratio is much below 3 in most businesses, it may be a sign that the company is not managing inventory efficiently.

In businesses with long assembly processes, turns might be 2–3 per year, whereas for a distributor of a commodity like coffee, turns might be 8–10 per year. A turns ratio of 1 indicates that the company completely changes its inventory only once a year. Consequently, if it must have an entire year's inventory on hand at all times, the capital of the business will be tied up. Conversely, a turns ratio of 12 indicates that the company has an entirely new inventory every month. This is a much more efficient use of money.

The inventory turnover ratio for Metro Printing is slightly over 13, indicating that Metro Printing changes its entire inventory 13 times per year! This seems like a good turnover ratio, but it should be examined in the context of similar companies before final judgment is made.

Another step that can (and should) be taken is the comparison of key financial data and ratios to that for companies in a similar line of business. Robert Morris Associates (RMA) Annual Statement Studies is the best source for this type of information. Robert Morris compiles and publishes lists by Standard Industrial Classification (SIC) code of financial data for businesses broken down by sales and assets each year. The RMA Annual Statement Studies volume is published each fall and is available at most libraries. Alternatively, you may order a copy directly from Robert Morris Associates. Other comparative sources can be found in Appendix A.

As with any analysis method, ratio analysis has its limitations. For one, there are no set rules for values of ratios in a given type of business. Second, as ratios are really a snapshot of the business, the snapshot may not be an accurate depiction if the business is in a particularly good or bad period. Nonetheless, ratio analysis is used by parties such as banks and analysts, so it will be good to become familiar with this aspect of business evaluation and financial management.

PRO FORMA STATEMENTS

Pro forma statements are operating statements that project future performance of the business. Pro forma income statements and balance sheets can be constructed based on your analysis of the historical financials and ratios. If you do not feel comfortable preparing these, your accountant or financial consultant should be able to prepare them for you. This is your opportunity to think about what the business might look like in your hands and adjust financial statements accordingly. Figure 6.5 gives the Metro Printing example. Note that these numbers are purely hypothetical and based on assumptions. The pro forma is the canvas on which you can paint different scenarios for the future. The pro forma income statement will be a very valuable tool as you move forward in your evaluation of the business, so you will want to construct it carefully. Use the percentages that you constructed as a guide to analyze the income statement and balance sheet, and then do some research regarding the projected state of the company's principal markets; future sales levels can be predicted according to movements in the company's end market(s). You should also consider changes that are likely to take place in either the raw materials that make up the company's products or in the costs required to deliver the product/service to the market. Include changes that could take place in manufacturing/service methods as well. All of these things will affect cost of goods sold and thus the gross margin that the company will earn. Your pro forma statements will rely heavily on the assumptions that you make in constructing them. Keep a record of your assumptions and carefully scrutinize them before you make additional changes in the pro forma.

The expense section of the income statement is often where you will have your chance to make changes to the business that affect its profitability. In analyzing expenses, you will want to make reductions where possible, but also add costs if your taking over the business will cause an increase in expense. For example, if the owner owns the building in which the business is housed, the business may have paid below-market rent, which will be increased when a new owner arrives.

The objective in constructing the pro forma income statement is to arrive at a figure for "free cash flow." (Figure 6.6) Free cash flow is the amount of cash the business is generating. To arrive at this number, determine the amount of non-cash expenses, such as depreciation and amortization. Next, analyze expenses, such as owner's compensation, travel, entertainment, subscriptions and auto. Small business owners often pay for such items as their car, travel, club dues and subscriptions out of the business. Additionally, they sometimes pay relatives or other people close to them out of the payroll

FIGURE 6.5 Metro Printing Pro Formas

	1992	1993	1994	1995	1996	1997
Revenue	$225,000	$255,150	$289,340	$328,112	$372,079	$421,937
Cost of Goods Sold	98,500	111,896	127,114	144,401	164,040	186,349
Gross Margin	$126,500	$143,254	$162,226	$183,710	$208,039	$235,588
Operating Expenses						
Supplies	$ 8,750	$ 9,940	$ 11,292	$ 12,828	$14,572	$ 16,554
Advertising	5,250	5,964	6,775	7,697	8,743	9,932
Rent	18,000	20,448	23,229	26,388	29,977	34,054
Insurance	2,000	2,272	2,581	2,932	3,331	3,784
Salaries	55,000	40,000	43,200	46,656	50,388	54,420
SG&A	17,500	19,880	22,584	25,655	29,144	33,108
Depreciation	2,500	2,840	3,226	3,665	4,163	4,730
Total Expenses	$109,000	$101,344	$112,887	$125,820	$140,319	$156,581
Earnings before Interest and Tax	$ 17,500	$ 41,910	$ 49,339	$ 57,890	$ 67,720	$ 79,007
Interest	720	0	0	0	0	0
Tax	6,125	14,669	17,269	20,262	23,702	27,653
Net Income	$ 10,655	$ 27,242	$ 32,071	$ 37,629	$ 44,018	$ 51,355

FIGURE 6.6   Metro Printing Free Cash Flows

	1992	1993	1994	1995	1996	1997
Net Income	$10,655	$27,242	$32,071	$37,629	$44,018	$51,355
+Interest	720	0	0	0	0	0
+Excess Owner's Compensation	25,000	10,000	13,200	16,656	20,388	24,420
+Depreciation	2,500	2,840	3,226	3,665	4,163	4,730
Free Cash Flow	$38,875	$40,082	$48,497	$57,950	$68,569	$80,505

of the business, when in fact these people do little or nothing. This is usually done in the case of a "C" corporation, where the owner is trying to avoid double taxation of the corporation's profits while simultaneously not increasing his own compensation or dividends. These payments will no longer exist when the new owner takes over, so this money can be used in other ways. When you have determined the amount of these "owner" expenses, subtract a reasonable salary for yourself and add the remainder to the non-cash expenses from above; then add the result to net income. This number represents free cash flow.

When this analysis is performed for Metro Printing, free cash flow is projected to increase from $38,875 in 1992 to $80,505 in 1997. If the entrepreneur bases his or her price on these projections, it is up to him or her to make them happen!

The free cash flow number you calculate is the amount of money that will be left over after all the operating expenses of the business. Thus it is the amount available for excess owner's compensation, return on equity, repayment of principal and interest, payments of acquisition loans, and such capital expenditures as new equipment or new products. Use of free cash flow in valuation is discussed in Chapter 8.

You should also construct a pro forma balance sheet for the business immediately after the acquisition. The principal concerns should be changes incurred during the purchase to the value of equipment and notes payable. A key consideration is how the balance sheet will look to banks in case further debt is needed either for working capital or for the acquisition of equipment or capital improvements. Include in this statement any capital-intensive programs you intend to undertake, such as advertising campaigns, investment in new equipment, or additional personnel you are planning to hire.

SENSITIVITY ANALYSIS

Since your pro forma projections are based on assumptions that you make prior to being involved in the business, there is a high margin for error in your results. Consequently, it is useful to perform a sensitivity analysis. A sensitivity analysis is just what the name suggests; it indicates how sensitive your projections are to changes in the underlying assumptions.

You can perform a sensitivity analysis by altering your assumptions and seeing how these changes affect your bottom line. For example, if you have chosen to increase sales at 10 percent per year for the next year, alter this assumption and see what would happen if sales remained flat or only increased by 5 percent. In order to do a complete sensitivity analysis, you should modify the key assumptions one at a time. This will help you determine how vulnerable your net income will be to any changes that might occur. Your computer and spreadsheet program are indispensable in performing this analysis.

BREAK-EVEN ANALYSIS

Another useful method of analysis using the cash flows that you have projected is break-even analysis. First, separate expenses into fixed and variable costs. Fixed costs are those that are totally independent of the volume that the business does—for example, interest expense and rent. Conversely, variable costs depend on the volume of sales—for example, the packaging or assembly costs of a product; these costs vary with the volume of product sold. To derive the amount of revenue required to "break even," you can construct a graph like that shown in Figure 6.7 or make the following calculation:

$$\text{Break-even} = \text{Fixed costs} \div (\text{Revenue per unit} - \text{Variable costs per unit})$$

If debt is used to purchase the business, fixed costs will rise, affecting the break-even point. Variable costs could also be altered by any changes you make to the business. By using a spreadsheet program to perform this break-even analysis, you should gain a better understanding of the sensitivity of the business to changes in

FIGURE 6.7   Metro Printing: Break-Even Analysis

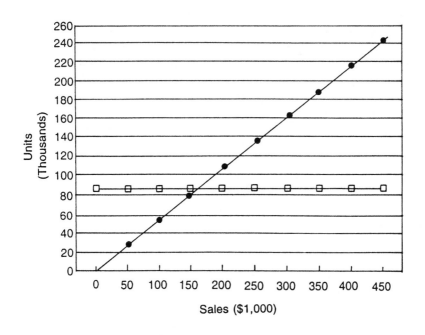

revenue, fixed costs and variable costs. This in turn will help you assess the riskiness of the business.

THE NEXT STEP

While managing a business is not purely a financial undertaking, the analysis of financials will help provide the realism and objectivity that is so important in the evaluation of a business. However, remember that there are many other aspects to investigate, as the following vignette illustrates.

While an investor was looking for potential acquisition candidates, she stumbled upon a small northeast wedding gown manufacturer that looked like a once-in-a-lifetime opportunity. It had a yearly cash flow of over $80,000. The owner wanted $150,000 for the business and was willing to take $50,000 down and finance the rest. In addition, the company's financials looked terrific. However, when she began to investigate the business further, she found out that it had only one customer—a designer whose sales were declining.

At this point you may ask yourself: "Now that I've done all this analysis, what do I do with it?" If the business still looks appealing after this analysis, then you should begin to look at the qualitative aspects, which we discuss in the next chapter. If you are no longer interested in the business, then cut your losses and return to looking at other deals.

CHAPTER SEVEN

Evaluating the Nonfinancial Issues

We have already discussed how to find a business and review its financial information. This chapter will focus on evaluating the nonfinancial aspects of a business so that you can determine whether or not you want to make an offer.

ANALYZING THE BUSINESS—WHERE TO BEGIN

Often a broker or owner will have prepared information on the business. Generally, you can obtain this information after you sign a confidentiality agreement (Chapter 5). This information can range from a full-blown memorandum of sale, which will include a description of the company's industry, markets, competition, products and services, operations, management and financials, to simply a set of financial statements. Use this information as a basis from which to build your analysis. Review it carefully, then prepare a list of questions for the broker or owner.

As you begin your evaluation, focus on the strengths of the business as well as its weaknesses. Prospective buyers tend to emphasize the problems that a business has and how they can solve them. It is just as important, perhaps more important, to discover what the company is doing well. These strengths may have kept the business going for years; if you buy the business and neglect to discover them, you could experience problems in the future.

We will now discuss each topic area that you should examine. Lists of relevant questions can be found after each section. These lists are not exhaustive; use them only as a guide in your information-gathering process. Each business you review will require a different set of questions and additional information tailored to its specific industry.

THE COMPANY

A good place to begin your review is the history of the company. The more that you know about the company's history, the better. In addition to gaining valuable information about how the company has operated in the past, you may also discover some problem areas that warrant further investigation. If the owner or broker hesitates when describing part of the history or brushes over it, this may be a warning signal. Keep your eyes open and listen carefully! At a minimum, you should have answers to the following questions:

- When was the business started?
- What does it do?
- Has it always been in this industry?
- How long has the current owner been active in the business?
- If he or she is not the original owner, how did he or she enter the business?
- Has the company operated uninterrupted up to now?
- Has it been involved in any bankruptcies, joint ventures or lawsuits?

INDUSTRY AND COMPETITION

When examining a patient, a doctor will review both the health of the patient's organs (how well his system functions) and the health of the environment in which he lives. Problems in either area will have long-term effects.

A business is not unlike a patient. When analyzing and trying to determine its current and long-term prospects, you need to review both its internal operations and the external forces acting upon it. The company may very well have profitable, well-managed operations, but if it is in a dying industry, its chances of survival may be slim. Consider a company manufacturing key-punch computer cards in the late 1970s. Although the company may have had efficient, profitable operations, the industry was moribund. If the company did not change its product, it would no longer have customers.

There are many external forces that affect a business. Michael Porter, in his seminal text *Competitive Strategy*, created a whole philosophy of business analysis around these five factors: buyer power, supplier power, competition, potential competition and substitute products. Two of the more important forces you should examine are the industry in which the company operates and its competitive nature. Understanding the way these forces affect a business under evaluation could help in the identification of areas that will significantly alter the competitive environment and thus the operations of the business. The following questions address some of the issues you should consider.

Industry

- Has the industry in which the business operates been expanding or contracting?
- What is the average size of a firm in the industry?
- Is the industry fragmented or concentrated—that is, do a few firms tend to have most of the market share, or is it well distributed among many firms?
- What external factors might influence the industry in the future (legislation, liability, new technology, etc.)?
- To what extent does foreign competition play a part in the industry?
- Is the industry regional or national?
- Is there an industry leader? If so, who is it?

Competitive Environment

- How many firms directly compete in the primary line of business?
- What is the principal base of competitive advantage (price, service, innovation, location)?
- Which of these strategies is employed by the industry leader?
- What barriers to entry exist to keep competitors from entering the business?
- Conversely, what barriers to exit exist?
- How is competition manifested in the marketplace (e.g., price wars, new product introductions, new service concepts)?
- What resources are necessary to participate in this competition (e.g., capital, creative prowess, salesmanship, etc.)?
- Are there any signs of collusion or cooperation among firms in the industry?

By thinking about these competitive and industry issues, you may be able to expose the strengths or weaknesses of the business and its competitors. If a weakness is discovered, try to determine if it is temporary or a permanent part of doing business. External forces are often the most difficult to manage, so caution should be exercised in planning the ongoing business on the assumption that these forces can be modified or mitigated.

PRODUCTS AND SERVICES

The core products/services compose the heart of the business. As with humans, the business cannot function without a heart. It is as important to identify the key products or services as it is to evaluate this condition. If there are problems with the products or services of the business, you will need to determine if they are acute or severe, and whether with treatment the business can recover. If you do not identify the key product or service early on, all your assumptions and strategies could be inaccurate.

Be aware that what the business sells is not always its core product. For example, while Domino's manufactures and sells pizzas, it could be argued that their key product is prompt service. People buy Domino's not because they are the best pizzas in town, but rather because they will be delivered within 30 minutes.

At a minimum, you should know how the product or service ranks in terms of quality, how it compares to other products and services on the market, and how it is received by the target market. The following questions can help you evaluate the product line or service that a company offers.

- What is the principal product/service?
- How many products/services does the company produce?
- What are their sales histories?
- Are some selling better than others?
- What are the competing products on the market?
- How do they compare to the company's product?
- Does the company have any proprietary products, such as patents, copyrights or trade secrets? If so, for how many years are the proprietary rights protected?
- Are product sales seasonal?
- How complex is the product or delivery of the service?
- What is the history of the product, both within the firm and in general?
- Are there any apparent liabilities associated with the product?
- What type of warranty is generally given on similar products?
- Are any fundamental technological changes about to take place or currently taking place that will significantly affect the way the product is manufactured/delivered?
- Do the company's products have substitutes? Complements?

In addressing these questions, you should try to develop a base level of understanding regarding the way the business derives its revenues. In doing so, try to think of things that could affect current lines of business and how sensitive revenues would be to such changes.

CONSUMERS AND MARKETING

The lifeblood of a business is its customers; many business people feel that understanding and satisfying this group is the single most important aspect of running a business. Ted Levitt, professor at Harvard Business School and former editor of the *Harvard Business Review*, stated that "The purpose of a business is to create and keep a customer."

It may be difficult to find out who the actual customers of the company are prior to making an offer. For competitive reasons, owners and brokers are generally reluctant to reveal such information. Often a business's customers do not know that the business is for sale. This is in the company's interests. If a customer knows that a supplier is for sale, it may perceive this as a risk to its supply channels and seek another supplier. As you investigate this element of the business, you should be careful not to reveal to the customer that the business is for sale. If you do so, you may alienate the owner and jeopardize his relationship with the client.

At the very least, try to identify the company's target market— whom they are trying to sell to. The key issues with which you should be concerned are whether any consumer has significant buyer power, whether the company has correctly identified its target market, and whether there is room for growth within the target market or by accessing other markets. The following questions should help.

- Who are the primary customers of the business?
- Are they individual or industrial consumers?
- If individuals, what are the demographics of the target market?
- If industrial companies, do you have a good understanding of their purchasing and decision-making process?
- If the customers are corporate, what size are they?
- Are any of the customers state, local or federal governments? (This requires submitting bids to get work.)
- What kind of credit history do these customers have? (An aging of the accounts receivable account can help you here.)
- Are any of the customers in a troubled industry (e.g., large retailers)?

- Are the majority of the customers in a growing, declining or stable industry?
- Has the company gained or lost a major customer recently?
- How often do the customers make purchasing decisions, and who is the decision maker?
- Does the company have any maintenance agreements or sales contracts? When do they expire?
- What percentage of revenue do the top ten customers account for?
- Is the business heavily dependent on any one of these customers?

Marketing is the way you communicate with and promote your products to your market. A company's marketing program can make or break its business. If the company is successful in identifying its target market and communicating the benefits of its product, it is a tremendous asset for the prospective buyer. If not, then there may be an opportunity for the prospective owner to increase revenues by fine-tuning the marketing and sales program. The prospective buyer should attempt to acquire an intimate knowledge of this aspect of the business. The following questions will help you in this process.

- Is demand for the company's product or service driven by basic necessity or is it created through marketing?
- Does the company have a formal marketing plan?
- Does the company have salespeople or manufacturer's representatives? How are they compensated?
- Has the company identified its target market? Has it been effective in reaching it?
- Are the segments well-defined and understood by current management?
- Is there more than one definable market segment?
- What kind of advertising is the company doing? Review any contracts carefully.
- What kind of literature does the company distribute (brochures, articles, etc.)?

- Have there been any articles or press releases about the company?
- What channels are used in delivering products to market?
- Is the company selling its products locally, regionally or nationally?
- Are changes occurring in the marketplace that may affect this?
- Who is currently performing marketing activities for the business?
- Will that resource be retained after the sale of the business?
- Are there other potential markets that the company could serve that it is not currently accessing?

As in the other areas of evaluation, the goal should not be to determine reasons why you should *not* buy the business (i.e., poor marketing), but to identify possible areas in which a basic change to the way the business is operating could have a significant effect on its results.

SUPPLIERS

Suppliers can have a dramatic impact on a business and, consequently, are an important part of your pre-acquisition analysis. If a company has one or two suppliers that account for a substantial portion of the company's raw materials, then the business is extremely vulnerable to any problems that the suppliers have. If they are unable to deliver product in a timely manner, then the business may not be able to meet its contractual obligations. The following questions provide information that you should gather about the business's suppliers.

- How many suppliers does the business have?
- Does any one supplier account for more than 10 percent of the company's raw material supplies?
- Are the suppliers in good shape financially?
- Do they deliver product in a timely manner?
- Does the business have a good relationship with its suppliers?

- Does the company have any outstanding contractual arrangements with it suppliers?
- What kind of payment terms does the business have with its suppliers?
- Has the company experienced problems with any of its suppliers?

If possible, you might even consider visiting the company's suppliers and reviewing their operations incognito. Through casual conversations, you may be able to discover some relevant information about the company.

MANAGEMENT

This area should be examined from two different perspectives: the nature of current management and how the management structure would change post-acquisition. The current management structure of the company may or may not involve the current owner. The prospective owner should ask himself if he envisions being involved in a similar fashion or if his involvement will take some different form.

Understanding the strengths and weaknesses of current management will help determine to what extent changes are possible. The most important issue you need to consider is whether the owner is the reason for the success of the business. If so, the company is extremely vulnerable to management changes. If he or she leaves, can you fill this role? Additionally, you should determine whether or not any employees are critical to the operations of the business. If a key employee leaves, what will happen? The following questions should help address this issue:

- Who is currently managing the day-to-day operations of the company?
- What is the organizational structure of the business?
- To what extent is the current owner involved in operations? Finance? Marketing?

- Does the owner play a crucial part in any aspect of the business (i.e., an area in which not only particular skills are involved, but also the particular personal resources of the owner, such as personal relationships)?
- Are there any specialized managers within the company?
- Do these people plan to stay after the acquisition?
- What is the general record of the current management team?
- Have they placed the company in a position of leadership in the industry?
- What is the nature of the relationship between current management and the owner?
- How well do your skills fit in with those of current management?
- Do resources exist to complement your weaknesses, or do you have specific strengths that will augment currently undermanaged areas?
- Has the company had any employee-related lawsuits?
- Do you plan to be an active owner or an absentee owner?
- How comfortable are you with the idea of managing this company?

Answering these questions should not only help you understand management aspects of the business, it should also help you understand your own skills and goals, how they will "fit" with current management, and the very nature of the business itself.

OPERATIONS AND FACILITIES

Whether the company is a manufacturing concern, retailer or service business, you should be concerned with its operations and facilities. A good quality control program and well-maintained facilities are indications of an efficient and effective organization. In contrast, if the business has no quality control program and operations management is poor, then the business may not be producing a competitive product. The following questions should assist you in your evaluation.

- Does the company have a strategic plan?
- Does the company have a quality control program?
- How does the company manage its operations?
- Does the company have modern operations?
- Are production/service delivery deadlines met?
- Does the equipment seem to be new and well-maintained?
- Where does the company buy its equipment? How is it serviced?
- Does the company own, lease or rent its facilities?
- What are the terms of the lease?
- What size facility does the company use?
- Can the business be moved?
- Are the facilities neat and clean?
- At what capacity utilization rate is the company running?
- How does the company measure productivity?

STAKEHOLDER ANALYSIS

Stakeholder analysis involves the consideration of various groups, both within and outside the company, and how they will be affected by the acquisition. Some of these groups and their concerns/motivations may be fairly obvious; others may not be as apparent. Considering the positions of the various groups and what they have to gain or lose from the acquisition can help you better evaluate the company and plan for post-acquisition success. Additionally, you may be able to influence the sale by appealing to groups other than the current owner. Support from various stakeholder groups may help you during the negotiation phase.

- What do current employees stand to gain or lose from the sale?
- What do suppliers and/or customers have to gain or lose from the sale (e.g., the owner may have been giving certain suppliers preference or giving customers below-market pricing, which might cause them to be opposed to a sale in which their advantage is eliminated)?
- Are there other groups that serve the business, such as lawyers, accountants, bankers and other professionals?

- What is the position of people close to the owner (spouse, family)?
- What is the main concern of the current owner—the ongoing success of the business? A fair price? Continued employment of current staff?

Understanding all of these viewpoints will help not only during your evaluation, but also in determining how to make an offer to the seller and what the important components of that offer might be. For example, an owner may be more flexible in terms of price if consideration is given to his employees. Also, the employees will be on your side if you take steps to ensure that they will be retained after the sale.

REASONS FOR SALE

It is important to know why the owner is selling the business. Ninety percent of owners will tell you that they are selling because they want to either retire or move on to something else. Few will tell you that they are selling because business is bad, products are not competitive, or qualified employees are too hard to find and retain. As a result, it is critical during your evaluation stage to determine the real reason for sale. Even if someone wants to retire, changes in the industry often precipitate the decision. Ascertain whether the reasons for sale are things that you can either mitigate or remedy.

- Have you talked to competitors or industry experts to determine if there are hidden reasons motivating the owner to sell? (Be sensitive to the fact that these groups may not know of the sale.)
- In your examination of the company, do the current owner's reasons make sense in light of your observations?
- Have you diligently spoken to suppliers, customers and employees to determine if they know of any reasons for the sale?

These issues are sometimes difficult to address, because they involve asking delicate questions. Nonetheless, if you do discover a hidden reason for the sale of a business, you may or may not decide to buy it, but you will certainly be happy that you were cognizant of the true motivations of the seller.

A young entrepreneur was evaluating the potential acquisition of a newsletter publisher. Everything looked great, and she was ready to sign a letter of intent to purchase until she began talking to some of the employees. After about an hour of conversation, they began to tell her about the "real" business, not the one the management had described to her. To begin with, they told her that she should look into the numerous lawsuits that had been filed against the company.

LEGAL AND TAX IMPLICATIONS OF THE SALE

Although legal and tax implications are discussed more fully in later chapters, it is appropriate to discuss these issues now. As will be emphasized often, without specific legal or tax training, the buyer should not try to act as a lawyer or tax accountant during the purchase of a business. However, it is important that, as the buyer, you are aware of the legal or tax issues that may come up during the sale so that you can take steps to eliminate them or use them as bargaining points.

Some of the legal and tax issues that you should explore include:

- Does the company have any contracts or other legal obligations?
- Do you plan to purchase the assets or the stock of the business? Purchase of the stock carries with it all liabilities—past, present, and future—of the business.
- Are there any current or pending lawsuits against the business that might prevent the transfer of operating assets?
- Do any of the assets of the business have a lien placed against them?
- What type of insurance does the company have?
- If the business is a corporation, what vote, if any, is required on the part of shareholders to sell assets of the business?
- What is the seller's tax position?

- How has the company been depreciating assets, and will there be any tax liabilities upon their sale?
- Who handles the taxes of the business?
- Who is the company's attorney?
- Do you know how earnings of the business flow through to the owner (salary, corporate profits)?

Again, the objective in evaluating these aspects of the business is neither to fully explore every legal and tax implication nor to find reasons to eliminate the business from your list of acquisition opportunities. Rather, the objective is to learn about outstanding issues that may affect the possible value of the business in your hands, so that you can call them to the attention of an expert and proceed accordingly during the negotiation.

OTHER ISSUES

There are a number of other issues that you should consider in your evaluation. These could involve practices on the part of the current owner that you will want to be aware of in the evaluation, valuation and negotiation phases of the purchase. Some of these issues are ethical (i.e., is the current owner doing anything that you consider unethical?) and some are managerial (i.e., what style of management does the current owner use, and is this congruent with the way you envision the business being managed?).

GATHERING ADDITIONAL INFORMATION: WHERE TO LOOK

In your evaluation it will be useful for you to have a good knowledge of the business section of the local library. Most large libraries contain an extensive amount of information regarding industries and specific businesses. Some texts and data bases contain information on private businesses. If you are lucky, you may find a detailed description of the company you are reviewing. Such information usually includes total sales, a list of executives, the company's SIC code and a description of the business. A source such as Dun & Bradstreet will give you some of this information and will list any liens or lawsuits that are pending against the company. Other texts and data bases can give you general market information, lists of competitors and industry forecasts. Appendix A lists a number of common reference texts and data bases that can assist you in your research.

In addition to researching texts and data bases, you may find it useful to search for articles on the company, its markets and competitors. Such online data bases as Wilson's Periodical Index and Dow Jones online text service can provide you with a recent list of articles on these topics appearing in newspapers, magazines and journals.

Before you begin your library search, you should be equipped with some information about the company. At the very minimum you should know its name, address and the industry in which it functions. It is also useful to know its Standard Industrial Classification code (SIC code). SIC codes are four-digit to eight-digit codes that were created by the government in the early 1970s and assigned to each industry operating at that time. Since many texts and data bases are indexed by SIC codes, they can be extremely useful in your search.

If you do not know the SIC code of an industry, it can be easily obtained. Most libraries will have a government-published SIC code book. These books contain lists of industries and their assigned codes. Be aware, however, that these codes have limitations. They were created in the early 1970s, and the face of U.S. industry has changed dramatically over the past 20 years. Rather than assign new codes, the government attempts to fit new industries into old codes, making the process of finding the right SIC code difficult.

SITE VISIT

Once you have done some research and prepared questions, you will want to visit the business. Visiting the business is an essential part of the review process. As you walk around the company, meet the employees and talk to the owner, the information that you have gathered will come to life. The better informed and prepared you are for this visit, the more you will get out of it. Use the previous sections of this chapter as a guideline and prepare questions for the owner. Remember that this will be the first impression the owner has of you. Your actions during this visit may affect any future dealings.

A buyer located a light manufacturing company in the northeast. Although the information she had received from the broker was sketchy, it sounded as if it would be worthwhile to investigate further. When the buyer actually visited the business, she realized that it had a number of fatal flaws, the least of which were that it was violating OSHA requirements, had illegal aliens on the payroll and was under-reporting income to the IRS.

Often one of the best ways to learn about both a business and its owner is by spending time there. This could mean simply watching operations, evaluating products, talking to employees and talking to customers.

Spend as much time as possible with the owner. If the owner is going to continue to be involved in the business, it will be very important that you are able to work together. Additionally, you should be able to learn a great deal about the owner simply through frequent interaction: is he or she honest, straightforward or noncommittal? The owner will also become more comfortable with you as you spend more time together.

In addition to the many detailed evaluation points raised, the most important thing to consider in the examination of a business is whether this is the right business for you. Three entrepreneurs obtained material on a bicycle shop for sale in the suburb of a major eastern city. On paper, the shop looked like a great opportunity. Cash flow was reasonable, it had been in the same location for 20 years and the owner owned the real estate as well. Additionally, the three entrepreneurs had an interest in bicycling and outdoor sports, so they were excited about the prospect of acquiring such a business. They decided that their first step should be to visit the shop to see what it was really like. Immediately upon walking in the door, they realized that this was not the right opportunity. Much of the inventory appeared old, and there was significant excess floor space that would be difficult to use for anything else. Upon leaving, they realized a very important point in business acquisitions: there is no substitute for actually visiting a business, no matter how good it looks on paper!

There may be a number of issues that will arise in your evaluation that were not mentioned in this chapter; do not brush these aside. Rather, determine how they affect you as a buyer and give them their proper weight in moving forward.

KNOWING WHEN TO STOP
GATHERING INFORMATION

One broker we spoke with stated that, based on his experience, aggressive people buy businesses. They recognize good opportunities and act upon them. For any given deal, there is a limited window of opportunity. If you spend too much time gathering and verifying information, the window may close before you have the opportunity to walk through it.

We are not suggesting that you immediately make an offer on a company merely because it looks good. Nor do we recommend that you go to the other extreme. Instead, you should gather enough information to decide whether you want to buy it, make an offer that is contingent upon the due diligence process (Chapter 14), and then verify as much information as you can after you have executed a purchase agreement with the seller.

YOUR NEXT STEP

At this point, you should know whether or not you want to make an offer on the business. Before you actually make the offer, however, you will want to know how much the business is worth. In the next chapter we describe how you can arrive at a value for the company.

■ CHAPTER EIGHT ■

Determining a Price

So far, we have discussed many of the issues that surround the evaluation of a business and considerations you will have as a potential buyer. While much of this analysis is qualitative in nature, one of the most important things to determine before you pursue an acquisition candidate is quantitative—the value of the business. Value is defined here as the price at which the business would sell in an open market. Valuing the business helps you determine the maximum amount you are willing to pay. If you pay more than the business is worth, you will have paid a premium for which you derive no benefit.

If you decide to make an offer, you should calculate the business's actual value. Don't depend on the owner's asking price; if you do, you may make an offer that is more than the business is worth. For instance, let's say the owner is asking $500,000 for the business. If you rely on this value, you may offer $450,000 and think you've gotten quite a deal when he or she agrees to $475,000. However, what if you later perform a valuation just to reassure yourself of the bargain you've gotten and determine that the business is actually worth only $400,000? Obviously, it would be too late to ask for a partial refund.

OPTIONS FOR VALUATION

A number of different options exist for determining the value of a business. If you are comfortable with numbers and financial analysis, you may wish to perform the valuation yourself. If you do perform the valuation, try to seek a second opinion from someone else who has some knowledge of finance. This person may find something in the business that you overlooked because of "buyer's myopia."

One option in determining value is to retain a professional business appraiser. Professional business appraisers make their living valuing small businesses, often in the case of the divorce or death of the owner, or for estate-planning purposes. If you decide to engage an appraiser, check his or her references and find out if the appraiser is a member of any appraisal organization or has any certification in business appraisal. Most states have regulations regarding who can call themselves an appraiser, but there are still individuals who will claim to be professional appraisers who do not have adequate training.

The Institute of Business Appraisers, Inc. (IBA) and the American Society of Appraisers (ASA) certify business appraisers. The IBA, founded in 1978, is the only society founded specifically to recognize business valuation as a separate discipline. It has members in 49 states and Canada, and offers periodic seminars and professional development courses for its membership. You can contact the IBA at (407) 732-3202.

The ASA is a multidisciplinary society. Its members include real estate appraisers, machinery and equipment appraisers, and business appraisers. The ASA has an accreditation program specifically for business valuation, and its members can be classified as Accredited Members or as Accredited Senior Appraisers. You can contact the ASA at 800-ASA-VALU (272-8258).

An appraiser's membership in either of these will at least assure you that he is aware of the standards governing business appraisal. These organizations can also refer you to members in your area and members specializing in specific business types.

You can also rely on the broker's or seller's appraisal of the business. This is probably the least desirable method of valuation;

both the owner and/or a broker have an interest in placing a high value on the business. If you must rely on this option for valuation, at least back it up with your own calculations.

PERFORMING VALUATION

The following sections discuss various methods you can employ to arrive at a reasonable value for the business. Being familiar with the terms used in valuation will help you as you evaluate businesses and converse with the small business community. Software is available. For more information see the end of the book.

A number of different valuation methods exist for small businesses. Most of them can be placed in one of two categories: asset-based valuation or income-based valuation. The use of different methods will result in different values for the business. Which value is most accurate? Neither is necessarily more accurate than the other. After all, the only important number is the price upon which you and the seller agree. Performing a valuation will merely give you confidence as you negotiate the purchase and may help you determine whether the owner has unrealistic expectations. Performing a valuation will also give you some idea of the "real" market value of the business, and will indicate whether you should walk away from a deal because the required purchase price does not make financial sense.

ASSET-BASED VALUATION

There are basically two components of value in an operating business: the assets used to produce income and the future cash flows produced by those assets. Asset valuation methods are based on the former. The basic premise in asset-based valuations is: What value can be assigned to the assets that will be acquired with the business? The prospective buyer of a small business must consider the current market value and the liquidation value of the assets, or what would happen if he or she were forced to sell the business immediately after buying it.

The first step is to disregard the book value of assets. The book value is the value listed on the company's balance sheet or, lacking a balance sheet, its list of assets. Because book value is based upon the original cost of the assets less depreciation, it is generally inaccurate. Depending on which depreciation method is used, the book value could significantly exceed the fair market value of the asset, or vice versa. Consider the following example.

A business purchases a new computer system for $15,000. Tax law states that computers fall into the "seven-year" class—that is, the value of the computer may be depreciated, or gradually written off, over seven years. Depending on the depreciation method chosen, the computer could be listed on the company's books at as much as 70 percent of its original value ($10,500) two years after purchase. Assets that are subject to rapid technological advancement, such as computers, tend to lose value faster than depreciation methods allow. In this case, the two-year old system might actually sell for only 50 percent of the original purchase price, or $7,500. If one were to rely on the book value of the asset, the actual value of the computer could be overstated by as much as $2,500 on the balance sheet. This may not seem like much, but if the example is extended to many computers or similar assets, the difference adds up quickly! As this example illustrates, you should consider the balance sheet more as a list of the items the company owns rather than an indication of their actual value.

You should also consider the assumption of liabilities. This largely depends on whether you intend to purchase the stock or the assets of the company. If you intend to purchase the stock of the company, then you must factor into your valuation the amount of money required to discharge financial liabilities, or specify in the purchase agreement that the discharge of liabilities is the responsibility of the seller. Considerations such as whether to purchase assets or stock are discussed more fully in Chapter 11, "Structuring the Deal."

Fair Market Value

The fair market value approach attempts to establish a price at which the assets of the company would sell on the open market.

Let's assume that you are considering the purchase of a printing business. Figure 8.1 shows the same sample (and simplified) balance sheet for Metro Printing as discussed in Chapter 6. To value this business based on its assets, examine each item in the balance sheet. Note that the value listed is book value, which should be considered only a guideline.

Each asset type demands different considerations when establishing value. Cash, of course, can be taken at listed value (keep in mind that later, during the due diligence phase, you will verify the accuracy of the figures on which you relied to establish a price, so you may assume for now that listed values are an accurate reflection

FIGURE 8.1   Metro Printing Balance as of 12/31/92

Assets	
Cash	$ 8,000
Accounts receivable	7,400
Inventory	7,800
Pre-paid lease	9,600
Furniture, fixtures and equipment	23,000
Pre-paid insurance	4,000
Lease-hold improvements	8,000
Other current assets	1,500
Total Assets	$69,300
Liabilities and Owners Equity	
Accounts payable	$ 6,500
Payroll taxes due	2,800
Note payable	7,000
Total Liabilities	$16,300
Owner's Equity	53,000
Total Liabilities and Owner's Equity	$69,300

of the book value). However, make sure that the cash is not restricted in any way. Some banks require a minimum cash balance for businesses to which they have loaned money; this may limit your options if you wish to use the cash for the acquisition, or for working capital after the acquisition. Additionally, the seller will often take all cash out of the business at the time of sale. If so, including the cash account in your valuation is not necessary. In the case of Metro Printing, assume that the cash will stay in the business and is unrestricted in use. Therefore, we can assign to it its full listed value of $8,000.

When valuing accounts receivable, consider the age and source of the receivables. Accounts receivable often includes "stale" customer accounts—those that are older than 90 days and realistically have little chance of being collected. Even if they are collected, it will likely be at a large discount (like 50 cents on the dollar). Many small companies keep receivables on their books for months or years, even after it has been determined that the receivable will not be collected. Public companies generally follow accounting conventions and SEC regulations that require them to remove old receivables from their books so as not to falsely inflate the value of assets. Small private companies are not subject to such requirements. So, owners of small companies sometimes have no reason to remove old receivables from their books. During the due diligence process, you will have a chance to verify that receivables actually exist and confirm their age, but a few simple questions early in the evaluation will help you avoid wasting time.

To determine the value of accounts receivable, inquire as to their age, or how long they have been on the books. Old receivables carry little value and are often a sign that the company has had trouble collecting in the past. If the company has never had a receivable that went uncollected and its customer base is relatively stable, then you can be reasonably sure that current receivables will be collected. However, make sure you know the nature of the relationship between the company and its customers. Does the current owner have a special relationship with customers that affects the speed and regularity with which they pay their bills? Or do customers simply follow the company's collection terms?

Another indicator of the value of receivables is the amount that a receivables lender or factor (someone buying the receivables) would advance for the receivables. Remember the "sell tomorrow" rule: If the seller maintains that the receivables are worth 100 percent of their listed value, but a factor will advance only 70 percent of the receivables, you may be overpaying.

In the case of Metro Printing, let's assume that the company has written off some receivables in the past (no more than 5 percent in any given year) and that a factor is willing to advance 80 percent of the value of the receivables. A reasonable value to assign to the $7,400 in receivables might be 80–95 percent of their value ($5,920–$7,030). Let's settle on $6,500.

Many of the considerations that apply to accounts receivable also apply to valuing inventory, specifically age and the price at which the inventory would sell if cash were needed. When examining inventory, determine in what form the inventory exists. Is it raw materials, work-in-process or finished goods? Raw materials are generally easy to value, because such material can readily be purchased at a specific price. Work-in-process is somewhat more difficult, because you must determine how much additional work would be required to convert the inventory into saleable goods, or whether the inventory has value in its current state. Check with other manufacturers of similar goods to determine if a market exists for partially finished product. Finished goods can generally be taken at their listed value and are often more valuable to a prospective buyer, because finished goods can be sold almost immediately and converted to cash.

It is also important to inquire as to the nature and location of all inventory items. One entrepreneur was examining the inventory of an industrial supply company only to find that the owner had included things on the book inventory like extension cords buried in desk drawers, the company's coffee maker and other trivial items. These items would probably sell for less than $1 at a garage sale, so valuing them at original cost on the company's books yielded an inflated inventory figure. For Metro Printing, let's assume that the inventory consists of $7,200 in raw materials (paper, ink, other supplies) that could generally be sold to another printer for an amount close to listed value. However, the remaining $600 is for calendars that were printed at the beginning of the year and have never sold. Because this balance sheet is dated 12/31/92, it is unlikely that the 1992 calendars are worth much to anyone but a recycler, so they should be omitted from your valuation of the inventory. Therefore, the actual value of the inventory to a buyer is approximately $7,200.

Prepaid items such as rents and insurance must also be examined closely. Often their value is dependent on whether the contract can be transferred in the event of a sale. Many leases and insurance policies are assignable—that is, the holder of the contract can assign (transfer) it to another party. If a lease or insurance policy is assignable, determine whether the rates offered by the contract are favorable or unfavorable. A simple example of a favorable lease rate is one in which the company holds an assignable lease at $5.50 per square foot per month, when the going rate for a similar location is $10. If the lease rate is favorable, make sure the term of the lease is long enough to make the lease worth something.

In a business one of the authors was evaluating, the seller had a very favorable lease with the landlord that was 50 percent below the going rate for retail space. The owner considered this a valuable company asset, but upon further inquiry it was discovered that the lease only ran for one more year, at which point the lease payment would most likely double! This not only made the prepaid lease less valuable, it also called into question the future ability of the company to make a profit.

On the reverse side, some companies have been acquired specifically for the leases that they hold.

Prepaid insurance policies are not as variable in value, but you should determine if the policy can be transferred to a new owner, and whether the existing policy rates are competitive.

In Metro Printing's case, let's assume that the lease is assignable and offers a competitive rate, and that the insurance policy can also be transferred to the new owner. We'll assign to these their full values of $9,600 and $4,000, respectively.

Furniture, fixtures and equipment are common asset listings. This asset class could include everything from the office copying machine to a lawnmower used to maintain the grounds of the business. It is important to ask for a detailed listing of the specific items that make up this asset category. The owner should at least have a list of the major assets and should be able to describe the condition of each. Make sure you also examine each asset to verify his claims about their condition. Assets in this category, such as furniture, often depreciate quickly. You should investigate the market for similar used equipment or fixtures to determine a good estimate of the assets' current value. Unless the equipment is highly specialized, it can often be acquired from another business or from an auctioneer. Fixtures used in retail stores are a good example. These fixtures are usually fairly expensive when purchased new, but a large secondary market exists for used retail fixtures because, unfortunately, many retail stores go out of business and have to liquidate all assets. Also check the equipment section of newspapers for equipment or have equipment appraised.

For Metro Printing, let's assume that the furniture, fixtures and equipment could be purchased on the open market for $17,000, significantly less than their book value of $23,000, so we'll assign to them a value of $17,000.

Leasehold improvements is a commonly listed item on the balance sheet of retail businesses that have made improvements to property they do not own. The real estate does not belong to the business owner, but improvements made to the site can be capitalized as leasehold improvements and depreciated gradually. This is another item that is often discounted from the value listed on the balance sheet. Find out how long ago the improvements were made and to what extent they are helping the business succeed. For instance, if the balance sheet lists leasehold improvements that are nothing more than custom doors installed in a warehouse that is no longer in use, then these will not have a great deal of value for the buyer of the business unless he intends to make use of the warehouse space.

Let's assume that Metro Printing recently made improvements to its facility that allowed for more revenue-producing equipment to be added. Because the new owner of the business would most likely derive some benefit from such improvements and would probably pay the same amount for the improvements today, we can assign a value of $8,000 to the improvements, the same value listed on the balance sheet.

Other current assets are usually items owned by the business that do not fall into any of the listed asset categories. Examine these closely; you should not pay for anything that is of no use to you.

For Metro Printing, let's assume that other current assets includes such items as the owner's personal bicycle and a stereo in the owner's office. The buyer does not wish these to be included in the sale, so the listed $1,500 should be omitted from the valuation.

These are just a few of the items that might appear in the asset section of a balance sheet; the important point to keep in mind is that when valuing a company, each item on the balance sheet should be examined closely to determine its true value rather than its book value. An additional point to consider in determining fair market value is whether the assets are actually earning money for the business. If they are not, then you may not want to include them in your purchase and thus in the determination of value.

To determine the fair market value of the business, simply add together the determined value of the listed assets. In the case of Metro Printing, we assigned value to the assets as follows:

Asset	Listed Value	Fair Market Value
Cash	$ 8,000	$ 8,000
A/R	$ 7,400	$ 6,500
Inventory	$ 7,800	$ 7,200
Prepaid lease	$ 9,600	$ 9,600
F, F & E	$23,000	$17,000
Prepaid insurance	$ 4,000	$ 4,000
Leasehold	$ 8,000	$ 8,000
Other assets	$ 1,500	$ 0
Total	$69,300	$60,300

Thus, the fair market value of the assets is estimated to be approximately $9,000 less than their listed values. If a prospective buyer were to rely on the listed value, he or she might offer too much for the business. Fair market values give us a more accurate representation of worth.

Depending on what the purchaser is planning to buy (stock or assets), the value of the liabilities of the company may need to be considered before final value is calculated. In the example of Metro

Printing, let's assume that the buyer of the business would be responsible only for the payroll taxes due and the accounts payable. Thus a fair value for the business might be $51,000, which equals the fair market value of the assets ($60,300) minus the sum of liabilities assumed ($9,300).

Would this necessarily be what the prospective buyer offers for the business? Not by any means. The owner may be asking twice this amount for the business. While the owner's asking price should generally be ignored in valuation (you don't want it to influence your valuation), you must consider it when determining your offer. If the business is selling for the book value of its assets and the replacement value of those assets is significantly less, there may be value in another aspect of the business, such as its name. Value in intangible assets such as a name is referred to as goodwill. Other factors such as the existence of goodwill, the needs of the seller, and the ongoing value of the business all come into consideration when the seller determines an asking price and when a buyer constructs an offer. These issues will be discussed later in this chapter and in Chapter 13, "Negotiating the Purchase."

Liquidation Value

The liquidation value of the assets is similar to the fair market value approach. It assigns the value most likely to be obtained if the assets of the business were immediately liquidated. The difference between liquidation and fair market value is that liquidation value will generally reflect the price that the assets could command if the seller were desperate to sell. Liquidation value establishes a floor price for the business; the seller has no reason to sell the business for its liquidation value unless he is desperate. If you could buy a business for below the liquidation value of the assets, then it would make sense to buy the company and immediately liquidate, keeping whatever profit is generated. Because the existing owner could sell the assets at liquidation value just as easily as you could, it is difficult to find a viable business valued anywhere near liquidation value.

Let's calculate a liquidation value for Metro Printing. We determined earlier that cash was worth its listed book value, and that still holds for liquidation value. In terms of accounts receivable, let's assume that if we needed to turn the receivables into cash right away, a factor would advance 50 percent of the value. The liquidation value of the receivables would be $3,700. Inventory, if sold at auction, would fetch approximately 80 percent of its book value (excluding the $600 worth of 1992 calendars), or $5,760. Someone might assume the lease for $6,000; the insurance is cancelable with a 20 percent penalty, so its liquidation value is $3,200. The furniture, fixtures and equipment might yield $10,000 if sold at auction, and assuming the leasehold improvements are not worth anything to anyone other than the operator of Metro Printing, their liquidation value is zero. We have already determined that the other assets are worth very little to the ongoing business, but let's assume that we could sell them for $400. If we were to calculate the liquidation value of the business, it would be as follows:

Asset	Listed Value	Liquidation Value
Cash	$ 8,000	$ 8,000
A/R	$ 7,400	$ 3,700
Inventory	$ 7,800	$ 5,760
Prepaid lease	$ 9,600	$ 6,000
F, F & E	$23,000	$10,000
Prepaid insurance	$ 4,000	$ 3,200
Leasehold	$ 8,000	$ 0
Other assets	$ 1,500	$ 400
Total	$69,300	$37,060

Thus, if you were interested in buying the business and then liquidating the assets, you should pay no more than $37,060, assuming our estimates of liquidation value are correct.

While liquidation value usually establishes a floor for the value of a business, this does not imply that it is an inaccurate or useless figure. In some cases, offering the liquidation value may be appropriate. For instance, what if the owner is desperate to sell and it is not clear whether the business can continue successfully without him or her? In this case, the owner may not be able to sell the business for much more than liquidation value.

Book Value

As mentioned earlier, book value is usually not reflective of the true value of the assets, and you should be skeptical of any proposed valuation that is based on the book value of any assets. Book value is most often used in the terminology of the public securities markets and in the analysis of the stock of publicly traded companies. Evidence exists even in these markets that book value is not necessarily an accurate representation of true value, as many companies trade at a discount to book value. For example, a company might have $1 million in assets and $500,000 in liabilities, putting the book value of the company at $500,000. If the assets were sold at book value and the liabilities satisfied with the proceeds, $500,000 would be left for the stockholders. If 5,000 shares of stock are outstanding, then each share is worth $100. However, the stock may actually trade at $75. The stockholders know that it is unrealistic to expect that assets can be converted to cash at book value. In this case, the market discounts book value by 25 percent.

The concept of book value can be extended to the example of Metro Printing. If all assets of the company were converted to cash at book value and the proceeds were used to satisfy the liabilities, $53,000 would remain for the owner of the company. Why is this unrealistic? Because it is unlikely that assets could actually be sold for book value. Our fair market value calculations indicated that if the assets were actually sold, they would generate approximately $60,300. If this were used to satisfy all the liabilities of the company (including the Note Payable), $44,000 would remain for the owner, not $53,000. As this example illustrates, book value might provide you with a reference point, but you should not base any of your valuations on it.

Asset-based methods are useful for establishing values that fall at the lower end of the range of values that you will calculate. Why? Asset-based valuations generally fail to take into account the intangible assets of the business. After all, what is the reputation of the company worth? How much would customer relationships be worth if sold? These items certainly have value, and their worth is one of the prime reasons that people purchase existing businesses rather than starting from scratch. However, their value is generally not listed on the balance sheet. The exception to this is if the business has been acquired before and the buyer assigned value to goodwill.

Goodwill

If you have followed the sale of businesses or are familiar with the structure of company balance sheets, then you probably understand the concept of goodwill. Goodwill is an intangible asset that accounts for the reputation, name recognition, customer base and going-concern value of the business. Goodwill deserves special treatment in this chapter because of the importance of the concept both in valuing businesses and, later, in structuring the deal.

If you have determined the value of a business using an asset-based method and the asking price exceeds the value of the tangible assets, the owner is factoring goodwill into the asking price. Goodwill can be used to justify a price over and above the value of the assets. It is unattractive to the buyer because, as we will learn later, it cannot currently be depreciated for tax purposes. Assets that cannot be depreciated, such as goodwill, cannot be deducted as operating expenses of the business.

How does one arrive at a value for goodwill when using an asset-based valuation method? Goodwill is a "plug" factor—the amount paid over the value attributable to assets must be attributed to intangible assets such as goodwill (there are methods for structuring the deal to avoid this, which are discussed in Chapter 11). If you are trying to buy a business and have calculated a value for assets, your best determination of goodwill will be the difference between the value of assets and the owner's asking price. In other words, you may not know until you start negotiating. Remember that the price the seller is asking is irrelevant. You need to make sure the business is worth what you pay.

While asset-based valuation approaches do not incorporate goodwill, income-based approaches do. How? As we will see, income-based valuation factors into the income stream that portion attributable to the intangible assets of the business, like reputation, customer loyalty and name recognition.

INCOME-BASED VALUATION

While asset valuations are useful, the prices of most businesses sold today are calculated using an income-based (or cash flow–based) approach. Asset-based approaches accurately value the assets of the business, but they do not address the ability of those assets to produce income. For example, while office furniture and a production machine might have the same value on the balance sheet, one produces income for the company while the other does not.

This disparity in the ability of assets to generate cash for the business is more accurately reflected by calculating a value based on the cash flows of the business—that is, the profits that the assets or goodwill of the business earn for the owner.

When a cash flow valuation is performed, the objective is to place a value on either the past or future cash flows of the business. In other words, what price do the historical cash flows support, or how much should a buyer be willing to pay for the right to collect the future cash flows generated by a business? To answer this question, it is necessary to briefly explore the concept of the time value of money.

TIME VALUE OF MONEY

The general premise of the time value of money is that a dollar today is worth more than a dollar tomorrow. Why? If you have a dollar today, you can make a decision as to what to do with that dollar. You can use it to buy goods and services. You can invest it and make money from your investment. You can hold on to it and use it later. The point is, holding money and having those options is something of value. That is why people are willing to borrow money for use today and pay it back, with interest, at some point in the future.

This concept influences the valuation of businesses because when buying a business, you will often give the owner money today for a right to future cash generated by the business (the exception to this is the transaction in which no cash changes hands; the owner is paid purely out of future cash flows). This tradeoff between receiving money today or at some point in the future works its way into many of the purchase considerations. One of the most prominent is that of valuation of the business.

CASH FLOW–BASED VALUATION

There are two main cash flow valuation methods: the multiple method and the discounted cash flow method. In general, the multiple method looks at historical cash flows, while the discounted cash flow method looks at future cash flows. Entire books have been written that address the valuation of businesses using cash flow. Our treatment of the subject here will be introductory in nature. Both of the methods discussed rely purely on the cash flow of the business; the value of assets and goodwill is accounted for by the earning power of both items.

Multiple Method

The multiple method is one of the most commonly used methods for valuing small businesses. Why? It is easy to apply, fairly straightforward, and relies to some extent on the sale of similar businesses; it reflects the changing nature of the business marketplace. The drawbacks to the multiple method are that it often relies on the observed multiple for other businesses, considers only historical cash flows and can be relatively subjective. The multiple method examines the most recent year's cash flow number. That figure is then multiplied by a somewhat arbitrary number, or "multiple," to arrive at a price for the business. The following example, using the income statement of Metro Printing, will illustrate the multiple method.

The first step in using the multiple method is to arrive at a number for the free cash flow generated by the business. This is basically the same number that was calculated in the evaluation stage and should reflect net (after-tax) profits with the following adjustments: excess owner's compensation, depreciation and amortization, interest expenses, increases/decreases in working capital, and investment. Figure 8.2 shows the income statements for Metro Printing for the past three years. Net income after tax for 1992 was $10,655. Of the $55,000 paid in salary to the owner, $25,000 was in excess of the amount necessary to pay a professional manager capable of managing the same business. There was $2,500 in depreciation charged, and the company paid $720 in interest. Assume that there was no change in working capital and no unnecessary investment. These three items will be added back into net income to arrive at a free cash flow for Metro Printing of $38,875. This is the number that will be used to calculate a price.

Next, a multiple must be determined. The multiple can be determined in any number of ways. Unfortunately, the most common way for sellers and brokers to determine a multiple is to look at the multiple of cash flow for which similar businesses have sold. Multiples of anywhere from three to ten are not uncommon. The variance usually occurs across dissimilar kinds of businesses rather than within similar types. For example, if most computer stores sell for a multiple of four to five, then it would be uncommon to find a computer store that is selling for a multiple of eight. However, it might not be uncommon to find two different retail stores selling for multiples of eight. Multiples vary for a number of reasons. The value and quality of assets in the business, the risk involved and the desire of the owner to sell can all affect the multiple of cash flow for which a business is sold.

If you are considering a business in a particular industry, talk with brokers and people who have sold businesses in that industry to determine if there seems to be a commonly cited multiple. As arbitrary as this seems, it is often the way the price for a business is set. For example, consider an owner who has owned his business for 30 years and has never considered selling. He knows that the business has provided him with a reasonable income, but he has no idea what a third party would be willing to pay for the business. When the owner begins to think of selling, he will probably speak with a broker or someone he knows in the same business. His question might be, "How much could I get for my business?" The friend or broker might reply, "Well, Jane sold a business like yours

FIGURE 8.2 Metro Printing Income Statements

	1990	1991	1992	1993	1994	1995	1996	1997
Revenue	$175,000	$195,000	$225,000	$255,150	$289,340	$328,112	$372,079	$421,937
Cost of Goods Sold	76,278	86,680	98,500	111,896	127,114	144,401	164,040	186,349
Gross Margin	$ 98,722	$108,320	$126,500	$143,254	$162,226	$183,710	$208,039	$235,588
Expenses:								
Supplies	$ 6,776	$ 7,700	$ 8,750	$ 9,940	$ 11,292	$ 12,828	$ 14,572	$ 16,554
Advertising	4,066	4,620	5,250	5,964	6,775	7,697	8,743	9,932
Rent	13,939	15,840	18,000	20,448	23,229	26,388	29,977	34,054
Insurance	1,549	1,760	2,000	2,272	2,581	2,932	3,331	3,784
Salaries	42,592	48,400	55,000	40,000	43,200	46,656	50,388	54,420
SG&A	13,552	15,400	17,500	19,880	22,584	25,655	29,144	33,108
Depreciation	1,936	2,200	2,500	2,840	3,226	3,665	4,163	4,730
Total Expenses	$ 84,410	$ 95,920	$109,000	$101,344	$112,887	$125,820	$140,319	$156,581
Earnings Before Interest and Taxes	$ 14,312	$ 12,400	$ 17,500	$ 41,910	$ 49,339	$ 57,890	$ 67,720	$ 79,007
Interest	720	720	720					
Tax	5,009	4,340	6,125	14,669	17,269	20,262	23,702	27,653
Net Income	$ 8,583	$ 7,340	$ 10,655	$ 27,242	$ 32,071	$ 37,629	$ 44,018	$ 51,355
Add-Backs for Free Cash Flow:								
Interest	$720	$720	$720	$0	$0	$0	$0	$0
Excess Owner's Compensation	12,592	18,400	25,000	10,000	13,200	16,656	20,388	24,420
Depreciation	1,936	2,200	2,500	2,840	3,226	3,665	4,163	4,730
Free Cash Flow	$ 23,831	$ 28,660	$ 38,875	$ 40,082	$ 48,497	$ 57,950	$ 68,570	$ 80,504
Net Present Value of 5-year Cash Flows:				$212,285				

for five times net income, so why don't you ask that much for yours?" The two businesses may have nothing more in common than providing the same goods or services, but the owner may have nothing else to use as a guide. If the multiple method is the only one the seller understands, he or she may be stubborn about changing that calculation of value, so arguing about the source of the multiple may be futile. For this reason, it is important to know that many businesses are priced using a multiple of cash flow even though this number may not be an accurate reflection of value.

What if, for example, the net income of a business has been declining for three years, and the owner insists on using a multiple for a similar business that has been growing? Herein lies one of the limitations of the multiple method. It primarily considers historical cash flows, which do not account for changes to the business or industry that may affect future value. It is best to understand the multiple method; but keep in mind that it is sometimes arbitrary and, if at all possible, should be double-checked with some other method, such as discounted cash flow.

Let's assume that we have spoken to owners of printing businesses similar to Metro Printing, consultants to the printing industry, and brokers who specialize in printing businesses. Based on these discussions, we have found that most printing businesses in the past year have sold for a multiple of five times cash flow.

Using this multiple and the $38,875 free cash flow we found, we can calculate a value for Metro Printing as follows:

Free cash flow	$ 38,875
Multiple	× 5
Calculated value	$194,375

This is the approximate price we would expect the owner to ask for the business if he priced it using the multiple method. He may be asking more or less than this figure. If he is asking less, you may want to investigate the business further to determine if there are any issues that would cause the owner to use a lower multiple than the recent average. If he is asking more, he might feel that the business warrants a premium beyond that asked for other businesses. No matter what the owner's justification, make sure you are comfortable with your own multiple-based valuation.

An extension of the multiple method is the capitalization rate method. In the capitalization rate method, the buyer sets a target rate of return to be earned on the price of the business. The cash flow number from above is then divided by this capitalization rate (or, conversely, multiplied by the inverse of the rate). Note the similarity to the multiple method. A rate of return is implicitly built into the multiple method, and applying a multiple simply implies the requirement of the rate of return indicated by the inverse of the multiple.

In the case of Metro Printing, we determined 1992 free cash flow to be $38,875. Based on conversations with people in the industry, we have determined that a capitalization rate of 20 percent is reasonable and has been applied to similar acquisitions. The capitalization rate method would be applied in the following manner:

Free cash flow	$ 38,875
Capitalization rate	÷ 0.2
Value of business	$194,375

Note that this is the same price that was calculated using a multiple of five. A multiple of five implies a capitalization rate of 20 percent. Therefore, the same caveats that were considered with the multiple method should be considered with the capitalization rate method. Additionally, the capitalization rate exposes an inherent weakness in both methods: the price is determined based on a return for the price of the business, but no consideration is given to the structure of the purchase. So if a buyer pays all cash, the capitalization rate applies to all of that equity. Conversely, if a buyer uses all debt to acquire the business, he or she will be earning the capitalization rate on almost no equity! Obviously, the same capitalization rate should really not be used for deals with different purchase structures, but it is.

Discounted Cash Flow Method (DCF)

Discounted cash flow is the method that most accurately places a value on the future cash flows of a business. That is, how much should someone be willing to pay today to receive the anticipated cash flows for upcoming years? Discounted cash flow is the method most often used by large investment banks, consulting firms and accounting firms. It is also the most technical and rigorous valuation method. It is generally not used by small business brokers or sellers (except the most sophisticated). One reason for this is that the method, while not complex, is often misapplied, which can result in inaccurate values.

The discounted cash flow method differs from the multiple method in that it depends on future, rather than historic, cash flows. The cash flows for each year are discounted back to the present to reflect the fact that a dollar tomorrow is worth less than a dollar today (time value of money principle).

The financial method most often used to calculate value based on future cash flows is present value. A present value calculation discounts all future cash flows back to the present based on some discount rate. The discount rate is determined by the return required on the assets, equity, and debt of the business, and by its riskiness.

Determining the proper discount rate takes advanced training in finance, and even then it is subject to question based on what assumptions are made. If you have used this method before, then we suggest incorporating it into your range of valuation methods. If you have not used it before, it may be safe to rely on the multiple and capitalization rate methods, or to consult a professional experienced with discounted cash flow–based valuation.

Let's value Metro Printing using a discounted cash flow approach. First, we need to project the operating results of the business for approximately five years. Why five years? Five years has become the de facto standard in valuations based on future cash flows. Venture capitalists generally use a five-year window when pricing an investment in a start-up company, and five years has become commonly used for existing businesses as well. You may have already projected results in the evaluation stage; if so, you should have three different scenarios for the business: worst case, nominal case and best case. These three scenarios come in handy during the valuation stage as well. The ability to calculate a range of values is one of the powerful features of the discounted cash flow method.

When using DCF, you may want to take a number of different approaches to the valuation. You can determine two things: what the business would be worth if the current owner continued to operate it, and what it might be worth in your hands. These could very well be the same thing, particularly if you are not planning to make major changes in the operation of the business. However, if you have ideas for how the operations (and, therefore, financial results) of the business could be improved, then the value of the business after those changes have been made might be quite different. The important distinction is that you should never pay for the value that you will be adding to the business. In other words, when you are ready to make an offer, place a value on the business that is representative of what would happen under *current* ownership, not what would happen if you were the owner.

A brief example might help to clarify this point. Let's say you have identified an attractive acquisition candidate that, based on current operations projected for five years, is worth $500,000. However, you know that if minor changes were made to the way the company operates, the resulting future cash flows indicate a value of $750,000. Do not offer the owner $750,000! You should not pay the current owner for value that you are going to create as the new owner. This distinction between the current value of a business and its value under new ownership is very important and will be discussed further later in this chapter.

To determine a value for the business as it exists today (without your future influence), project the financial results of the business for five years based on past results; i.e., if revenues have been increasing at 4 percent per year, project that they will continue to do so. Do the same with the expense items of the business; project them to increase at their historical rate. Calculate the projected net income for the business and add back any noncash expenditures, such as depreciation and excess owner's compensation. This will give you cash flow numbers for the future, which can then be discounted back to arrive at a reasonable price in present dollars. This price reflects the value of the business in the hands of the current owner and might form a good basis from which to establish an offer.

Let's consider the example of Metro Printing again. By examining the income statement, we can determine growth trends for revenue and expenses and project those into the future. Doing so yields the income statement shown in Figure 8.2. Next, we must determine the free cash flow of the business for the same five years, as we will use that to establish a value. Free cash flow is listed as the last item in the projected income statement.

Once cash flow figures are calculated, we must determine a discount rate to use in our present value calculation. This requires some subjectivity. How do you determine what discount rate to use? The discount rate you use should be based on the riskiness of the business and your opportunity cost of capital—the return that you can earn by investing your money elsewhere. The discount rate should factor in the interest rate you are charged on debt (ROD) and your required return on equity (ROE); also consider the time value of money as well as inflation expectations. For example, consider the determination of a discount rate for a business purchase in which half of the purchase price is financed with debt at an interest rate of 10 percent, and the required return for the other half of the deal is 30 percent. You can estimate the discount rate (DR) using the following weighted-average formula:

$$DR = ROD \times \text{Percent debt} + ROE \times \text{Percent equity}$$

In this example, the percent debt and percent equity are both 50 percent; by plugging these figures into the equation, the discount rate can be calculated to be 20 percent:

$$DR = (10\% \times 50) + (30\% \times 50) = 5\% + 15\% = 20\%$$

If you are not comfortable estimating your own discount rate, you could consult a finance professional who knows how to calculate discount rates for particular lines of business. This too, however, will depend on how you are planning to structure the acquisition in terms of debt and equity. The lesson is, there is no simple method for determining a discount rate, which is one of the primary reasons for the discounted cash flow method being misapplied. Perhaps you will simply need to use a rate that seems reasonable to you.

Make certain that your discount rate appropriately compensates for the riskiness of the venture. The stock market is priced based on discount rates and present value calculations; however, there are two fundamental differences between investing in a public company and purchasing a smaller business. First, your investment will not be liquid. When you invest in a public company, you can buy and sell shares of the company easily. If you wake up one morning and no longer believe that the future prospects for the public company are promising, you can call your broker and sell your stock in the company. You can also look in the newspaper daily to see how much your investment is worth. In contrast, when you invest in a small business your investment is not liquid, and it is difficult to accurately estimate the value of your investment. It could easily take six months to a year to cash out of your business, and the actual price for which you sell it will be negotiated.

The second fundamental difference is that if you invest a large portion of your net worth in buying a small business, your investment will not be diversified. You will be putting all your eggs in one basket. With the stock market it is easy to be diversified, even with a small amount of money. For example, you can invest $1,000 in a mutual fund and be fully diversified.

Whether you invest in the stock market or in the purchase of your own small business, you should seek to earn a return on your investment. However, it is important to realize that, for the reasons mentioned above, acquiring your own small business is riskier than investing in the stock market. Therefore, your discount rate should be higher than those normally used for similar public companies.

If we assume that Metro Printing has a capital structure similar to the example above, a discount rate of 20 percent seems reasonable. Once the discount rate is determined, we can use a spreadsheet program or a financial calculator to discount the future cash flows back to the present. This is generally done by calculating the net present value of the future cash flows. Performing this calculation for Metro Printing results in a value of $166,036. What does this number mean in terms of the cash flows? If someone were to require a return of 20 percent on their money, they would be willing to pay

$166,036 to purchase Metro Printing today in exchange for the estimated future cash flows. This represents the value of the business in the hands of the current owner and is thus a good starting point for establishing a possible offer.

If you would like to examine what the business might be worth under your ownership, project revenue and expenses as above, factoring in the effects of changes you would make as the new owner. Almost every increase in revenue has some associated cost, even if it is a "soft" cost, such as increased time devoted to a task by a staff member. Remember to include these costs as you establish financial projections for the business. When you have projected scenarios under your ownership, calculate the present value of cash flows to determine the value of the business with your projections. You might want to project results for three different scenarios: best case, most likely and worst case. This will help you understand the sensitivity of the value to changes in operating results. This may also prove useful if you write a business plan either for investors or for your own use. Remember, you should not use these values as the basis for your price, because you don't want to pay the owner for value that you are going to create.

What you offer for the business may or may not be the value you have calculated for the business. This depends on your assessment of the seller and on your intent to acquire a business. Buyers generally fall into three different categories: those who seek to purchase businesses for less than their true value; those who are willing to pay actual market value and are satisfied with their return on investment; and those who are willing to pay actual value and expect to increase that value by making changes as the owner. What you do after determining a value will depend on your profile as a buyer.

If you are interested in acquiring a business (or businesses) at below-market value, you need to accurately calculate its value, then determine what discount from this value would be necessary for you to meet your financial objectives. Because the market for small businesses is not fully efficient—sellers and buyers do not always have the same information—opportunities for this type of acquisition do exist.

Alternatively, you may be searching for a business that offers a reasonable return on your investment when purchased at or near market value. In this case, you need to be especially confident about the price you pay, because a slight change in the company's operations or results could significantly affect your return. For example, if an entrepreneur buys a business for $200,000 in cash and expects to take $50,000 a year out of the business, this 25 percent annual return could be seriously affected by an additional $30,000 in annual costs.

The third type of buyer is the one who seeks to buy a business that is accurately valued, then add value to the business by making changes to its operations or structure. In this case, the buyer is counting on operational changes to increase his initial return on investment.

GENERAL CONSIDERATIONS IN VALUATION

Valuation of a business basically provides the prospective buyer with an approximate range of what he or she should be willing to pay for a business. Using asset-based methods such as fair market value and liquidation value, we found the value of the assets of Metro Printing to be $60,300 and $37,060, respectively. Using income-based methods such as multiple, capitalization and discounted cash flow, we determined a range of value of $166,036 to $194,375. Why are the asset-based values so much lower than income-based values? The asset-based values only considered the tangible assets of the company; no consideration was given to valuing goodwill and other intangibles in the business. One way to think of this is that it might cost someone only $60,000 to enter this business, but what is the guarantee that he or she will succeed? How will a customer base be built? How will people know that the business offers a quality product or service? The value of many of these things is reflected in the ability of the company to earn a profit for the owner based on the use of assets.

By considering the figures arrived at using the various valuation methods, you should be able to determine a fair offering price. Once you have made an offer, you can begin negotiating with the seller to determine whether you are able to purchase the business at a mutually agreeable price. Remember, however, that sellers are often not sophisticated in valuation techniques, so if you try to defend an offer the seller believes to be too low by justifying or explaining your valuation method, you may be fighting a losing battle.

■ CHAPTER NINE ■

Financing the Acquisition

Before you decide whether or not to buy a business, you must determine if it is possible to secure the capital needed to consummate the transaction. First, you should analyze the company to be purchased (Chapters 6 and 7). Second, you need to determine the amount of capital necessary to accomplish your goals. Finally, you should evaluate what financing alternatives will be available. If you determine that financing can be secured and the target is worth pursuing, you should prepare a business plan that can be used to help secure the required capital. The business plan should explicitly tie the financing needs of the company to its milestones and stages of development.

FINANCING ALTERNATIVES

The two basic types of financing available for acquisitions are debt and equity. Debt can be defined as any loan made to the business. Debtholders generally have first right to the assets of the business, but do not have any ownership claims. In contrast, equity can be defined as any capital contributed to the business in exchange for a percentage of ownership. Equity holders own "stock" in the business and share equally in its profitability and risks.

The actual characteristics of the financial instruments can vary considerably. For example, debt can be recourse or nonrecourse, convertible or straight; payments can be at variable or fixed interest rates, or contingent on profits or earnings; and the payment schedule can be interest only or amortizing over various periods of time. Equity investments can be structured in a number of ways, too. The number of financing alternatives is limited only by the creativity and willingness of the parties involved in the structure of the transaction.

There are four main sources for acquisition financing: seller financing, third-party debt, third-party equity and the entrepreneur's personal savings.

Perhaps the easiest way to obtain capital for an acquisition is to convince the seller to finance as much of the business as possible. The extent to which the seller will finance the acquisition and the deal structure he will require will depend on his needs, tax considerations, cash requirements and his confidence in your ability to operate the business. Seller financing can be structured as consulting contracts, covenants not to compete, straight debt or debt paid strictly out of operating profits.

Third-party debt can be obtained through banks, the Small Business Administration (SBA), Small Business Investment Companies (SBICs) (see Appendix C for listings), credit corporations, commercial finance companies and factoring firms. The amount of financing available will depend on the operating cash flow and history of the business, the quality of the collateral pledged as security, and the strength of the borrower's personal guarantee and creditworthiness.

Third-party equity can be found through venture capital companies, private investors, business associates and family or friends. If you happen to raise capital from individual investors, consult an attorney to make sure that you comply with securities laws and that you do not misrepresent the investment opportunity. You should also consider the form of the business entity: a partnership, an "S" corporation, a "C" corporation or a limited partnership. Choice of business entity is detailed in Chapter 10.

The amount of personal equity invested in the deal depends on the entrepreneur's personal savings. The entrepreneur must consider how much capital he is willing to risk in such a business venture. If he contributes capital, the investment will seem more credible to the other participants and it may, therefore, be easier to raise money.

DETERMINING CAPITAL REQUIREMENTS

Determining the financial needs of the acquisition requires careful planning. Financing requirements should be matched with the planned development of the firm. This will help determine the exact amount of money needed and when it should be raised. For example, an entrepreneur may be able to purchase a company for $100,000; however, an additional $50,000 may be needed for working capital, and an additional $100,000 may be required in two years for capital asset purchases (the entrepreneur must plan ahead). Since the business will require additional funding in the near future, the entrepreneur must be careful not to structure the acquisition financing in a way that will inhibit the future availability of capital.

In assessing the acquisition's financial needs, you should be careful not to undercapitalize or overcapitalize. Being undercapitalized can put a serious strain on the business; it can inhibit growth and make it difficult for the company to pay suppliers and other creditors in a timely manner. Being overcapitalized can also be a disadvantage; highly leveraged transactions are sensitive to changes in the company's performance, and excess equity capital will serve only to dilute the owner's interest in the company. If a business is overcapitalized and earnings fall, it may not meet its debt payments.

Before deciding on a capital structure—the mix of debt and equity used to finance the acquisition—consider the requirements, liabilities and restrictions of the different options. A number of financing alternatives are available to the resourceful entrepreneur, and each with its advantages and disadvantages. The following section discusses several in detail.

SELLER FINANCING

It is often hard to beat the terms that owners will provide in order to sell their business. Not every seller will provide financing; however, the majority realize that by providing financing, they increase the odds of selling their business. Seller financing can be structured in a number of different ways, depending on the seller's financial needs, tax position and confidence in the new management team. The better you understand the needs of the seller, the better chance you have of structuring mutually beneficial financing. Prospective purchasers should consider the following when negotiating different options with the seller.

- How much cash does the seller need upfront in order to sell his business?
- What are the future cash flow needs of the seller, and for how long is the seller willing to stretch out the payback schedule?
- Is the seller willing to have debt service payments contingent on future profits?
- Will the seller require personal guarantees?
- If the seller requires a lien on the assets of the business, will he subordinate his lien to other sources of financing?
- Is the seller willing to structure the financing as a noncompete agreement, employment contract or consulting agreement? These agreements and contracts have scheduled payment terms that are similar to typical loans; however, they have tax benefits that straight debt does not. These items are discussed in detail in Chapter 11.
- What are the seller's tax considerations, and how will these affect his willingness to structure the deal as you would like? Conversely, what are your tax considerations?

A buyer and seller were negotiating the purchase of a quick-lube oil business. They had agreed upon a sales price and on all terms of the sale except for the issue of personal guarantees. The seller agreed to provide $450,000 in financing of the $650,000 purchase price, to be paid back over 12 years at an interest rate of 8 percent. These terms were much better than any financing available from a third-party lender, especially since there were not many hard assets to pledge as collateral for the loan. Unfortunately, however, the buyer refused to personally guarantee the financing.

Discussions with the seller revealed that he had recently bought out a partner for $250,000 through a noncompete contract paid out over seven years. The seller had pledged a building as collateral and had personally guaranteed the noncompete contract. It was later agreed that a reasonable compromise was to have the purchaser personally guarantee $250,000 of the $450,000 seller financing.

DEBT FINANCING

If the seller is not willing to provide all the financing necessary to acquire the company beyond your own contribution, you will have to seek money from other sources. Before doing so, you should understand and consider the available options. Focus on the following issues:

- What are the advantages of debt versus equity?
- Does the business have machinery and equipment or real estate that can be pledged as collateral for a loan?
- Are the receivables and inventory financeable? Can the receivables be factored?
- Are the assets of the company pledged as security for seller financing, and if so, will the seller subordinate his lien priority to some other lender? (When someone subordinates a lien, he or she agrees to give another lender priority on the collateral.)
- Is there any existing financing that may be assumable, or can any existing relationships be called upon to provide additional financing for the acquisition?
- How much cash flow is available for debt service, and how much do you want to leverage the company?
- Can any suppliers or customers help finance the acquisition?
- What types of institutions or government agencies would consider financing your acquisition target?

Using debt financing has certain advantages. First, debt is considered a cheaper source of capital than equity, because the entrepreneur does not have to share the potential upside with creditors. Second, debt can leverage the equity investor's return on investment and thereby increase the likelihood of attracting such capital. Third, debt financing is easier to obtain than equity financing; however, creditors should be approached after the equity has been secured.

Finally, interest payments on debt are a tax-deductible expense of the business.

Debt financing also has some drawbacks. When an entity borrows money, it generally must make regular payments of both principal and interest according to a set schedule, regardless of the profitability of the company. This can strip the business of money needed to expand and grow. A creditor might also have covenants in the lending documents that will impose restrictions on the operations of the business. Creditors will usually require personal guarantees. The amount of personal liability the borrower assumes depends largely on the quality of the collateral pledged as security, the amount of equity in the company and the acquisition management team's track record.

RECOURSE VS. NONRECOURSE DEBT

A recourse loan requires the entrepreneur to personally guarantee that the loan will be repaid. If the business does not make the debt payments, the lender has the legal right to seek repayment of the loan from the guarantors. For example, if a company defaulted on a $100,000 loan secured by $60,000 worth of equipment and the personal guarantees of the business owners, the creditor would seek to obtain a deficiency judgment against the owners for $40,000—the difference between the amount of the loan and the value of the equipment repossessed.

In contrast, a nonrecourse loan does not require that the loan recipient personally guarantee the loan. If the example above was for a nonrecourse loan, the creditor would not have any claim against the owners for the $40,000. Usually a nonrecourse loan is secured by tangible assets, such as equipment or real estate, that have a value in excess of the loan amount. In the event of a default, the creditor will be able to recoup his investment by repossessing and selling the collateral. The borrower should avoid recourse loans; from a practical standpoint, however, this is not always possible.

SOURCES OF DEBT FINANCING

There are a number of different sources for financing an acquisition: accounts receivable and inventory lenders; factoring companies; equipment finance and leasing companies; unsecured lenders like banks and thrifts; real estate lenders; Small Business Administration (SBA) lenders; and Small Business Investment Companies (SBICs).

Each type of lender has its own investment criteria, based on a business's cash flow, creditworthiness and quality of available security. Terms of available financing, such as interest rates and payment schedules, also vary considerably among lenders.

Shopping for the right lender, or combination of lenders, will depend on the specific details of the acquisition and the financial resources and desires of a purchaser. If a purchaser has plenty of cash available to buy a business, he or she may shop for the financing alternatives with the lowest interest rates and best terms in order to leverage return on investment. In contrast, another purchaser may be concerned about securing just enough money to close the deal. In this case, rates and terms will not be as important as the amount of money that will eventually be provided.

No single type of financing suits all situations. This is why there are so many different types of lenders; each specializes in fulfilling distinct needs of business owners. In this section, we will explore what financing alternatives are available and how one gains access to such sources.

Unsecured Lenders

Banks and other lending companies provide unsecured loans that are primarily based on the amount of cash flow that a company has available for debt service. In order to determine the amount of financing available and the terms of the loan, banks rely on five underwriting criteria: (1) the cash flow generated by the business; (2) the debt-to-equity ratio; (3) the type of available collateral; (4) the credit of the borrowers; and (5) the financial strength of the borrowers.

Unsecured lenders focus on the cash flow generated by the business. They look for businesses with strong cash flows and high debt service coverage ratios. The debt service coverage ratio is derived by dividing the cash flow generated by the business by the debt service payments. For example, if a company generates $100,000 of annual cash flow and the debt payments of both principal and interest equal $60,000, the company will have a debt service coverage ratio of 1.67 percent ($100,000 divided by $60,000). Common coverage ratios range from 1.25 percent to 2.5 percent.

Lenders also consider the regularity of the business cash flows. They examine the seasonal needs of a business and the past history of the company to identify how predictable and stable future cash flows might be.

Lenders like to see companies with healthy debt-to-equity ratios. While an aggressive lender might allow a 3:1 or 4:1 ratio to exist, most consider a 2:1 debt-to-equity ratio to be reasonable. Lenders will limit loan amounts based on this ratio.

The type of assets within your company will also be a consideration for a typical bank lender. The term *unsecured lender* can be misleading, because these lenders will seek to secure their loans if there is collateral available, especially if they make a nonrecourse loan.

Lending institutions will also run a credit check on all borrowers who are purchasing the business and a Dun & Bradstreet or a Standard & Poor's report on the business itself. Each institution has its own credit criteria; however, a history of late payments, outstanding judgment liens or a prior bankruptcy filing will hinder the chances of securing financing.

Borrowers with a substantial net worth are more likely to secure financing than those with little or no financial strength. Lenders like to see that borrowers have liquid assets, such as cash or marketable securities, plus a steady income.

SBA Lenders

SBA lenders provide long-term financing to small businesses under the guidelines of the U.S. Small Business Administration loan guarantee program. The government established this program to help fuel the growth of the economy by providing term loans to small businesses. SBA lenders will provide favorable financing for acquisitions.

Loans are funded based on the health and viability of a company. Most SBA lenders require collateral, either in the form of machinery, equipment or real estate, plus sufficient cash flow to service debt payments.

Business acquisition loans have a maximum amortization period (loan term) of ten years, and 70 percent financing is available. Equipment can be 100 percent financed for ten years if there is sufficient cash flow to service the debt. Working capital loans are for shorter terms, usually seven years. Loans are usually reasonably priced at spreads of 1.5 percent to 3.5 percent over prime.

If the acquisition target has good cash flow but insufficient collateral to qualify for a loan, the purchaser may want to pledge personal assets. For example, in order to qualify for a loan, the purchaser may have to pledge his house as collateral. Most entrepreneurs would prefer not to pledge personal assets; however, it may be necessary.

Shop around for a good lender. Some SBA lenders will provide better service and loan terms than others. The best place to start is the SBA regional office; find out which lenders are most active in your area, and try to get the names of some loan officers to contact. A list of regional offices is included in Appendix C.

Accounts Receivable and Inventory Lenders

Accounts receivable loans are revolving loans that are repaid as the business receives payments from its customers. New advances are funded against new account sales and secured by the accounts receivable. There are no regular repayment schedules for accounts receivable loans, and balances fluctuate with sales; as sales increase, so do accounts receivable and loan advances. Accounts receivable financing is a good way to meet the financial needs of a growing company or seasonal business.

The first priority of an accounts receivable lender is the financial health of the borrower. If the borrower is not in financial trouble, then the lender will review and qualify the borrower's accounts receivable. There are no hard and fast rules about how lenders underwrite a receivable loan; the following are some of the issues that a lender will consider:

- Is there one customer, or a small group of customers, that represents a large percentage of the total outstanding receivables? What is known about these customers' payment history and creditworthiness?
- Are there many small accounts under $100? Lenders perceive that it is hard to collect on these accounts.
- Do the accounts receivable represent a large enough group so that the lender's risk is sufficiently diversified?
- What are warranty policies for the borrower's products? Are many products returned under warranty, and if so, what does this reflect about the quality of the products being sold?
- Are there "contra" accounts—accounts receivable from one customer that can be offset against accounts payable to the same customer? Contra accounts are not accepted as collateral for a loan.
- Is the reserve for bad debts adequate in relation to historical results?
- How does the accounts receivable turnover ratio (net credit sales divided by accounts receivable) compare with industry averages?
- What are the ages of the accounts? If more than 15 percent are over 90 days past invoice date, lenders may not be willing to make a loan.

After reviewing the receivables and determining if you can finance them, you should consider if you will need additional short-term funding. Additional funds can be secured by pledging inventory as collateral.

Inventory lending is riskier than receivable lending. The value of receivables is easily ascertainable, whereas the value of the inventory is not. Generally only a portion of the inventory is finished product, and the rest is work-in-process and raw materials. In addition, if a borrower defaults on an inventory loan, the lender must repossess the inventory and then liquidate it, possibly incurring substantial costs. For example, the lender may have to pay shipping costs for relocation purposes and rent for a warehouse to store the goods. As a result, the proceeds that a lender nets from the liquidation of inventory is usually at a substantial discount to cost.

Since there is more risk involved in inventory lending, most lenders will not lend on the inventory alone; they will also require the accounts receivable lending business of the company. Some of the underwriting considerations for inventory lenders are as follows:

- Does the raw material have a resale value in the condition in which it is purchased? Is the value readily available and determinable—e.g., commodities?
- What percentage of inventory is raw material, work-in-process and finished goods?
- Does the work-in-process have any resale value during any stage of the manufacturing cycle? Work-in-process usually has little or no collateral value.
- How large of a market is there for selling the finished goods?
- Is there strong demand for the product, or will large discounts be necessary to dispose of the inventory?
- How does the inventory turnover rate (cost of goods sold divided by inventory) compare with industry averages?

Receivable and inventory lending requires constant monitoring and supervision of the collateral. The associated costs are expensive, so it does not pay for these lenders to finance small loans. The best candidates for accounts receivable and inventory loans are manufacturers and distributors/wholesalers who sell to a wide customer base and have average annual borrowing of at least $250,000. Financing service companies is less desirable for receivable lenders.

Accounts receivable and inventory lenders usually determine the interest rates they charge based on three factors: their cost of capital (the rate at which they borrow money); the amount of work needed to supervise and monitor the loan; and the perceived degree of risk based on the quality of collateral and advance rates. Most accounts receivable loans float at from 1 percent to 10 percent over prime rate.

Accounts receivable loan advance rates—the amount of money a lender will advance expressed as a percentage of acceptable accounts—vary depending on industry type, customer type, and the quality of credit and collection policies of the company. Typical advance rates are between 60 percent and 90 percent of the accounts receivable within 90 days of invoice date.

Inventory loan advance rates can range from 0 to 65 percent of the cost of qualified assets. Actual advance rates vary depending on inventory salability and liquidation values. Advance rates and interest rate spreads are usually negotiable.

Factoring Lenders

Accounts receivable lenders fund loans backed by a security interest in a company's accounts receivable. In contrast, a factor actually purchases the accounts receivables from the company on a daily or weekly basis. Factors collect receivables directly from the customers. Once a factoring relationship has been established, the company's invoice will explicitly state that all payments are to be made directly to the factor.

A factor's expertise in credit review and account collection enables it to set credit limits and terms for each of the client's customers. Consequently, a factor generally is more liberal when extending credit than the business owner. Some companies find it more cost-effective to use a factor rather than establish their own credit and collection department. This would allow a company to focus on production of goods and promotion of sales, rather than the collection of accounts receivable.

There are two types of factoring relationships: maturity factoring and old-line factoring. In maturity factoring, the total amount of the invoice, less a factoring fee, is advanced within ten days after maturity date of the invoice. For example, if the invoice terms are net 30, then the factor will advance money to the company within 40 days of the invoice date regardless of whether the invoice has been paid by the customer. The company must have sufficient working capital to operate under these payment terms. If capital is tight, sometimes the company can pledge the amount due from factors as collateral for a revolving bank line.

Old-line factoring enables a business to borrow against the invoices before the maturity date. The borrower pays interest for any money drawn against its account. When the invoices reach maturity, the factor pays the borrower the amount of the invoice less advances, factoring fees and interest charges. Old-line factoring is better suited to undercapitalized companies—businesses that have a shortage of money for day-to-day operations—than maturity factoring.

Since factoring companies actually purchase receivables, they are concerned with the credit and payment histories of a company's customers, warranty policies and product quality, return policies and invoice terms. Factors usually charge fees that range from 1 percent to 6 percent of the invoice amount; they pay 94–99 percent of the invoice amount for the receivable.

Equipment Finance Lenders and Leasing Companies

Equipment finance companies lend money to businesses and secure their investment by placing a lien against equipment. In comparison, leasing companies purchase equipment and then lease it back to businesses. There are numerous types of finance companies that seek to secure their loans with equipment liens. For example, banks, subordinated debt financiers, SBA lenders and SBICs all prefer to have their investments secured so that they can reduce their risk of losing money if the company has financial problems.

Equipment finance companies are concerned with the financial health of the borrower and the quality and salability of the equipment that is being pledged as security. The following are some of the considerations of equipment lenders.

- How old is the equipment and what is its physical condition?
- Is it obsolete, or is it likely that it will be obsolete before the term of the loan is over?

- What type of equipment is being pledged? Lenders prefer to have security interests in equipment that has a determinable value and that is readily marketable.
- Are there numerous small pieces of equipment or is the value concentrated in larger items? For example, lenders prefer industrial machinery to office furniture and fixtures.
- Will it be difficult to repossess the equipment if there is a default? It can be difficult to collect from a borrower who pledges cars, vans, trucks and other items that are easy to move or relocate.
- What discount will the equipment sell for at an auction or liquidation sale? This information will likely be determined by an appraiser before a loan is advanced. Appraisers usually determine two values: a going-concern value and a liquidation value.

Equipment lenders determine loan amounts by considering the information above and the cost of repossessing and liquidating equipment in the event of a default. The lender will want to secure his investment, even under a worst-case scenario. Advance rates for equipment loans usually vary between 60 percent and 100 percent of liquidation values; interest rates range from 1 to 10 percent over prime.

There are no set lending terms and rates. For example, an asset-based lender that bases loan amounts strictly on the value of collateral may lend at an 80 percent advance rate against the liquidation value of equipment. However, some lenders are much more flexible. SBICs might be willing to advance twice the value of equipment for the opportunity to share in the equity appreciation of a business.

Small Business Investment Companies

SBICs are venture capital companies licensed by the federal government. The federal government founded the SBIC program in 1958 to stimulate the economy by making money available for investment in small companies. The program's objectives are job creation, an increase in the general wealth of the economy and increased tax revenue for the government. SBICs are privately owned companies with investment funds created by coupling private capital with money borrowed from the government (see Appendix D for a list of SBICs).

There are essentially three types of SBICs: straight debt lenders, equity investors and those that fund loans with equity features. SBICs that make regular loans usually follow underwriting criteria similar to equipment finance or real estate lending companies; they require the value of collateral pledged as security to be sufficient to protect their investment in the event of a default. Sometimes SBICs will fund loans based on criteria similar to unsecured lenders, where the availability of a company's cash flow is the major concern.

SBIC loans are at least five years in duration, and interest rates, which are regulated by the SBA, cannot exceed certain limits. Maximum rates usually fluctuate between 15 percent and 17 percent, depending on current market conditions.

While SBICs provide acquisition financing and term loans to growing companies that cannot be funded elsewhere, they require appropriate compensation for assuming this risk. They usually structure their investments as loans with warrants. Warrants are options to purchase stock in a company for a prespecified price, no matter how high the stock value rises. The better the company's performance, the more valuable your warrant.

When an SBIC makes a loan with warrants, it charges a lower coupon interest rate than it would charge on a straight loan. To compensate for the increased risk, however, the SBIC will attach "call" and "put" options to the loan. A call option gives the borrower the right to purchase the warrants from the SBIC at prices that are either set in advance or are calculated based on the company's performance. An SBIC may set call prices in advance to guarantee a certain return on investment that compensates for the risk. With set call prices, however, the SBIC has only a limited share of the profitability of a company; if the business performs better than projected, the call prices will not change.

Conversely, if call prices are based on the performance of the company, the SBIC's return on investment will reflect that performance. For example, an SBIC may set call prices equal to a percentage of a company's value, estimated as a multiple of earnings or earnings before interest and taxes (EBIT).

The business owner will have an opportunity to exercise the company's call options at various times throughout the term of the loan. However, if at the end of the loan term the call option has not been exercised, the SBIC has the option to "put" the stock back to the company. The owner has a choice of either paying the put price for the SBIC's shares or relinquishing some ownership in the business. The put price will be a percentage of the company's value, just like some call prices. Put prices are structured in such a way that the business owner should exercise his call option, unless his business is performing substantially below projections.

SBICs want a reasonable return on investment; they are not interested in taking control of companies. However, if the company is performing poorly, an SBIC lender may gain a controlling interest in the business by exercising its put option. The amount of ownership will vary from loan to loan and will be stipulated in advance in the loan documents. SBICs also make pure equity investments, but these are less frequent.

EQUITY FINANCING

Equity financing will be a critical component of the capital structure of the acquisition. The optimal mix of debt and equity will depend on both the short-term and long-term capital needs of the company.

There are a number of advantages to equity financing. First, it is a permanent source of capital and does not require scheduled repayments of fixed charges, such as principal and interest payments. Second, it adds to the firm's net worth by increasing the assets without increasing the liabilities. This will increase the company's creditworthiness, which can result in better payment terms with vendors; an increased confidence in the company's ability to remain in business; and an increased availability of, and better terms for, financing and equipment leasing. Finally, equity investors do not require the entrepreneur's personal guarantee or security interests in the assets of the company. These factors also increase the entrepreneur's chance of obtaining nonrecourse debt financing, because the assets of the corporation can be pledged as collateral for a loan.

There are also a number of disadvantages to equity financing. First, it dilutes ownership and reduces the profit potential for the entrepreneur. Second, equity is more expensive than debt; equity investors require greater returns, because they assume more risk than secured lenders. Third, equity investors might require the entrepreneur to relinquish control of the business, or at least certain operating responsibilities. If the company does not perform as well as projected and investors have a controlling interest in the company, they may take over management. The investors become, in essence, indirect partners in the business. In order to regain control, the entrepreneur may have to buy out the equity investors, which can be expensive. Finally, obtaining equity financing can be difficult and costly.

SOURCES OF EQUITY AND
OTHER CONSIDERATIONS

Equity, above and beyond the entrepreneur's contribution, can be raised from business associates, friends, relatives, private investors or venture capital companies. When deciding which source of equity funding to use, you should consider nine factors.

1. Determine whether potential investors have the ability to contribute additional money for future capital requirements. When you acquire a company, unforeseen obstacles and hidden costs often appear post-acquisition. You should consider how you will finance these unexpected capital needs. Finding investors who have the money available and are willing to contribute capital to meet future needs is an excellent way to infuse cash into the business.

2. Consider the securities issues and other legal implications connected with raising capital. (See Appendix C for detailed information on this subject.) These issues will have a significant

impact on your decision regarding equity sources. You should retain an attorney to advise you on this subject.

3. Determine the number of equity investors you will seek. If you have too many investors, you may violate securities regulations. In addition, the more investors you have, the more difficult it will be to serve their needs. For example, if you have 20 equity investors who are mostly family and friends, and they question you endlessly about their investment and expect you to keep them up to date on the day-to-day performance of the business, your relationships can become strained—especially if things don't turn out as planned.

4. Think about the investor's required rate of return. Venture capital companies and sophisticated private investors will probably require higher rates of return than friends and family members. Venture capital companies and private investors look for investments daily and will have a number of alternative investment opportunities to consider. Friends and family members might not have as many investment options. For example, a friend who has $10,000 to invest might consider mutual funds, the stock market or CDs. The opportunity to support a friend by investing in his business, however, might be a rare and exciting alternative.

5. Determine how much control you are willing to relinquish. As the purchaser, you should attempt to retain control of the company. In order to do so, you will want at least 51 percent of the equity. If you will be the sole owner, this may not be of concern to you; if you have to raise equity capital, however, you will have to give up some control. If ownership is to be divided 50-50, it will be difficult to resolve any disputes, because no one investor will have a dominant ownership position.

   A recent MBA graduate purchased a stake of exactly 50 percent in a gourmet food retail and distribution company in Atlanta, Georgia. After the transaction was completed, he described it to one of his old professors at the university, an Entrepreneurial Law teacher, who immediately responded, "Didn't you learn anything in my class?" The MBA answered, "YES! I put a binding arbitration clause in the shareholder agreement." Absent such a clause, the entrepreneur may have had difficulty resolving disputes because he and his co-owner held *exactly* the same stake.

6.   Consider the personal and emotional problems you might experience if the business venture fails. Although equity investments from friends and relatives may appear to be the least expensive, most readily available and most flexible source of capital, this is not necessarily true. There is an inherent cost in doing business with friends and relatives.

   One entrepreneur raised equity capital from a number of friends for a start-up business venture that failed. Prior to this incident, he had been extremely successful in his other ventures. However, after the business failed, the entrepreneur was overcome with guilt and depression. Finding it difficult to face his friends, he moved to a different part of the country.

7.   Consider seeking sophisticated investors. Sophisticated investors require less hand-holding than unsophisticated investors. In addition, they can be a valuable source for advice and business insight.

8.   Think about the contacts your investors have. Contacts can help establish or improve relationships with financial institutions, suppliers and customers. You might need such contacts to help secure acquisition or future financing. However, do not rely on an investor solely to capitalize on his or her contacts. Even with a vested interest in the company, investors may be reluctant to introduce you to their contacts.

9.   Consider the credibility of your investors. If you can convince someone who is reputable and well-known to invest in your business, others will perceive the opportunity to be more credible. This will make it easier to raise capital, both debt and equity, and it can help relations with suppliers and customers.

UNDERWRITING CRITERIA FOR
EQUITY INVESTORS

By understanding the needs and investment criteria of investors, you will improve your chances of securing financing. Usually you only have one chance to convince an investor to contribute capital, so you should be prepared to answer all of his or her questions.

Although there are venture capital companies that seek to invest in acquisitions, it is unlikely that you will receive financing from a venture capital company. However, a brief overview of venture capital firms and their investment criteria can provide insight to an equity investor's concerns.

The venture capital industry is composed of three types of investing entities: (1) independent private venture capital firms, (2) Small Business Investment Companies (SBICs) and Minority Enterprise Small Business Investment Companies (MESBICS), and (3) venture capital subsidiaries of large financial institutions and industrial corporations. *Pratt's Guide to Venture Capital Sources* has an extensive list of venture capital companies and facts about the industry, including how venture capital firms price investments.

Venture capital firms make investment decisions based on the growth potential of the company, management's level of experience and the company's product or service. They finance start-up or rapidly emerging companies and generally do not invest in leveraged buyout transactions or in mature private companies. These firms anticipate investing for a period of at least two years and an average of four to five years. They target an annual net return on investment (ROI) of 30–50 percent. Figure 9.1 presents how venture capital firms ranked the importance of seven variables that contribute to a company's success, based on a 1984 survey by Boissiere.

Private investors will tend to invest using criteria similar to those of venture capital companies. The required rate of return for an equity investor will depend on his or her perception of the risks and potential rewards of the investment. An investor contributing capital to a small business acquisition may be satisfied with lower returns than those typically required in start-up financing, since purchasing a company is perceived to be less risky than starting one. Carefully consider the returns that you offer investors. Often there is a great disparity among investors' required return on investment.

One entrepreneur who recently purchased a company had two types of private investor financing. Both investment options were structured as debt so that he could retain full ownership. However, the returns he offered to one group were dependent on future profits.

FIGURE 9.1   Venture Capital Criteria to Success

Rank by Importance to ROI	Mean Rank	Variable
1	1.4	Investing in companies with strong management
2	2.3	Investing in companies serving in substantial and rapidly growing markets
3	3.6	Investing in proprietary technology
4	4.6	Providing assistance and contacts (recruiting, customers, suppliers, etc.) to portfolio companies
5	4.9	Actively helping to manage portfolio companies
6	5.2	Investing in conjunction with reputable venture capital firms
7	5.5	Concentrating portfolio investments in specific industries or geographic areas

There was potential for a 20 percent return if the business performed well; if the company did not do well, the investors would earn less than 10 percent. The other investor group's financing was structured as debt, with interest accruing for two years at 12 percent, then changing to a regular amortization schedule for five years. At the time, the entrepreneur felt that he needed to offer investors an abnormally high return; however, looking back, he realized that he was much too generous with the first group of investors.

In order to gain credibility with investors, you may need to invest some of your own money in the deal. In addition, be aware that an unreasonable salary and unnecessary perks may make investors uncomfortable and weaken your credibility. Finally, construct a good-quality business plan; it also can help you gain credibility.

SUPPORTING DOCUMENTS

Just as you need to review certain information to determine whether a business meets your acquisition requirements, lenders and equity investors need to review similar information to determine whether they are interested in financing the purchase. For best results, you should put together a professional package that contains all the information that an investor will want to review. In doing so, be aware of the needs of your prospective financiers. For example, a friend or relative may invest without seeing any formal business plan or offering memorandum. However, a more sophisticated equity investor will want to see a well-organized business plan with a concisely written executive summary. If the executive summary does not catch their interest, then chances are they will not even read your business plan.

Most lenders and sophisticated investors will tell you what information they want to review. The following is a list of standard information that is commonly requested:

- *Financial statements for the past three years plus a current year-to-date statement.* Some lenders may require audited statements. Others may settle for a review or compilation.
- *A breakdown of the accounts receivable and inventory.* Even if the lender is not an accounts receivable lender, reviewing these documents can provide valuable information on the company's collection policies and payment histories of customers.
- *A list of machinery, equipment and real estate that indicates estimated values—include appraisals if applicable.* Term lenders will be especially interested in this information. They may have appraisers verify the information you provide.

- *A description of the management team.* Give details on the education, professional experience and age of the managers.

✓• *Financial projections.* Map out the future of the company. Be sure to include a list of assumptions so that an investor can understand and follow your forecast.

- *A complete description of the use of funds.* The more explicit the better.

- *Personal financial statements of the borrowers and guarantors.*

This list represents the minimum information you should supply to prospective financiers. Some lenders will review loan proposals without a complete business plan; others will not. How you proceed to secure financing is up to you; however, remember that you may only have one chance to sell yourself and the viability of your acquisition.

THE BUSINESS PLAN

The importance of a good business plan cannot be overstated. It will help secure financing; define company strategies, objectives and needs; and provide a benchmark by which to measure and monitor progress after the acquisition. Beyond the plan's inherent value in forcing the entrepreneur to analyze all aspects of the business, a plan is absolutely essential to attract the attention of investors. Your business plan must be excellent to obtain financing.

Preparing an in-depth business plan is a significant undertaking. If you have not written a business plan, you should purchase a book on the subject. You may choose to hire someone to prepare the business plan for you. This could cost from $2,000 to $10,000. Regardless of who prepares the plan, you should be actively involved in assembling the document. This will force you to closely analyze the business.

The business plan should start with an executive summary. The purpose of this summary is to describe concisely, in one or two pages, the components of the plan. The plan itself should be 20 to

50 pages in length, including appendices. Seven specific elements should be included in your business plan:

1. **The Company**

   This section should describe, in detail, the experience, background and ages of the management team. Which employees are staying with the company after the acquisition? Do key employees have employment contracts? What is the age distribution of the management team? If the entire management team is in their 50s or 60s, who will the successors be? You should also forecast how the future management team will be structured to meet financial projections.

2. **The Market and Competition**

   Investors want to know about the market for the business's products or services. For example, a small acquisitions firm in San Francisco seeks to acquire manufacturing companies that distribute to large warehouse retail stores, such as the Price Club, because of the rapid growth of these distribution sources. By having a specific acquisition strategy focused on a growing market, the firm successfully located investors who financially support their efforts. What market share does a company have within its industry, and how competitive is the business?

3. **The Products or Services**

   Discuss the main theory of operation and why your company is different, or how you can make it different. Does the acquisition target have any proprietary knowledge or patents? What are the company's competitive advantages? Provide specifics that can substantiate your claims.

4. **Selling**

   Explain the current selling methods, their adequacy and what you plan to change in the future. Be specific about selling methods, in-house sales support, distribution outlets, product pricing, sales contracts and warranty policies.

5. **Manufacturing**

   The plan should explain the manufacturing process and facilities. Is the process state-of-the-art or antiquated? Will capital expenditures be required to bring the facilities up to current standards? Is there a quality control program? What are the staffing requirements? What are the major purchasing issues? What is the capacity of the facilities, and is it adequate to support the financial projections?

6. **Financial Data**

   The plan should include at least three years of financial statements, a balance sheet describing the company at the time of purchase, and projections. The projections should account for all anticipated capital expenses and future financial requirements. Additionally, projections should incorporate the proposed capital structure and forecast equity investors' returns.

7. **Investment**

   If the business plan is being used as a selling memorandum to raise equity capital, the deal structure should be explained as well as the use of proceeds. Be sure to fully disclose the risks of the investment to all potential investors.

Take the time to prepare a good business plan that is realistic and clearly identifies the benefits and risks involved in the acquisition. Don't present an incomplete or sloppy business plan to potential investors; it will turn them away. The time invested in preparing a solid business plan will provide excellent returns.

CONCLUSION

Regardless of the eventual capital structure of a business, it may be possible to successfully acquire a company and have it prosper with "seat of the pants" financing. The entrepreneur must be resourceful and willing to take some risks. Consider the following episode.

A recent MBA graduate wanted to purchase a retail ice cream and candy store in New Haven, Connecticut. The company was being offered for sale for $135,000. The entrepreneur, however, had just graduated from business school and had no money, only outstanding student loans. Regardless, he decided that it was too good an opportunity to pass up, so he proceeded to write a business plan that outlined how he intended to purchase and operate the business.

By presenting the business plan to friends, family and business associates, he raised $97,000 from 11 investors. He also secured a $20,000 loan from a local banking institution. To raise the remaining capital he invested $15,000, which he personally borrowed from a finance company at an interest rate of 18 percent. The net result is that he was able to purchase the business.

If the entrepreneur cannot obtain financing, he should consider a contingency plan. Sometimes there is a less capital-intensive approach to financing the acquisition and its subsequent growth that can still result in a very profitable investment.

CHAPTER TEN

Choice of
Business Form

If you have decided to purchase a business that you have evaluated and valued, you must now consider what business form your acquisition vehicle will take. To a certain degree, the business form will be influenced by whether you purchase the assets or the stock of the target company (see Chapter 11). If you acquire the stock of the target company, you assume the existing business form, a corporation. However, if you purchase the assets of the business, you must determine the business form that your acquisition will take. Your acquisition vehicle can take one of four forms: a sole proprietorship, general partnership, limited partnership or corporation.

Each business form has advantages and disadvantages. When deciding which choice of entity is best, you must consider your specific needs. For example, a corporation may be best if your main concerns are the flexibility to structure financing and limiting personal liability for the business's obligations; however, with a corporation you may be subject to double taxation, whereby the company's income will be taxed at the corporate level and dividends taxed at the personal level. Figure 10.1 summarizes the liability and tax characteristics of business forms.

You should consult with your advisers before you decide which form of entity to use in your acquisition. However, the following discussion of typical choice-of-entity considerations and a brief explanation of the different business forms will help you better evaluate your needs.

FIGURE 10.1　Partnership versus Corporation

		Taxes	
Business Form	*Legal Liability*	*Income*	*Dividends*
Partnership			
General	Unlimited	Personal level	NA
Limited	Limited[1]	Personal level	NA
Corporation			
C	Limited	Corporate level	Personal level
Sub. S	Limited	Personal level	Personal level

[1]Liability is limited only for *limited* partners in a limited partnership.

SOLE PROPRIETORSHIP

A sole proprietorship is the simplest type of business form. It is a business that is owned and operated by a single individual. To create a proprietorship, you have to register a company name with the appropriate state agency and purchase the assets of the business in your own name. This structure offers a number of advantages, such as simplicity and complete control over the business. However, these are outweighed by the disadvantages. As the sole owner, you will be personally liable for all debts and other liabilities of the business. In addition, your access to capital will be determined by your personal wealth and what you are able to borrow; you cannot issue stock or have partners.

GENERAL AND LIMITED PARTNERSHIPS

There are two types of partnerships: general partnerships and limited partnerships. *General partnerships* can be formed with few legal formalities. By definition, a partnership is formed when two or more people are engaged in a venture for profit (by either an oral or written agreement, "Articles of Partnership").

The Uniform Partnership Act (UPA) governs general partnerships. The UPA, which has been adopted by almost all 50 states, states that each partner will share equally in the profits and losses of the venture; will have equal control over the management and operations of the business; will have unlimited liability for partnership debts, contracts and torts; and is jointly and severally liable. The assets of the business are owned by the partnership, not individually. In addition, partners are bound by a fiduciary obligation to one another. This is a duty of the finest loyalty, and each partner is expected to put the interests of the partnership ahead of his own interests.

The terms of the general partnership agreement take precedence over UPA regulations. However, if any terms of the partnership are not explicitly stated in a partnership agreement, the rules of the UPA will govern.

To form a *limited partnership*, you must file a limited partnership certificate in the county in which business is conducted and with the secretary of state. A limited partnership's governing law is the Uniform Limited Partnership Act (ULPA). ULPA divides limited partnerships into two components: general partners and limited partners. The limited partners are, essentially, passive investors who share in the profits or losses of the company, while maintaining limited liability for the obligations of the business. The limited partner may not participate in the management operations of the business. In fact, if a limited partner participates in the control of the business, he will lose his right to limited liability. A limited partner is not liable for more than the amount of his capital contribution. The general partner is subject to unlimited liability.

Each partner, general or limited, is taxed on his share of profits that have been allotted by means of the general or limited partnership agreement. Partnership profits are taxed once at the individual income tax level.

The costs associated with forming a general partnership will vary depending on the contents of the partnership agreement. Generally, it will cost more to draft a partnership agreement than it will to form a sole proprietorship or corporation. The most expensive choice of entity to form is a limited partnership. Limited partnership agreements are intricate and detailed. They must comply with certain state standards that dictate issues to be addressed within the contents of the document.

CORPORATIONS

To form a *corporation,* you must follow a statutory procedure. This is a process that your attorney should be able to carry out for a reasonable fee—$150 to $1,000. Corporations are governed by state laws, which vary considerably. The state of Delaware is well-known for having the most liberal and pro-business state corporate laws. For this reason the majority of large public companies are incorporated in Delaware. If you anticipate purchasing a business in a state that has restrictive corporate laws, you may want to consider incorporating in a state that better fits your needs.

The owners of a corporation are actually shareholders, and the title to all company assets are in the corporation's name. This allows all the owners to have limited liability and a form of ownership that is freely transferable. The benefit of freely transferable ownership can be illustrated with the following story.

A married couple purchased a computer business in New England. The acquisition was structured as a stock purchase whereby the husband and wife each owned 50 percent of the stock of the company after the deal was consummated. After six months, they decided to bid on some government contracts to provide computer services and supplies. However, in order to be eligible to bid on these contracts, the company needed minority status—the majority of the company had to be owned by a person who was a minority. Since women are considered minorities, the husband sold 1 percent of the company to his wife so that she would own 51 percent of the business and could bid on these contracts. It is relatively easy to sell shares in a corporation.

There are two types of corporations: subchapter "S" and "C" corporations. Typically, a shareholder in a C corporation is subject to double taxation. Taxes are paid once at the corporate level and then again when the earnings are distributed to the shareholders. One way of avoiding double taxation is to take most of the profits out of the business as salary. You must be careful, however, because if it is obvious that you are being paid more than "reasonable" compensation, you may be double-taxed anyway. Another way to avoid double taxation is to own property and lease it to the business, which enables you to recoup profits through the lease payments. In both cases, the "profits" that you take out of the business will be taxed only at your personal income level, not at the corporate level and then again as dividends. Both the salary and the lease payments will be expenses of the business and, as such, will decrease corporate profits and consequently corporate tax liability.

Double taxation can also be avoided by filing for subchapter-S status; S corporations are exempt from this policy. To qualify as a subchapter S corporation, the business form must meet six requirements: (1) it must be a domestic corporation; (2) there can only be one class of stock, although it can have different voting rights (this might impose limitations when you are trying to structure the financing); (3) there cannot be more than 35 investors; (4) corporate shareholders are not allowed; (5) there can be no nonresident alien (foreign) shareholders; and (6) the corporation cannot be part of an affiliated group of corporations.

Subchapter S corporations are easy to form, and they enable business owners to avoid double taxation while retaining the other benefits of incorporation. For these reasons, this is often a logical business form to use for an acquisition.

WHEN TO DECIDE ON A BUSINESS FORM

You may want to decide on a business form before you locate an acquisition candidate. This can help streamline the acquisition process, because it may take a while to form your acquisition vehicle. Setting up an entity requires deciding on a name and filing a business name certificate with the appropriate state agency. This process can be time-consuming.

Figure 10.2 is a list of issues that should be considered by an entrepreneur when he or she decides what choice of entity best suits his or her needs.

FIGURE 10.2 Issues To Consider When Choosing Form
of Business

1. Tax treatment of the entity, its owners and its employees

2. Liability of the owners for the obligations of the entity, or limitations thereon

3. The extent to which the entity lends itself to centralization or decentralized management

4. The extent to which the entity lends itself to free transferability of ownership interests or the restriction of such transferability

5. The extent to which the entity lends itself to continuity of existence of the enterprise or limitations thereon

6. The expense of formation and maintenance of the entity

7. The legal requirement that the type of business must be conducted in a particular form

8. The number of co-owners of the entity

9. The extent to which the entity lends itself to a complex capital structure or the issuance of different kinds of securities

10. The extent to which the entity facilitates various types of employee compensation

11. The extent to which the entity lends itself to a public offering of securities or other subsequent financings

12. The ease of formation and the time required to organize the entity

13. The clarity of the rules relating to the formation and operation of the entity and the resolution of conflicts among its constituents

14. The extent to which the entity lends itself to estate-planning goals

15. The nature of the duties of the constituents to the entity and to other constituents of the entity

16. Rules relating to deadlocks in the management of the entity

17. Rules relating to the dissolution or termination of the entity

18. The ease with which the form of the enterprise can be subsequently changed

FIGURE 10.2   Issues To Consider When Choosing Form
of Business (continued)

19. The extent to which the entity is subject to statutory reporting and record-keeping requirements

20. The extent to which consultation with professionals will be required in connection with the organization and operation of the entity

21. The extent to which the entity lends itself to anonymity of ownership

22. The extent to which the form of entity is influenced by custom or tradition

Reprinted with the permission of the publisher from *Start-Up Companies: Planning, Financing and Operating the Successful Business,* planned, edited and co-authored by Richard D. Harroch, published and copyrighted by Law Journal Seminars-Press, 111 Eighth Avenue, New York, New York 10011. All rights reserved.

This list of questions is not exhaustive; however, it does cover the major issues to be considered. After you review this list, you should consult a lawyer and an accountant on the best acquisition vehicle for you.

CHAPTER ELEVEN

Structuring the Deal

So far we have talked about the personal motivations and considerations of the small business buyer, the structure of the search process, evaluation of candidates, and the possible methods of financing a purchase. At this point, you should know whether or not you want to make an offer on a business. If you do, the first step is deciding on a possible structure for the deal.

This chapter describes the tax and legal considerations of structuring a deal. Tax considerations affect the amount of income tax that the seller will pay and when he will pay it as well as the future ability of the buyer to write off a portion of the purchase price as expenses of the business. In addition to minimizing current and future tax liabilities, the buyer will also want to protect himself from assuming any legal liabilities, while the seller will want to absolve himself of all liabilities connected with the business, adding yet another dimension to the purchase structure.

WHY IS DEAL STRUCTURE IMPORTANT?

It is essential for you as a buyer to know how various deal structures affect the value of the business before you make an offer. Both you and the seller will have specific needs in terms of cash flow, income tax considerations and legal issues, all of which will be affected by the eventual structure of the deal. Once you have evaluated the various options, you will be much better prepared to make an offer that is advantageous to you and acceptable to the seller.

You should start to consider deal structure early in the process of making an offer. The intended structure should be outlined in the letter of intent (Chapter 12). If the seller feels strongly about a particular issue but it is not raised until late in the negotiations, the entire process could be stalled while one point of contention is resolved—or, in the worst-case scenario, an agreement may not be reached.

Recently, one of the authors was called by a business broker who sought counsel in structuring a deal. The buyer and seller had agreed on a price, the buyer had conducted due diligence and the seller was ready to relinquish the business. Unfortunately, one minor point—a loan guarantee—arose late in the negotiations, and the purchase was stalled for a number of months while the broker tried to structure a deal that was acceptable to each party. If the buyer had outlined the terms of loans in the letter of intent, the buyer, seller and broker might have been spared much agony later in the purchase process.

Once you reach the advanced stages of negotiation and due diligence, you will have spent a great deal of time and money investigating the business. Walking away may be difficult after these investments, so it is preferable that you anticipate points of contention before entering this phase. If the seller has a clear understanding of the intended deal structure as soon as you are prepared to outline your intent, then you might avoid any last-minute problems.

Additionally, contemplating possible structures for the deal will give you a good idea of your financial position and that of the company after the deal is consummated. One of the most important considerations you will have as a buyer is whether there will be adequate working capital in the business after the acquisition. The structure of the deal will affect this, particularly when the stock of an incorporated business is purchased. If you are to provide working capital for the business, outlining structure ahead of time will allow you to decide whether the deal is feasible for you financially. It would be a shame to purchase a business only to run out of cash during the second month of your ownership because you did not properly structure the deal.

THE IMPORTANCE OF PRICE VERSUS TERMS

If someone were to offer you $1,000 for the shirt you are wearing, would you accept his or her offer? Most of us would jump at the chance. However, what if the $1,000 would be paid out over 1,000 years? The deal is not as appealing. This example, while probably both extreme and simplistic, demonstrates an important point: the terms under which a sale is consummated are often more important than the amount of the sale itself.

When evaluating the terms of a deal, you should consider the price paid, how it will be paid, and the duration and interest rate on any seller financing. All of these variables can be tailored to your needs and those of the seller. You can also use them as negotiating points if the seller is unwilling to yield on the actual dollar figure assigned to the sale.

Price is usually the most visible and explicitly negotiated aspect of the purchase agreement. Buyers and sellers often focus on one number—what they can pay or are willing to accept, respectively—and feverishly negotiate to get the other party to concede. The buyer usually wants to minimize either the total amount paid for the business or the cash required to consummate the deal. By carefully structuring the deal, however, many buyers can achieve a price that is both acceptable to the seller and advantageous to them. A number of methods exist for accomplishing this. Two of the most common are the earn-out and seller financing.

In an earn-out, a portion of the purchase price depends on the future performance of the business. Suppose a seller is asking $400,000 and, based on your financial analysis, you have determined that this is a fair price as long as the business meets projections in the next three years. Make a portion of the purchase price, perhaps $100,000, dependent on the performance of the business. This would both reduce the cash required to complete the deal and eliminate some of your future risk. By including an earn-out, you also delay the payment of a portion of the price.

Seller financing is another popular means of structuring a deal and is used in approximately 90 percent of deals completed today. With seller financing, the seller takes back a portion of the purchase price in the form of a loan or promissory note. This minimizes the amount of cash required and allows you to pay for a portion of the business in the future.

If the seller is willing to finance part of the purchase, the financing instrument you choose will generally be paid out at a certain rate over a certain length of time. By negotiating these two parameters, you can effectively alter the price of the business as measured in today's dollars.

For example, a seller might accept a non–interest-bearing note for the portion of the purchase that is seller-financed. If a seller is asking $200,000 and agrees to accept a $100,000 down payment plus $50,000 per year for the following two years, assuming a 10 percent discount rate, you have effectively only paid ~$187,000 ($100,000 plus the present value of the two years of cash flow). So, by offering the seller $200,000 with a portion paid out over two years at zero interest, you have reduced the effective price of the business by $13,000.

Most sellers will seek a short payback schedule and a high interest rate for any seller financing. As the above example illustrates, as a buyer you should seek a long repayment period and a low interest rate. By doing so, you can minimize your costs.

Keep in mind that if the interest rate that you offer on seller financing is lower than that available in the open market, the seller would be better off demanding cash than financing your purchase of the business. For instance, what if you offer to buy a business for $500,000 paid over ten years at an interest rate of 5 percent, but the seller can make 7.5 percent by investing cash in government bonds or treasury bills? The seller would much rather receive cash, because the sum of the difference in payments implied by a 2.5 percent difference in interest rates over ten years is quite significant!

Another method for deferring payment is to promise the seller a portion of the future profits of the business. For instance, you might offer a cash down payment plus 10 percent of the profits of the business for the next three years. This arrangement worked very well for an entrepreneur who purchased a publishing company. The seller agreed to accept a small down payment plus a portion of the future profits of the business. Without this arrangement, the deal would not have been possible for the buyer, who did not have access to a lot of cash.

When you are structuring the purchase of a business, consider the many ways that you can offer a price with which the owner is comfortable, yet also allow terms that make the deal work for you. Some options might be:

- to stretch out the duration of a note payable to the seller;
- to negotiate a below-market interest rate on the loan; or
- to rent the facility from the owner at below-market rates.

By structuring these aspects of the deal with care, you can often satisfy the seller's requirements while also minimizing both the amount of cash required for the deal and your risk.

WHAT SHOULD I BUY? ASSETS VERSUS STOCK

One of the most fundamental decisions in a business acquisition is whether to purchase the assets or the stock. If the stock of a business is purchased, everything the business owns (and owes) becomes the property of the new owner of the stock. This implies that all assets of the company transfer along with all liabilities. If the assets of a business are purchased, only title to those assets transfers to the new owner, not the liabilities of the business.

Buyers and sellers have distinctly different motivations in attempting to structure a purchase. Most owners want to sell the stock of the business. This usually releases them from liability for past actions of the company. Additionally, if stock is sold, the seller has only one level of tax to pay—a capital gains tax on the difference between the sale price of the stock and its original basis. (The capital gains rates may influence the desire of the seller to sell either stock or assets.)

In contrast, the buyer generally prefers to purchase the assets of the business. This allows him to avoid liability for past actions of the company. Sellers generally dislike this arrangement, because they maintain liability for the past actions of the company and must pay two tiers of tax on the sale. First the company pays a tax on the sale of the assets; then the company makes a liquidating distribution to the shareholder—the owner—who must pay tax on the dividend (assuming a gain).

The following section discusses strategies for acquiring either the assets or stock of a business. The first case treated is that of the sole proprietorship, which does not have stock, but does have assets and goodwill. The next section discusses the purchase of businesses that have been incorporated and the advantages and disadvantages of each method.

Many small businesses are sole proprietorships and thus have neither a corporate charter nor stock. In these cases, the owner can only transfer the assets of the business or goodwill. A payment by you personally to the owner will simply be a payment for the right to take over the business and will not be deductible either by you or by the ongoing business. You will have made the payment out of your own personal after-tax dollars.

If you form a company with your capital and then purchase the business from the owner, the effect is much the same, as your holding company will have simply purchased the assets or goodwill of the business. With the sole proprietorship, title to these assets can be transferred by the owner.

Before the Tax Reform Act of 1986, assets could be purchased and "written-up" to fair market value without incurring a tax liability. Under current law, if the assets are written-up in value after the purchase, a tax will be paid by the purchaser. Therefore, you should seek the seller's agreement on value (and hence price paid) for each asset. It is risky to value assets at much above their fair market value, as the IRS may hold that amounts paid over the fair market value are attributable to goodwill. Therefore, don't be too aggressive in valuing assets; all or part of the remainder of the purchase price could be allocated to either a noncompete agreement, a consulting contract or a customer list (which we discuss later), providing you with the tax-deductible expenses.

If a business is incorporated, the choice of what to purchase becomes more complex. Not only are there financial considerations, there are legal issues as well. In addition, you now will be dealing with a corporation with at least one and perhaps many shareholders. Purchase of either the stock or assets of the business may require a vote of the shareholders, depending on the nature of the sale (liquidating versus nonliquidating) and the form of conveyance (stock, cash or other).

Purchasing assets from an incorporated business can be attractive because it enables you to write-up the value of the assets, which will provide you with subsequent depreciation. Also, you may still have either noncompete agreements or consulting arrangements with one or several stockholders. If you buy the stock of the corporation, you will have to make an election to "step-up" (increase) the value of the assets, thus incurring a sizable tax liability.

While buying the stock may be attractive because it will save you the expense of setting up your own corporation, there is an excellent reason to avoid such an arrangement. When you purchase the stock of a company, you also assume all past, present and future liabilities incurred by the business. As the owner, you could lose all the assets and earnings of the business if a judgment is levied against the company.

Let's say, for example, you purchase all the stock of a small paint company that appears to be well-run. Two years after the purchase, a lawsuit is filed against the company for improperly disposing of toxic waste 15 years earlier. Your first reaction may be that you are not liable, as you had nothing to do with the company then. However, if you own the stock of the company, the company is liable. This does not mean that you are personally liable, but all of the company's assets are at risk.

Hence you should adopt the following rule: buy assets, not liabilities!

ALLOCATION OF PURCHASE PRICE

Many people think about buying a business but do not think about what they will actually be getting for their money. An ongoing business consists of many things—customers, inventory, products, processes, employees, suppliers and so on. While all these things are components of the business, the problem for you as a buyer arises when you attempt to allocate the price you are willing to pay to the various components of the business. Your main concern is how payments to the owner will affect the financial condition of the business after it has changed hands. You should allocate as much of the purchase price as is reasonable (and legal) to items that are deductible as business expenses. This increases the value of the business to you by decreasing the amount of taxes that will be paid from profits. Certain expenses, such as depreciation and interest, are often referred to as "tax shields," because their payment results in less tax being paid by the business. While we cannot stress enough the importance of adhering to both state and federal tax law, you should take advantage of those provisions that are advantageous to you as a buyer.

The purchase of a business is one of the events that can cause a "resetting" of tax shields. In the leveraged-buyout craze of the 1980s, buyers found that businesses were worth more when debt was used for the purchase than when the company had only equity. Tax shields offered by the interest payments on debt increased the value. Likewise, when a business is purchased, the buyer is able to reestablish the value of its assets, thus providing tax shields on future depreciation. While the technical details differ in each case, this is true with both asset and stock purchases.

When the stock of a company is purchased, it is transferred to the new owner for some consideration—usually cash or notes equivalent in value to the agreed-upon sale price of the business. The company will have some stock value assigned on the balance sheet based on the par-value at issue and additional paid-in capital by the owner. This establishes the basis of the owner's stock. When you buy the business, you will establish a new basis for the stock, which will be retained until you in turn either sell the stock or liquidate the company. In most cases, the amount you pay for the stock will be in excess of the owner's basis. The implication of this is that the value over and above the book value of the company (assets less liabilities) will be attributed to goodwill.

Consider the following example using the summarized balance sheet of a fictional industrial supply company. Assume that all the owner's equity represents par-value of the stock or additional paid-in capital (i.e., there are no retained earnings) and that the business is to be sold for $150,000. In this case, owner's equity will increase by

$70,000 and, barring alternatives, the amount of the purchase over the value of the assets will need to be attributed to goodwill:

	Pre-Acquisition	*Post-Acquisition*
Assets	$100,000	$100,000
Goodwill	0	70,000
Liabilities	20,000	20,000
Owner's equity	80,000	150,000

Under current law, goodwill is considered an intangible asset without a demonstrable useful life. The IRS has held that intangible assets that do not have a demonstrable life cannot be gradually depleted, or amortized.

If the $70,000 were allocated to equipment with a seven-year useful life, the equipment could be depreciated over seven years, implying a legitimate business expense of $10,000 per year for each of the seven years. This would create a tax shield decreasing the profits of the business and would not require a cash payment by the business—it is a noncash expense. If the $70,000 were allocated to goodwill, it could not be depreciated at all under current tax law.

As of June 1992, the U.S. Senate was considering a tax provision that would allow goodwill to be amortized over 16 years. The House of Representatives was also exploring ways for goodwill and other intangible assets to be amortized. If such a tax provision is enacted into law, the effect on business acquisitions will be significant, but more so in the stimulation of greater acquisition activity than in the structure of deals. With a 16-year amortization period, goodwill will still be one of the least desirable components to which to assign value in a business purchase. A 16-year amortization period is longer than the depreciation period of almost all assets and offers less control to the buyer than noncompete, employment or consulting agreements.

In the transaction above, in addition to goodwill arising from the transaction, the value of assets did not change. The book value of the assets may be below their fair market value. If so, it would be advantageous to the buyer to write-up the value of the assets to fair market value, thus providing greater future tax shields. This is one disadvantage of the stock purchase. In a stock purchase, the value of the assets will remain the same unless the new owner makes an election to step-up their value, which could trigger a tax liability because of past depreciation taken (known as "recapture"). If the buyer does elect to step-up the basis of assets, he will be afforded future tax benefits but will incur a current tax liability.

In the case of the sole proprietorship, the sale of assets is the only title transfer that can occur. In this case, the basis of the assets is automatically stepped-up to reflect the purchase price of the business. However, the new basis of the assets should not exceed their fair market value. In such a transaction, the seller will realize a gain on the sale of the assets in the amount of the difference between the selling price and the old basis of the assets. The buyer does not incur a tax liability by stepping-up the basis of the assets, as this is achieved without election by the buyer.

You can also purchase the assets of a corporation. This allows the buyer to establish a new basis for the assets, which would be the lower of fair market value or the total price paid for the assets. However, remember the two levels of taxation that occur when a corporation sells its assets: the corporation's tax liability on any gain realized in the sale, and the shareholder's (the owner's) tax liability when the proceeds from the asset sale are distributed. While this is not true in all situations (such as if the corporation has declared Subchapter S status), it is usually the case in the sale of corporate assets. Depending on the structure of the business to be sold, there will generally be a preferred method of structuring the deal in terms of tax liabilities for both buyer and seller and in terms of the basis of assets after the purchase.

No matter what the structure of the entity to be sold, one main consideration almost always arises as a result of the sale: the price paid for the business is generally above the fair market value of the assets. To what should this excess value be attributed? For example, if you are going to buy a business for $1 million and the fair market value of the assets is $400,000, what is being purchased for the remaining $600,000? First of all, writing-up the value of the assets from their depreciated value to fair market value will allow you to depreciate them over their useful lives. But if the remaining $600,000 is allocated to goodwill, the intangible value of the business, then it will have to be capitalized and will, for tax purposes, remain on the books at its original value for the life of the business (for accounting purposes, goodwill may be amortized over 40 years).

To what do you allocate the remaining $600,000 of the purchase price? Ideally, the buyer would like to assign value in excess of the fair market value of assets to items that are depreciable or can be written off as expenses of the business. Three items are commonly used for this purpose: agreements not to compete, consulting or employment contracts and customer lists. The first two are contracts rather than assets; you pay the owner an agreed-upon amount for his fulfillment of a contract. This amount can be paid in one lump sum when the business is acquired or as a series of payments. The third item, the customer list, is an actual asset of the business and thus is included as part of the bill of sale.

When considering the use of these components in an acquisition, keep in mind that few businesses truly have *no* goodwill. If your deal structure were to be challenged by the IRS, the absence of any goodwill at all in the purchase of an ongoing business might seem curious. Thus, consider allocating some value to goodwill. A deal structure that makes sense from all aspects will be much easier to defend should the need arise.

NONCOMPETE CLAUSES

One of the most common elements included in the purchase agreement of a business acquisition is the noncompete clause (Figure 11.1). A noncompete clause is basically a contractual agreement by the seller not to compete directly or indirectly with the business that he or she has just sold. The purpose of a noncompete clause is to protect you, the buyer, from having the owner sell the existing business to you, then start an identical business shortly thereafter, taking substantially all of the customers and/or employees of the existing business. Another useful aspect of the noncompete clause is that it can be written off as an expense of the ongoing business by amortizing the value of the contract over its life or by making periodic payments to the seller.

FIGURE 11.1 Restrictive Covenant Agreement

THIS RESTRICTIVE COVENANT AGREEMENT is made this _____ between _____, _____ corporation with offices at _____ (hereinafter called the "Company"), _____, of _____ (hereinafter called "Seller"), and _____ of _____ (hereinafter collectively called "Purchaser").

WITNESSETH:

WHEREAS, pursuant to a Purchase Agreement dated _____, all of the shares of the Company owned by Seller are being acquired by Purchaser; and

WHEREAS, as a condition to such acquisition, the Seller is required to enter into this Agreement with the Company; and

WHEREAS, the Company and the Purchaser desire to assure themselves that the Seller will not compete with the Company;

NOW, THEREFORE, in consideration of the premises and mutual covenants hereinafter set forth, the parties hereto agree as follows:

1. <u>SELLER WILL NOT COMPETE</u>. During the term hereof and for the entire period of five (5) years from and after the date of closing, in consideration of the compensation set forth in paragraph 2, Seller will not, for any reason whatsoever, engage directly or indirectly in any way either as principal, agent, manager, employee, consultant, owner, partner (dormant or otherwise), lender, stockholder, director, or officer of a corporation, in any business or activity which is competitive with or in the same line or lines of business as any business being conducted by the Company on the date of closing within the state of _____; and during the same period, the Seller will not endeavor to entice away from the Company any customer, employee, or salesman of the Company, whether on the Seller's own behalf or on behalf of another, in either case, unless the Company acting on the authority of its Board of Directors shall have given its prior written consent thereto.

FIGURE 11.1   Restrictive Covenant Agreement (continued)

The Seller does hereby acknowledge that money damages alone would not adequately compensate the Company in the event of breach by the Seller of the foregoing restrictive covenant, and therefore, the Seller does hereby covenant and agree that, in addition to all the other remedies available to the Company at law or in equity, the Company shall be entitled to injunctive relief for the enforcement thereof.

2. <u>PAYMENT</u>. In consideration of this Agreement, the Company hereby agrees to pay Seller the sum of _____, of which _____ shall be paid upon execution of this Agreement and the balance of _____ shall be payable in equal, consecutive, quarterly installments of _____ for a period of _____, the first such payment being due on _____, and thereafter, payments shall be due on the first day of each succeeding quarter until _____. In the event of a default in the payment of the aforesaid installments or in the payment of the consulting payments as provided in a certain Consulting Agreement between the parties of even date herewith, which default shall continue for a period of 15 days, then the entire amount of the remaining installments shall be immediately due and payable without further notice or demand. The Company further agrees to pay any and all costs of collection, including reasonable attorney's fees, incurred in any action to collect the aforesaid payments.

3. <u>GUARANTY</u>. The payment of quarterly installments and all other obligations provided in paragraph 2 is hereby personally guaranteed by the Purchaser. In accordance therewith, _____ is hereafter joined in the execution and delivery of this Agreement for the express purpose of being personally liable, jointly and severally, for the performance of the said obligations and payment of indebtedness as hereinabove provided. Guarantors will not cause a sale of a substantial portion of the assets of the Company nor transfer more than forty (40) percent of the outstanding stock of the company without first paying the entire amount of the remaining installments due hereunder.

4. <u>SEVERABILITY</u>. It is the intention of the parties that the provisions of this Agreement and particularly paragraph 1 hereof shall be enforceable to the fullest extent permissible under applicable law, but that the unenforceability or modification to conform to such law of any provision or

FIGURE 11.1 Restrictive Covenant Agreement (continued)

provisions hereof shall not render unenforceable or impair the remainder thereof. If any provision or provisions hereof shall be deemed invalid or unenforceable, either in whole or in part, this Agreement shall be deemed amended to modify, as necessary, or if modification is not feasible, to delete the offending provision or provisions and to alter the bounds thereof in order to render it valid and enforceable.

5. <u>WITHHOLDING AND OFFSET</u>. In the event the Purchaser claims a right to indemnification as provided in the Stock Purchase Agreement, then, after 15 days' written notice to the Seller, in addition to any other rights and remedies which Purchaser or the Company may have, the Company may withhold payments next due Seller under this Agreement in an interest-bearing escrow account and shall pay the withheld amount with interest upon final determination as provided in the Stock Purchase Agreement, and Purchaser shall further have the right of offset equal to the amount of the claim so determined as provided in the Stock Purchase Agreement.

IN WITNESS WHEREOF, this Agreement has been duly executed by the parties as of the date first written above.

By _____
Its _____
_____

While it may seem unlikely that the owner will have the energy or desire to start over in the same business (especially in the case of older or retiring owners), it does happen. Often the owner will tell you that he or she only wants to sell the business in order to retire and have nothing but free time. However, in many cases the owner has spent years building the business, and it is difficult for him or her to realize the void that will result. In some cases, the owner will have planned for retirement and be prepared to go without the business in day-to-day activities. In other cases, the owner may be happy spending time on the golf course for a short period, then decide that he or she really misses the excitement and satisfaction of running a business. If the owner returns to that line of business, you will have a very experienced competitor who not only knows more about the business than you, but also must compete against you for his livelihood.

While retiring owners have been used as an example here, the same thing can happen with sellers who are young but give you assurances that they are "quitting the business" or have no interest in being involved. We know of one instance in which a buyer bought a government-document expediting service, only to have the seller go into competition with the buyer within six months of the sale despite the existence of a noncompete clause. This situation is best avoided, so the inclusion and proper structuring of a noncompete clause should be a paramount consideration in the structure of a business sale.

The terms of the noncompete agreement are mutually agreed upon by the buyer and seller and should be explicitly stated either in a clause of the purchase agreement or in a separately executed contract. The tax courts have consistently upheld that if the covenant is not explicitly agreed upon and the terms noted, the costs to the buyer may not be deductible as business expenses. The most important elements of the agreement are the duration, scope and conveyance. These elements outline the protection you will receive as a buyer, as well as the compensation the seller will receive. The courts examine duration and scope when determining whether a covenant not to compete is enforceable. In most states, for the noncompete covenant to be enforceable, it must be reasonable in both duration and scope.

The duration specifies the amount of time for which the seller will not compete with the business. Duration will depend to a large degree on the nature of the business, the number of customers, the customer turnover and the knowledge required to compete in the business. A noncompete clause cannot have an indefinite period for two reasons. First, federal and state governments prefer competition among businesses. This is best for the consumer in terms of price and service (assuming an "open market" is best for the consumer). Second, the noncompete clause must be valued for purposes of the purchase, and for tax reasons the clause, like other depreciable assets, must have a useful life in order to be valued.

You should choose a duration for the noncompete clause that is reasonable relative to the seller, industry, business and competitive environment. An example of an unreasonable noncompete clause might be one that restricts the owner for 25 years when the owner is already 82 years old. Statistically, it is not very likely that this owner will be competing with the business in even 10 years, regardless of the absence or presence of a clause.

The scope of the noncompete clause defines the geographical areas and lines of business in which the seller agrees not to compete. The geographical area is usually specified relative to the business to be purchased. For example, if you were buying a glass distributor in Salt Lake City that sold products throughout the Rocky Mountain region (i.e., Denver and Cheyenne), you would want to make sure that the noncompete clause covered not only Salt Lake City but also the other cities in which the business was active. Sometimes the geographical scope will be defined as an area surrounding the business—i.e., within ten square miles. If a company is doing business on a worldwide basis, then it is reasonable to ask the seller not to compete anywhere in the world.

The line of business specified will, in the most simple case, be the principal line of the existing business to be sold. However, you may want to specify other lines that you feel are close substitutes or are closely related to the business and represent possible areas of expansion. For example, if you were buying an industrial printing shop, you might want to specify that the seller is not only restricted from competing in industrial printing, but he is also restricted from competing in commercial printing, which represents an area you would like to pursue.

The conveyance specified for the noncompete agreement is simply what you give to the seller as consideration for agreeing not to compete with the business. Because the noncompete agreement compensates the seller for giving up the business, the consideration given is often cash. However, there are no limitations as to what must be conveyed to the seller, as long as it has value (e.g., stock, assets of the business). If the consideration given does not have value, the tax courts might disallow the noncompete agreement and allocate its assigned value to goodwill.

The important thing to remember in structuring a noncompete clause is that it should protect you, the buyer, from having the seller destroy or diminish in value any part of the business that you have purchased. The noncompete clause should serve to protect the goodwill of the business. While this is the objective for the buyer, it should be emphasized that in terms of public policy, noncompete clauses may be undesirable if they restrict competition and free commerce in the state. Again, the test most courts would apply is whether the covenant is reasonable in both scope and duration. If it is not, it does not mean that the clause is illegal; it only means that you may not be able to enforce it if the seller does indeed decide to start or join a competing business.

Prior to the Tax Reform Act of 1986, sellers were reluctant to enter into noncompete agreements, because the tax code stated that amounts received by the seller in return for such agreements were considered ordinary income. This is in contrast to goodwill, on which the seller would recognize either a capital gain or loss (most likely a gain). Prior to 1986, the tax rate for capital gains was 20 percent, while that for ordinary income was as high as 70 percent. Thus most owners strongly preferred to sell the goodwill of a business.

The Tax Reform Act of 1986 made the the top personal income rate and the capital gains rate approximately the same. As of 1992, the capital gains rate was 28 percent and the top personal income rate was 31 percent, so sellers now are not as concerned about the classification of part of the selling price as an agreement not to compete.

As the tax laws governing capital gains and ordinary income tax rates change, there may be changes in the motivation of both buyers and sellers in business acquisitions. It would be wise to stay abreast of potential changes by maintaining a close relationship with a tax professional or by reviewing the tax column in the Wednesday edition of *The Wall Street Journal*.

CONSULTING AND EMPLOYMENT CONTRACTS

Often one of the most valuable assets of many small businesses is the owner. As a buyer, it will be in your best interest not only to prevent the seller from competing with you, but also to keep him involved in the operations of the business. There are two popular methods of accomplishing this: the owner can remain a part of the active management of the business either for a definite or indefinite period of time, or the owner can act as a consultant to you and the business.

If the owner would like to play an active role in the business, it is up to you as the buyer to determine what that role will be; once the business formally changes hands, you will be the previous owner's boss. Consider this as you structure the seller's future involvement. He or she may not appreciate being managed, particularly in "his" or "her" business. Retaining the owner as an employee or contractor could be valuable; you can direct his or her efforts to those areas of the business that you feel are strong, and direct your own attentions to those that you feel need a fresh or different perspective. It may be difficult, however, for the owner to participate only in certain aspects of something that he or she has nurtured throughout the years.

The period of time for which the previous owner is involved is up to you. You may wish to have the owner there for a minimum of three months, then available on an as-needed basis. It is advisable to have the owner involved for at least a month, depending on the complexity of the business. Make sure you have an agreement as to the period of time for which the owner stays on, either paid or unpaid. Otherwise you may be surprised, as was one entrepreneur we know of. He had a longstanding working relationship with the owner of an industrial printing business, and after much thought and discussion with the owner, he decided to purchase it. After all the formalities were taken care of, he went to the office for his first day, expecting that the owner would at least help him get started. Unfortunately, when he arrived the owner simply handed him the keys to the building and walked out!

In order to keep the owner involved, you can make some of the down payment money contingent on his or her participation for a specified period of time. You can place the money in escrow for a certain period after closing—perhaps 60 days. As long as the seller meets conditions specified in the purchase contract, the money can be taken out of escrow.

Sometimes the owner is interested in selling either to reap the rewards of having built the business or simply to eliminate the personal responsibility of being the owner, but is not necessarily interested in quitting. If this is the case, you may be interested in keeping the owner on as a full-time manager. As the new owner, you can make changes as you see fit, but you will not need to devote your attention to day-to-day management issues.

One very successful entrepreneur employed this type of arrangement when purchasing an electrical contracting business in the southwest. The seller's health was deteriorating as a result of the pressures of owning the business, but he was not ready to step out completely. The buyer purchased the business and assumed responsibility for management of the overall business; the seller was able to maintain an active role as president. The seller was extremely happy with the new arrangement and returned to good health shortly after selling the business. The business prospered with the experience of the previous owner, and the new buyer was able to better manage the broader issues of the business.

Often the owner wants to sell, but not immediately. This can be beneficial to both you, as the buyer, and the owner. It may give you the opportunity to work in the business for a predetermined amount of time—perhaps one year—then have an option to buy the business at a previously agreed-upon price. If the business is not what you hoped for, you can walk away. If it is still attractive, you will have gained at least cursory knowledge of most aspects and will be better prepared to take over as the new owner.

The above examples represent methods of keeping the seller actively involved with the business. Sometimes the seller simply wants to walk away, as in the example of the industrial printing business above. While you may be able to handle most issues that arise, it is strongly advisable that you not let the seller walk away without any obligation to you or the business.

The most common method of keeping the seller involved on a passive basis is to include in the sales contract a consulting agreement for the seller (Figure 11.2). Such agreements generally specify that the seller will be available for a minimum number of hours per week or month as a consultant to the business.

In one acquisition, the buyers structured a deal so that one of the previous owners retained 10 percent of the stock in the company. They also entered into a consulting agreement with him. As a result of this arrangement, the seller had incentive to stay involved with the business and had a stake in its future success. The business is prospering and the former owner has been able to make significant contributions, particularly during the transition stage.

Consulting agreements are excellent for you as a buyer because, while the seller is available when necessary, you are able to take control of the business immediately. Additionally, payments to the seller for consulting services are an expense of the business, making them very attractive from a tax standpoint. The payment to the seller could be in one lump sum or paid out over a number of periods.

Like the noncompete agreement, consulting arrangements became much more attractive to sellers with the adjustment of the capital gains and personal income tax rates in 1986. However, like the covenant not to compete, the terms of the consulting agreement must be specified explicitly either in the sales contract or in a stand-alone contract for the consideration paid to be classified as an expense of the business for tax purposes. If the consulting agreement is not found to be valid, amounts paid under it (in excess of the net worth of the business) will be considered goodwill.

In summary, you should do whatever possible to keep the seller involved in the business for some period of time following your acquisition. The seller is one of the most valuable assets of many businesses, and ongoing involvement even after the sale is completed will greatly enhance your chances for success. Including such an arrangement is often advantageous from a tax standpoint, as expenses paid to the seller as a consultant or an employee are usually deductible as business expenses. Such arrangements help you minimize the portion of the purchase price that must be allocated to goodwill.

FIGURE 11.2   Consulting Agreement

This consulting agreement is made this _____ day of _____,
between _____, a _____ corporation with offices at _____ (hereinafter called the "Company"),
and _____ of _____ (herein-
after called "Consultant").

WITNESSETH:

WHEREAS, pursuant to a Stock Purchase Agreement of even date, all
of the shares of the Company owned by Seller are being acquired by
_____; and

WHEREAS, as a condition to such acquisition, the Consultant is
required to enter into this Consulting Agreement with the Company; and

WHEREAS, the Company desires to assure itself of the continuance
of the Consultant's technical, marketing, and operation guidance, expertise, and advice;

NOW, THEREFORE, in consideration of the premises and mutual
covenants hereinafter set forth, the parties hereto agree as follows:

1. ENGAGEMENT. The Company hereby engages Consultant, and
Consultant hereby accepts said engagement as a consultant, to provide
technical, marketing, and operational guidance, service, and advice to and
for the Company's employees and business as provided herein for a term
of one year following the date of closing of the sale of his stock to the
Purchasers.

2. DUTIES. Consultant agrees to be available by telephone to the
Company and its employees during normal business hours throughout the
entire one-year term of this consultancy. Consultant agrees that unless
otherwise excused by the Company, he will be required to be physically
present at the business premises to render his services for not more than
thirty-five (35) hours per week during the first month of the consultancy.

Consultant shall also assist the Company in the collection of those
accounts receivable which existed on the date of closing to the extent that
any such accounts are more than ninety (90) days old.

FIGURE 11.2 Consulting Agreement (continued)

3. <u>ADVISORY COMPENSATION</u>. During the term of consultancy, Consultant shall receive for all services to be rendered to the Company a one-year advisory compensation fee of _____ payable as follows:

a. Payable upon the signing of this Agreement........

b. Payable in equal installments............................

4. <u>EXPENSES</u>. Consultant is authorized to incur reasonable expenses for operating and promoting the business, reputation, and goodwill of the Company including expenses for entertainment, automobile, travel and similar items so long as such expenses are preapproved by the Company. When Consultant is traveling on engagements and trips devoted to the Company's business, goodwill and reputation, Consultant is expected to render bills for transportation, communications, hotel accommodations, meals, entertainment and the like, all of which shall be paid by the Company as expense items. Further, the Company shall reimburse Consultant for all such expenses upon presentation thereof by Consultant to the Company from time to time of an itemized account of such expenditures.

5. <u>NONDISCLOSURE</u>. The Consultant expressly covenants and agrees that he will not, at any time during or after any termination of this Agreement, reveal, divulge or make known to any person, firm or corporation any secret or confidential information whatsoever in connection with the Company, any affiliate of the Company, or their respective suppliers or customers or their businesses, or anything connected herewith, including, but not limited to, copyrights, production or testing data, financial information, trade secrets, processes, formulae, know-how, improvements, inventions, applications, engineering and marketing techniques and data, sales and other techniques, customer and prospect lists, sales know-how and product information, and Consultant agrees to refrain from using any such information other than in the course of the Consultant's activities as a consultant of the Company and from disclosing such information to anyone (other than authorized personnel of the Company) without the Company's prior written consent.

FIGURE 11.2   Consulting Agreement (continued)

6. CONSULTANT'S REPRESENTATIONS AND WARRANTIES. The Consultant represents and warrants that he is not a party to or otherwise subject to or bound by the terms of any contract, agreement or understanding which in any manner would limit or otherwise affect his ability to perform his obligations hereunder. The Consultant further represents and warrants that his consultancy with the Company will not require him to disclose or use any confidential or proprietary information belonging to other persons or entities.

The Consultant represents that his experience and capabilities are such that the provisions of this Agreement will not prevent him from earning his livelihood and he acknowledges that it would cause the Company serious and irreparable harm not compensable in monetary damages if the Consultant were to otherwise breach the obligations contained in this Agreement.

7. TERMINATION. It is understood and agreed that this Agreement may be terminated by the Company in the event Consultant violates his covenant of nondisclosure, violates the provisions of paragraph 5, or refuses to render reasonable advisory or consulting services as herein provided. In such a case, upon 15 days prior written notice to Consultant, the Company shall have the right to refuse to pay any monies due the Consultant hereunder and shall have the additional right to offset against any monies due Consultant under a Restrictive Covenant Agreement provided under the Stock Purchase Agreement of _____.

It is understood and agreed that this Agreement may be terminated by the Consultant in the event the Company, without cause, refuses or fails to pay any quarterly installment of the advising compensation fee or quarterly payments due under the aforementioned Restrictive Covenant Agreement within FIFTEEN (15) days from the date that it is due. In such a case, the entire balance of the installments shall become immediately due and payable without further notice or demand, and such sum shall accrue interest at the rate of _____ annum.

8. MODIFICATION. This Agreement may only be modified or amended by a writing executed by Consultant and the Company.

FIGURE 11.2 Consulting Agreement (continued)

9. ASSIGNABILITY AND BINDING EFFECT. This Agreement shall not be assignable by Consultant but shall be binding upon and inure to the benefit of any successors or assigns of the Company.

10. SEVERABILITY. It is the intention of the parties that the provisions of this Agreement and particularly paragraph 6 hereof shall be enforceable to the fullest extent permissible under applicable law, but that the unenforceability or modification to conform to such law of any provision or provisions hereof shall not render unenforceable or impair the remainder thereof. If any provision or provisions hereof shall be deemed invalid or unenforceable, either whole or in part, this Agreement shall be deemed amended to modify, as necessary, or if modification is not feasible, to delete the offending provisions and to alter the bounds thereof, in order to render it valid and enforceable.

11. COUNTERPARTS. This Agreement may be executed in duplicate or more counterparts and each of such counterpart shall be deemed an original. Further, it shall be binding upon all of the parties when each party has signed at least one counterpart even though all signatures may not appear on any particular counterpart.

12. ATTORNEY'S FEES, COURT COSTS AND DISBURSEMENTS. In the event that any action is taken by either party to enforce any rights or remedies under this Agreement, it is hereby agreed that the successful or prevailing party shall be entitled to receive any costs, disbursements and reasonable attorney's fees.

13. SALES TAX. The Company agrees to pay the _____ sales tax due in connection with this transaction, which shall be billed separately to the Company by the _____.

IN WITNESS WHEREOF, this Agreement has been duly executed by the parties as of the date first above written.

By _____

Its _____

CONSULTANT

_____

CUSTOMER LISTS

Placing value on a customer list is not as popular as the use of either noncompete agreements or consulting contracts, but it is a perfectly legal and accepted method for allocating part of the purchase price to something other than goodwill. It is more difficult to demonstrate the value and/or useful life of a customer list than the other items discussed. For this reason, even if an asset such as a customer list does have an assignable value, it may be difficult to depreciate or amortize it. In a number of cases the U.S. Tax Court has ruled that customer lists are depreciable assets. In the words of the U.S. Tax Code: "The depreciability of assets of [an intangible] nature is a factual question, the determination of which rests on whether the taxpayer establishes that the assets (1) have an ascertainable value separate and distinct from goodwill, and (2) have a limited useful life, the duration of which can be ascertained with reasonable accuracy."

Examples of those cases in which the taxpayer has been able to prove both distinct value and limited useful life of a customer list include that of a laundry operation, a linen supply company and a fuel-oil supply business. However, in each of these cases only a portion of the value of the customer list was allowed to be depreciated, as the taxpayer was unable to prove that the entire list would lose its value over time.

As with the agreement not to compete and the consulting contract, it is important to include the assignment of value to the customer list as a point of discussion in striking a deal with the seller, and to include an agreed-upon amount and useful life in the sales contract. While this will not expose the seller to any liability, the fact that it was discussed in the negotiation of the sale will significantly enhance your chances of successfully defending depreciation deductions taken against it. Payments to the seller in consideration of a customer list will be part of the purchase, and following the acquisition the customer list will be an asset of the business.

SAMPLE DEAL STRUCTURES

There are many options when it comes to structuring a small business acquisition. There are numerous legal and tax-related considerations, and tools such as the noncompete agreement and consulting contract add another level of complexity. The eventual structure of an acquisition is arrived at only by examining different scenarios for the particular business at hand. In addition to your own wishes regarding structure, you will need to consider the needs of the seller. He or she may not even be aware of things like noncompete clauses and consulting contracts. The deal structure that you propose may be radically different from that which is necessary to consummate the deal. The important thing is for you to be aware of various options and how their use will affect your eventual ownership of the business. As long as you are aware of these considerations, you can make an informed decision regarding the structure of the deal and its effect on both you and the seller.

The following hypothetical examples of deal structure will help demonstrate some of the concepts discussed in this chapter. Each scenario considers the organization and nature of the business to be acquired, the age and financial needs of the seller, and the financial condition of the buyer.

SCENARIO 1

Type of Business: Valve manufacturing shop; sole proprietorship

Owner Profile: Retiring after sale; has substantial retirement fund

Buyer Profile: Leaving job to purchase, has $100,000 for down payment

Financial Details: Agreed-upon price of $350,000; fair market value of assets, $225,000

■ ■ ■

In this business, a sole proprietorship, it is only possible to purchase the assets; stock does not exist. The buyer, therefore, should be able to escape liability for past actions of the business. Of the purchase price, $225,000 can be attributed to the assets, providing future tax shields from depreciation. The seller might consider making a down payment of $75,000, securing outside financing of $100,000 against the assets of the business, and asking the seller to finance the remaining $175,000. Of the $125,000 that cannot be attributed to assets, the buyer might allocate $25,000 to a noncompete agreement and pay the owner $25,000 per year for four years as a consultant, assuming both of these sums are reasonable when the business is considered. The remaining $25,000 could be attributed to goodwill. ▪

SCENARIO 2

Type of Business: Wholesale food distributor; incorporated

Owner Profile: Interested in starting new business; high tax-bracket; will not sell assets

Buyer Profile: Young, borrowing most of down payment of $50,000 from friends and family

Financial Details: Agreed-upon price of $190,000; book value of assets, $40,000; fair market value of assets, $75,000 (much of which is inventory)

▪ ▪ ▪

If the buyer is intent on buying this business, there are a few things he or she will have to accept. The seller will not sell assets, so the buyer will have to be content with a stock sale and try, during due diligence, to uncover any liabilities that might exist. The buyer is also making a down payment of slightly more than 25 percent of the purchase price, so his or her bargaining position may not be as strong as it could be if the down payment were larger. The buyer might consider borrowing money against the inventory of the business to increase the down payment. In terms of components to include in the deal, a noncompete clause is almost essential. With the seller interested in starting a new business, the buyer needs to protect the business being purchased. After the purchase, only $40,000 can be attributed to the assets, so the buyer should seek to assign significant value to the noncompete agreement, and might also consider offering the seller a consulting or employment contract. Because the tax implications of the noncompete agreement, gain on sale and employment contract are similar, the seller should not be averse to any of these. Assigning value to a customer list might also be explored in this deal. A wholesale food distributor most likely has fairly steady customers, which makes a good case for assigning value to the customer base. ■

SCENARIO 3

Type of Business: Retail gift shop, two locations; incorporated

Owner Profile: Tired of being a business owner; some need for immediate cash

Buyer Profile: Experienced entrepreneur has made other acquisitions; adequate liquidity to purchase for all cash

Financial Details: Agreed-upon price, $175,000; fair-market value of assets, $80,000

■ ■ ■

The buyer in this case might consider offering the seller an employment contract; the seller may be tired of owning a business, but could be willing to continue managing the business. If the buyer is an experienced entrepreneur, absentee ownership might be appropriate for managing this acquisition. In terms of deal structure, the buyer should seek to purchase assets, assuming the buyer is not completely opposed to this. Remember that it is almost always preferable to buy assets rather than stock, even in the case of an incorporated business. By buying the assets of the business and writing them up to fair market value, the buyer can benefit from the future tax shields from depreciation.

If the buyer has adequate cash to purchase the business outright, should she necessarily do so? Not always. If the seller is willing to finance a portion of the business at below-market rates, the buyer should consider seller financing. For instance, the buyer might offer $100,000 in cash, $80,000 of which would be for the assets and $20,000 for goodwill. The other $75,000 could be paid out either in fulfillment of a noncompete agreement or as part of an employment contract; this would help the buyer avoid excess goodwill. Depending on which method is used, it might also give the seller a stake in the ongoing operations of the business. ▪

While these examples of deals and possible deal structures are illustrative, they are by no means comprehensive. The types of deals and deal structures that exist are at least as numerous as the different businesses and owners that exist. Each deal will have its own specific considerations, and each seller will have his or her own unique requirements. The best approach is to determine what is acceptable to you in terms of deal structure, and work to reach a mutually beneficial arrangement with the seller. This will help you as a buyer and might make the selling process easier for the seller.

■ **CHAPTER TWELVE** ■

The Letter of Intent

After you locate a business that you want to purchase, your next step is to make an offer. Your offer should be presented to the seller in a letter of intent (see Figure 12.1). A letter of intent specifically states all the material terms of the deal structure. The letter of intent is not a final proposal and will be subject to further negotiations.

Before drafting a letter of intent, you should understand the seller's motives. What kind of a deal structure will he or she consider reasonable? Propose a deal that accounts for all your needs and as many of the seller's needs as possible. The seller may not receive his or her ideal offer, but will have an opportunity to negotiate.

Once a negotiated agreement is reached, the buyer and seller will have agreed in principle to all material terms of the acquisition.

This chapter will provide prospective purchasers with an understanding of when to use, and what to include in, a letter of intent.

PURPOSE OF LETTERS OF INTENT

A letter of intent is the first formal offer and step toward a preliminary agreement of sale. It outlines a *proposed* purchase arrangement including the price, the terms, what you expect from the owner, and what he can expect from you. It is subject to negotiation and due diligence.

FIGURE 12.1   Letter of Intent

January 2, 1993

Dear _____:

This letter evidences the intent of _____ and/or its Assignee (the "Buyer"), to purchase substantially all of the assets of _____ (the "Company") in accordance with the following provisions:

1. <u>ASSETS TO BE SOLD</u>. All of the assets of _____, as a going concern, including but not limited to machinery, equipment, furniture, fixtures, leasehold improvements, accounts receivable, vehicles, tools, supplies, inventory, work-in-process, the name _____, contract rights, books, records, trade secrets, technical information and general intangibles. Excluded assets will include cash on hand or on deposit and any other assets specifically agreed upon by both parties.

2. <u>PURCHASE PRICE</u>. The purchase price for the assets shall be $ _____ payable in cash on the closing date.

3. <u>LIABILITIES</u>. The sale of the assets shall be made free and clear of any and all liabilities, liens, encumbrances and security interests of every kind, including the security interest of _____; but excepting the liability to _____, which liability the Buyer agrees to assume.

4. <u>CONDITIONS TO CLOSING</u>.

(a) <u>Lease</u>. A satisfactory new lease of the premises must be negotiated between the Buyer and the owner of the premises.

(b) <u>Technical Information Evaluation</u>. A satisfactory evaluation of _____ technical information must be made by the Buyer's engineers and patent attorneys in order to determine technical feasibility and potential exposure for infringement of existing patents.

(c) <u>Environmental Audit</u>. A satisfactory environmental audit of the premises and operations of _____ must be made to determine the presence of hazardous wastes and toxic substances.

FIGURE 12.1   Letter of Intent (continued)

   (d) <u>Employment Agreements</u>. _____ must enter into one
(1) year employment agreements with the Buyer upon mutually acceptable
terms.

   (e) <u>Covenants Not To Compete</u>. _____ must agree that
during your employment with the Buyer and for a period of two (2) years
thereafter you will not compete with the business of the Buyer.

   (f) <u>Assumption of State Loan</u>. The Buyer must be able to assume the
indebtedness to _____.

   5. <u>CLOSING DATE</u>. The closing of this transaction must occur not
later than December 31, 1990.

   6. <u>BULK SALE</u>. The parties agree to comply with the provisions of
the Pennsylvania Bulk Sales Law.

   7. <u>FULL DISCLOSURE</u>. _____ shall make full and complete disclosure to Buyer and its accountants, attorneys and banker of its
business, technical and financial information reasonably required to verify
representations made as to the business and assets to be sold. All such
information shall be held in confidence.

   8. <u>APPROVAL OF TRANSACTION</u>. It is understood that this transaction is subject to the approval of _____, and the Board of
Directors and shareholders of Buyer and _____. Both parties
agree to seek such approvals as soon as possible.

   9. <u>ASSIGNMENT</u>. The Buyer intends to assign this Agreement prior
to closing to a subsidiary corporation to be organized in _____
for the purpose of owning and operating the assets to be acquired from
_____.

   It is understood that both you and we will keep this Letter of Intent
confidential and, except insofar as it may necessarily relate to obtaining
the approvals mentioned above and our due diligence investigation, neither
of us will make any disclosures of the proposed transaction.

FIGURE 12.1   Letter of Intent (continued)

It is further understood that this is a Letter of Intent only and that this Letter of Intent *does not* create a binding obligation upon either the Buyer or _____, which can only arise if and when a definitive Asset Purchase Agreement has been negotiated, reduced to writing, approved by our respective counsel and executed. Such agreement will contain *inter alia,* the representations, warranties, covenants and conditions which are appropriate and usual in transactions of this magnitude.

If you agree with all of the above, please so indicate by dating, signing and returning a copy of this letter, upon receipt of which we will undertake to proceed as rapidly as possible to a closing of this transaction.

Sincerely yours,

The main purpose of a letter of intent is to determine whether you can reach an agreement with the seller about the price and terms of the sale. Use it to discover whether a deal is worth pursuing further before wasting too much time and money in pursuit of the acquisition candidate. If you find that the best deal you can negotiate with the seller is not good enough to justify pursuing the acquisition, focus your energy on searching for another target.

A letter of intent also sends a signal to a business owner that you are serious about buying his or her business. Sellers are more willing to negotiate with a purchaser they believe to be credible and serious; they perceive "shoppers" as a waste of time. Additionally, a letter of intent gives the owner an incentive to provide more information to a prospective purchaser. Some owners will not provide prospective buyers with complete information until they ascertain the buyer's level of commitment.

CONTENT OF LETTERS OF INTENT

The actual content of a letter of intent may vary depending on the needs of the buyer and seller and the type of business being sold. All key terms and issues should be included in the letter of intent, because it will be difficult to bring these items up after you have reached an agreement in principle. Strategically, it may makes sense not to include sensitive issues in the letter of intent. If the seller is immediately put off, he or she may not want to proceed. For example, indemnification clauses or representation and warranty clauses should be only vaguely discussed in the letter of intent and detailed in the purchase agreement. If you go into too much detail in the letter of intent, you may scare the seller out of doing business with you.

You should include the following key issues in a letter of intent:

Structure, Price and Terms

Tax, legal issues and the availability of money determine what deal structure makes sense for the purchaser. The seller has similar concerns, and should know exactly how you intend to structure the deal. That way, the seller and his or her advisers can determine if the proposed deal is satisfactory.

The letter of intent should indicate whether you intend to purchase stock or assets of the business. If you intend to purchase the assets, the letter should state which assets will be purchased and which will not; it should also indicate liabilities to be assumed as well as liabilities that will not.

The letter of intent should also include the price that you propose to pay for the business and the terms of your payments. Specifically, the letter should state:

- how much money will be paid upfront;
- how much will be paid as noncompete, employment or consulting contracts, and under what terms;
- what assets will be pledged as collateral for the seller financing;
- the extent of personal guarantees;
- what money will be held in escrow for earn-outs; and

- how the sales price will vary with the financial position of the company at the time of closing.

You should carefully map out every issue. For example, for an earn-out, where a portion of the purchase price paid to the seller is contingent on the future performance of the company, the letter of intent should state how the performance will be measured (based on profits or gross revenues, etc.); who will audit or verify the financial performance; how much money the purchaser will place in escrow to assure the seller that earn-out purchase money is in a safe place; and what role the seller will play during the evaluation or earn-out period.

Closing Conditions

The closing conditions portion of the letter of intent is extremely important. It should limit the conditions whereby the seller can abandon the sale, while maximizing the purchaser's ability do so. If you cannot obtain financing, or if your due diligence process reveals unforeseen problems with the business, you want to be able to back out of the transaction without violating a legal obligation.

This section should identify what issues the sale is contingent upon. If you must obtain governmental, third-party or internal corporate approvals before the deal can close, state that the sale is dependent on obtaining such approvals. If you need third-party financing, negotiate for a clause stating that the purchase is contingent on your ability to secure the financing needed to consummate the transaction—and state the amount of financing you need to secure.

It is also critical to include a clause stating that the business cannot be altered, and if it is, the purchase price will adjust accordingly. You should stipulate that no increases in compensation will be paid to employees, and that certain key personnel will remain with the company. If you purchase the stock of the company, make certain that the company does not pay dividends between the time of your letter and closing. Also, restrict the company from incurring any new debt, selling assets or depleting inventory. If the value of the company changes between the time you agree upon the price and terms of the sale and the closing of the sale, adjust the deal structure to reflect the current value of the business.

Sellers often want to close the deal as soon as possible; they may want to retire or move or the business may have been on the market a long time. If you have the wherewithal to close the deal quickly, you may have a competitive advantage over other potential purchasers. If so, state in the document when you intend to close—for example, 30 days after executing a purchase agreement. Try not to state specific dates, because you do not have control over how long the negotiations will take.

A seller may ask for a "time is of the essence" clause in the purchase contract. This clause stipulates that the closing must take place by a specific date or else the purchase contract becomes null and void; often the seller must forfeit the deposit. Avoid these clauses if possible. Many factors you cannot control affect when you will close.

Representations, Warranties and Covenants

In general, you should address representations, warranties and covenants in the acquisition agreement and should not include these in the letter of intent. The letter of intent should state this fact and that details will be based on standards for similar transactions.

There are exceptions, however. When a seller makes claims about *critical* components of the business, you should explain how the deal structure will change if his representations are not true. For example, if you are purchasing a retail store that has a great location, the lease terms will be a critical issue; the success of retail stores depends on their location. If the lease expires shortly after the scheduled acquisition and the seller claims he can get the lease renewed before the deal closes, the letter of intent should have a clause that stipulates that if the lease is not renewed, the purchase price will be adjusted accordingly. In such a case, be as specific as possible about the type of adjustment to be made. The best adjustment may require a *holdback,* or holding some of the purchase money in escrow. The amount of money advanced to the seller can depend on the performance of the business in its new location.

If the seller will not agree to a holdback, you could arrive at a reasonable adjustment by considering the following:

- The rental rate on a new lease at a different location compared to the old lease
- The moving costs and downtime
- The quality of available locations compared to the old location, and impact on future sales and profits

Aside from specific issues that significantly affect the business—like expiring leases or sales contracts—the letter of intent should state that the acquisition agreement will include representations, warranties and covenants that are standard for similar transactions. The acquisition process will run smoother if you do not discuss these general issues until you are further along in the process.

Due Diligence Arrangements

After the terms of a letter of intent have been agreed to, the buyer should thoroughly investigate the business to verify all claims the seller makes. This is known as due diligence. The letter of intent should state that access to the company's books, records, facilities and offices must be granted to the purchaser and his or her advisers. You should specify that you intend to do a complete review of the business and that you expect the seller to cooperate fully. If your due diligence reveals misrepresentations, you can choose not to purchase the business or use this information to restructure your offer. If you decide to purchase the business at the end of the due diligence period, the letter of intent will serve as a preliminary draft of the purchase agreement. (The due diligence process is discussed in detail in Chapter 11.)

Indemnifications

You should defer the general details of indemnification to the acquisition agreement. However, if specific issues are critical to the deal, you should explain them in the letter of intent. For example, if you know that the company has some environmental problems with a specific property, you should state in the letter that you will be indemnified from this liability.

Environmental problems with real estate can be major liabilities, and cleaning up the property can be extremely costly. By being indemnified, you attempt to avoid financial responsibility for cleaning up the property; the seller agrees to assume sole responsibility for the environmental damage that occurred prior to the acquisition. But be careful; if the seller cannot assume the entire financial burden, you might have to pay for the damage.

No-Shop Clause

A *no-shop* clause prevents the seller from soliciting acquisition bids from interested parties while you complete your due diligence and enter into a binding acquisition agreement. This is an issue where your interests are diametrically opposed to those of the seller. Obviously, you want to be the only prospective buyer reviewing the business. However, it is in the seller's interest to have others looking as well. First, it is risky to deal with only one prospect. You may walk away from the deal and he or she will be without a purchaser. Second, the seller might be able to get a higher price or better terms by creating a competitive bidding situation. Consequently, he or she will want to limit the period of time of the provision. Some sellers may even want to keep their business on the market so that they can search for a better deal.

The actual duration of the provision will be open to negotiation. Obviously, you should get the seller to agree to keep the business off the market for as long as possible.

THE FINAL DRAFT AND SIGNOFF

The final draft of the letter of intent should reflect the price and terms of the acquisition that have been agreed upon by both buyer and seller. Before proceeding further with the acquisition, both parties should sign the final letter in order to formalize their agreement.

You can prepare your own letter of intent; it does not have to be prepared by an attorney. However, have your attorney review and comment on your document to make sure you covered all the important issues. If you are not comfortable drafting the letter of intent, assign the task to your attorney.

CHAPTER THIRTEEN

Negotiating the Purchase

The negotiation process begins long before a purchase agreement is drafted; it starts the moment you look at the business. Your actions from that point on will set the tone for future negotiations. While you look at the business, try to build a strong relationship with the owner, understand his or her needs and desires, and impress upon him or her that you are serious about buying the business.

This process can be complicated, involving both technical and psychological dimensions. Valuing the business and determining the highest price that you will pay requires technical skills. In contrast, negotiation of the purchase price and terms involves psychological skills, such as understanding the seller's motivations. This chapter describes how the prospective buyer should approach a negotiation. It begins with a discussion of how to prepare for the negotiation and then reviews common negotiating techniques and mistakes often made in the process.

There are several good books on negotiation. One of the best is *Getting to Yes: Negotiating Agreement Without Giving In,* by Roger Fisher and William L. Ury (Penguin Books, revised edition, 1991). Another fine book is *Judgment in Managerial Decision Making,* by Max H. Bazerman (John Wiley & Sons, Inc., 1990).

PREPARING FOR THE NEGOTIATION

Negotiating the purchase of a small business requires a substantial amount of preparation on the part of the prospective buyer. The more knowledge you have going into the negotiation, the better off you will be. At a minimum you should try to understand the business, the person selling it and yourself. The more thorough your understanding of the business, the better able you will be to value it. As the following vignette illustrates, the better your valuation, the better able you will be to evaluate the seller's proposals.

One entrepreneur felt that the asking price for a retail business was too high. In order to confirm his suspicion, he spent several days calling business brokers and stating that he was interested in selling a business with revenues of $600,000, a cash flow of $200,000 and inventory valued at $150,000. He then asked them what they thought the business was worth. In total, he spoke with ten brokers. He used the valuations he obtained to substantiate his offer to the seller. Although his offer was lower than the asking price, the seller gave it serious consideration, because it had been confirmed by numerous outside sources as a fair value for such a business.

In addition to understanding the business, an understanding of the seller—his or her needs, objectives and personality—will give you a stronger negotiating position. If you hope to influence the seller, then you should understand his or her point of view. Finally, a thorough understanding of your motivations, strengths and weaknesses may prevent you from making mistakes during the negotiation that may cost you money and might cost you the deal.

KNOW THE SELLER

The best way to learn about the seller is to spend time at the business and ask questions. Demonstrate your interest in the business and indicate that you would like to structure a deal that accommodates the seller's needs. If the owner recognizes your interest and sincerity, he or she will be more willing to speak with you and, in the process, reveal valuable information. You should try to discover the answers to the following questions:

Why does the owner want to sell? What does he or she intend to do after the business is sold? The answer to this question will give you an indication of some of the key negotiating points. If the owner started the business 20 years ago and over time has made a substantial amount of money from it, then the price of the business and the terms of payment may be minor issues. In fact, the owner could be more concerned with the type of person who takes over the business and his or her ability to make it a long-term success.

You can gather much of this information by spending time with the owner, the employees, the broker and customers. Spend as much time as possible at the business. If you can, talk to the employees. Often they are more than willing to discuss their jobs and the business, particularly if they don't like the current owner. In some instances this may not be a viable option. As we have stated in earlier chapters, some business owners will not tell their employees that the business is for sale and will not want you to spend much time there.

What does the seller want out of the deal? You should identify the seller's interests before the negotiations begin. The following questions provide you with an outline of what you need to know:

- Does the owner really want to sell?
- Does the owner want to work in the business after it is sold?
- Will employment contracts with current employees be a requirement of the sale?
- Is the reputation of the business an important factor?
- Is the owner emotionally attached to the business?
- Does the owner need money (immediate payment) or is he or she more interested in having free time and being rid of the responsibilities of the business? (If the latter, he or she might be willing to receive payments in installments or provide seller financing.)

- Is the safety and security of the employees and customers important?

All of these issues and more may enter into the negotiation. You should identify them beforehand and try to gain a thorough understanding of the seller's stance on each. The more information you have at your disposal, the more creative and effective you will be as a negotiator.

What will the seller do if he or she does not sell the business to you? In negotiation jargon, this is known as identifying your opponent's Best Alternative to a Negotiated Agreement, or BATNA. If the seller desperately needs to sell and has no other prospects, you will have the advantage and may be able to negotiate more favorable terms. In contrast, if there are other interested buyers, you may lose the opportunity to buy the business by haggling over minor points. In evaluating the seller's BATNA, you should consider the following issues:

- Will the seller be able to sell the business if you do not purchase it?
- How long has the business been on the market?
- Are there any other prospective buyers?

Who are you negotiating against? An analysis of the seller's personality can provide you with insight about his or her negotiating style. While you spend time at the business, watch and listen. How the owner interacts with customers, suppliers and employees can tell you a great deal. If he or she takes a hard, tough stance in business dealings, there is a good chance you will be up against a tough negotiator. How the owner might negotiate should influence the negotiating style you intend to use.

Can you build a relationship with the seller? Some sellers are more concerned with the person buying the business than the price. In such instances, you should show the seller that you can run the business and will make it a success. If you build a "mentor" relationship with the seller or create a bond by demonstrating interest in the business, then he or she may be more likely to grant you larger concessions during the negotiation process. In fact, if you have built a strong relationship with the seller, he or she may *want* you to buy it and be more eager to structure a deal that will allow you to do so.

An entrepreneur in New York wanted to purchase a finance company from an owner nearing retirement. The entrepreneur knew that the business owner's wife had recently passed away and that his children had no desire to take over the business. In addition, he knew that the seller was emotionally attached to his business and wanted to continue to work on a part-time basis.

Recognizing the opportunity, the entrepreneur decided to work with the owner as a part-time consultant. During his time at the business, he realized that the seller's primary concern was to find a successor; price was not a critical issue. After six months, the owner asked the entrepreneur to take over the business. He offered the entrepreneur equity and agreed to relinquish control within three years. He also agreed to an earn-out; no down payment was necessary. The entrepreneur would not have had the chance to capitalize on this opportunity if he had not built a relationship with the seller and understood his needs.

ISSUES AFFECTING THE SELLER'S VALUATION

In addition to understanding the seller's personality, you should also be aware of some issues that may influence the way the seller values the business. Since the seller has an intimate knowledge of the business and its operations, he or she has *asymmetric information,* or information that the prospective buyer cannot obtain. As a result, the seller may place a higher or lower value on the business than would the buyer. Unfortunately, the prospective buyer often must depend upon information from the seller and has no way of knowing whether it is complete. Consequently, a prospective buyer should evaluate everything the seller provides and attempt to substantiate it, rather than accept it blindly.

The *endowment principle* may also influence how the seller values the business. The endowment principle suggests that an owner of an object tends to attribute a higher value to that object because he owns it. Consequently, the owner of a business may think that the business has a higher value than it actually does, merely because he or she started it, nurtured it, etc. You should take this into account if your valuation falls far below the owner's asking price.

KNOW YOURSELF

Understanding the business and the seller will not guarantee a strong negotiating position; you must also understand yourself and your negotiating strengths and weaknesses. First, you must identify how you negotiate. If you have a tendency to set objectives and not move from them, then you are a tough negotiator. In contrast, if you have a tendency to make concessions easily and give up too much surplus, then you are a soft negotiator. Be aware of these traits and watch for them during the negotiation.

COMMON NEGOTIATING TRAPS

In addition to understanding how you will act during the negotiation, you should also understand the most common negotiating mistakes that people make. They include anchoring, representativeness heuristic, confirmation trap, curse of knowledge and winner's curse.

Anchoring occurs when the first price proposed influences one or both parties. For example, if the seller asks for $1 million for the business, and prospective buyers "anchor" to the number, using it as a reference point for the negotiation. However, the seller's reservation price—the lowest price he or she will take for the business—may be substantially lower. Although the seller may ask for $1 million, he or she may, in fact, settle for $500,000. As a result, a buyer who anchors to the $1 million asking price may pay more for the business than he or she should.

The prospective buyer should also be wary of adhering to a *representativeness heuristic,* or letting the asking prices of similar companies influence how he or she values the business. Because similar companies are being offered for X amount of dollars, you may believe the company you are purchasing has a comparable value. This could be far from the truth. Although two businesses may be the same size and in the same industry, their values may vary tremendously. One could be very profitable and the other could be close to bankruptcy. It is extremely difficult to find truly comparable companies. You must consider the value of any business on a case-by-case basis.

Another common negotiating mistake is falling into the *confirmation trap.* If the seller's stated asking price is comparable to that of similar businesses, then the price will be confirmed in the buyer's mind. Remember, you can determine an appropriate value for a business only through a careful analysis of its operations and financial statements, not by comparing it to other businesses.

The *curse of knowledge* may also affect the prospective buyer. A sophisticated buyer dealing with an unsophisticated seller often tends to believe that the seller has more information than he or she actually does. For example, this type of buyer might perform a discounted cash flow analysis of the business and find that it has a value of $1 million. If the seller has not stated an asking price at this point, the buyer might assume that the seller understands the concept of discounted cash flow valuation and might believe that the seller has also valued the company at $1 million. However, the seller may have no knowledge of this type of valuation and may have valued the company much lower—say, $500,000. If the buyer then makes an offer of close to $1 million based upon such erroneous assumptions, he or she will have made an offer well above the seller's reservation price and will end up losing quite a bit of surplus.

Finally, a buyer who actually does buy a business may be a victim of the *winner's curse.* If the buyer is in competition with other prospective buyers and really wants the business, he or she may make a bid simply to win—and could pay considerably more than the business is worth in the process. This is known as the winner's curse.

Like the buyer, the seller may fall prey to these tendencies during the negotiation—and you may be able to use them to your advantage. For example, if you know that people are influenced by the first deal that is constructed, you can make the first offer through your letter of intent and try to get the seller to anchor to it. Take these into consideration while plotting your negotiation strategy.

PLANNING YOUR NEGOTIATION STRATEGY

Once you have gathered the information described above, you should create a negotiation strategy. This will entail determining your reservation price, identifying the issues that are most important to you, identifying the issues that you are willing to concede, and analyzing how the seller may react to you.

1. Determining your reservation price Your reservation price is the most you will agree to pay for the business. It should reflect the value of the business as it stands today, without attaching any premium for what you might add to it in the future. (Chapter 8 discusses valuation.)

When determining your reservation price, you should always disregard the seller's asking price. As one seasoned buyer puts it, "What the seller wants and what the seller gets are two different things."

2. Identifying key issues You should identify the key areas of concern to the seller and the issues you can negotiate, such as price, payment period, noncompete clauses, consulting contracts, etc. Once you have listed these, you should identify the most important issues, the least important issues and how far you would move on each. You should also attempt to determine which issues will be the most important to the seller. If you understand this prior to the negotiation, you can focus on what is important to you and make concessions on the least important issues.

3. Choosing your negotiating style The way in which you negotiate the deal should be based upon your opponent, the circumstances and what you think the most effective negotiating style will be. Negotiating tough on the issues and easy on the seller is the best strategy.

In the case of partnered negotiations, where you are working with someone else, a "good guy/bad guy" strategy often works well. In such instances one person plays the role of the "good guy," or the person who makes all the concessions and tries to smooth things over during the negotiations, while the other person takes on the role of the "bad guy." This person asks all the difficult questions, refuses to move from his or her stance and plays the foil for all the problems in the negotiation.

4. Anticipating the seller's response Once you have determined your position, weighed the various alternatives and plotted your strategy, you should consider the seller's possible responses to your offer and negotiating style. If you can anticipate his or her response and be prepared to counter, you will have a tremendous advantage. As in a game of chess, if you can anticipate your opponent's moves, then you are better able to counter them.

NEGOTIATING THE PURCHASE

There are no hard and fast rules about how to be a successful negotiator. More often than not, success is a function of being prepared and of experience. However, there are some guidelines you can follow in order to make yourself more effective during the negotiation.

1. Focus on the issues During the negotiation, you should focus on the issues of the negotiation instead of on the seller's position. For example, if the seller is concerned with the price and will not budge, agree to the price but try to negotiate the terms of the sale. If the seller wants $1 million, see if he or she will take it in $50,000 payments over 20 years. (Note that there is a substantial difference between paying $1 million in the first year and paying it over 20 years.) In both cases you are meeting the seller's price; however, in the second case it is on terms that are more favorable to you. As the saying goes, "Seller's price, buyer's terms."

2. Try to get the seller to anchor to your offer   As discussed earlier, both the buyer and the seller tend to anchor. If you can get the seller to anchor to your offer, you will have a tremendous advantage during the negotiation. You can do this in your letter of intent. If you put together an attractive, somewhat detailed offer in your letter of intent, you may be able to use it as the draft for your purchase agreement. If the purchase agreement will be based upon your letter of intent, the seller will be anchoring to your deal structure.

3. Search for solutions that provide mutual gain   You should pursue a "win-win" negotiation strategy: try to structure a deal that satisfies both your interests and those of the seller. You can do this by identifying shared interests and areas of mutual gain. For example, if the owner would like to stay in the business, but in a limited role, and does not want immediate payment, he or she might accept a percentage of future profits as a part of the payment for the business. This has several advantages for both the buyer and the seller. First, the seller becomes a stakeholder in the future outcome of the business, and thus will be more willing to help the buyer make the business a success. Second, it gives the seller a potentially larger (or smaller, depending on the deal structure) price and allows him or her to stay in the business.

4. Remember that this is a multi-issue negotiation   That being the case, you may be able to gain ground on one issue while conceding on another. The key will be to concede on the issues of least concern to you and gain ground on the issues of most concern to you. For example, if you understand which issues are most important to the owner (e.g., employee security and involvement in the business), you may obtain a concession on price in return for guaranteeing employee job security with employment contracts and offering the owner a role in the new business.

Be careful. Don't attribute your own needs and priorities to the seller. Price may be the most important issue to you, while employment contracts are the most important issue to the seller.

5. Do not go beyond your reservation price Knowing when to walk away from a negotiation is as important as knowing when to close the deal. If during the negotiation you realize that you and the seller will not come to an agreement, then walk away from the negotiation. If you continue to negotiate simply for the sake of making the deal, then you will make concessions that in retrospect you would not make. This is known as *escalation of commitment*. Once a person is committed to a course of action, he or she is inclined to continue along the course rather than end it, despite the outcome.

By walking away from a negotiation like this, you lose nothing but the time and money you have spent looking at the business. These are "sunk costs"; they have already been incurred and should not be factored into a decision to leave or stay at the negotiating table.

CONCLUSION

Negotiation is an art rather than a science. No two negotiations are the same. Every negotiation will be a function of the negotiator, the issues and the circumstances. Consequently, there is no right or wrong formula for negotiating a business purchase.

The best advice we can offer is to gather as much information as possible. The better prepared you are, the better able you will be to move the process in your direction.

CHAPTER FOURTEEN

Due Diligence, Purchase Agreement and Closing the Deal

In Chapters 6 and 7, we discussed the importance of doing preliminary due diligence in order to determine whether to pursue an acquisition candidate. Once you have made that decision and have sent the owner a letter of intent, you will be ready to perform final due diligence. You will use this examination of the business to determine whether the representations that have been made to you about the business are, in fact, accurate, and whether you still want to purchase it. If the results of this investigation are positive, then you will be ready to draw up a purchase agreement and close the deal.

This chapter outlines the process you should follow in your final due diligence proceedings and describes the essential elements of a purchase agreement and closing the deal.

DUE DILIGENCE

There are three types of due diligence that should be performed on your acquisition candidate: business, financial and legal. The purpose of this process is to ascertain whether or not you will receive the assets you expect in the condition you expect, to insure that the business will not be subject to any unexpected liabilities, and to verify that there will be no additional unexpected expenses post-acquisition.

It is extremely important to plan your due diligence proceedings prior to undertaking them and to get the assistance and advice of your advisers throughout the process.

Coopers & Lybrand's publication *Checking into an Acquisition Candidate* can be helpful in your planning. It provides a list of questions you should have answers to prior to making an acquisition. Using this publication or a similar one as a guide, you should prepare your own checklist based on the specifics of the company. First, it will help you keep track of the information you receive. Second, it will ensure that no vital information is overlooked. Third, after you have finished preparing your list, you should have an idea of how long the process will take.

The business portion of your due diligence review will encompass the operations of the company, its assets, its history and its industry. You will want to examine the company closely to ensure that what you think you are purchasing is indeed what you are purchasing. Your investigation should include several visits to the plant and/or facilities of the business. At a minimum, you should examine the following topics:

- Background of the company
- Operations
- Product lines
- Service lines
- Market
- Customers and customer relationships
- Management and employees
- Competition
- Facilities
- Assets, such as inventories, equipment, etc.
- Planning and internal controls
- Marketing
- Internal reports
- Environmental problems and/or liabilities

The financial review of the business will require verifying the quantitative information you have been given about the company. Your accountant should assist you. You not only need to obtain the numerical data on the business, you also need to substantiate it. For example, if accounts receivable is represented on the balance sheet of the company as $100,000, you should estimate whether or not 100 percent of the accounts are collectible. It could be that 50 percent of the accounts receivables are over 90 days old and are, in fact, not collectible. If this is the case, the accounts receivables will only be worth $50,000, rather than the $100,000 that is on the books. You may have a similar problem with inventory. Although it may be on the books with a value of $120,000, some of the inventory may be ten years old and not sellable. At the very least, you should investigate the following items in detail:

- Financial statements
- Assumptions regarding the financial statements and a review of the accounting principles being used
- Terms of any loans, leases, etc.
- Financial stability of the company
- Accurate value of assets
- Financial risk evaluation
- Health and pension benefits
- Cost allocation

One entrepreneur who purchased a restaurant in Connecticut encountered some problems with hidden costs that were overlooked during the financial review of the business. Connecticut charges a property tax based on the value of equipment. As it turns out, the seller had reported the value of the equipment as $24,000 on the company's state tax returns and $60,000 on the federal returns. She depreciated the equipment at the higher value for federal tax purposes, and paid taxes to the state based on the lower value. The net result was that the entrepreneur's state taxes increased by $2,300 after the acquisition. Luckily, the entrepreneur protected himself from being liable for the seller's questionable business methods. (The seller is currently being audited by the Internal Revenue Service.)

In some cases, a thorough review will help you avoid purchasing a business that is destined for bankruptcy. In the mid-1980s an entrepreneur considered purchasing a food-processing company in

Philadelphia. A preliminary financial analysis indicated that the company was worth close to $5 million. However, during the due diligence process the entrepreneur discovered that the company's pension plan was underfunded by almost $10 million. The entrepreneur concluded that there were greener pastures elsewhere. The processing company was eventually purchased. However, as a result of this pending liability, the acquiring entity declared bankruptcy.

In your legal due diligence, you will need to examine all the legal liabilities of the company and any contractual agreements. You want to verify that the owner has the legal authority to sell the business, that all contracts and agreements and their terms have been disclosed, that title to the assets is clear, and that the business has no legal liabilities that have not been disclosed. As mentioned in Chapter 4, your lawyer should be able to provide a legal due diligence checklist that can help you in this process. It is imperative that your lawyer assist you throughout this section of the review. The value of good legal advice during this process cannot be overstated. It can save you time, money and lawsuits. You should investigate the following documents in this review:

- All corporate documents
- Charter amendment
- By-laws and minutes of meetings
- Contracts with suppliers, customers and employees
- Any financial or loan agreements
- Leases, deeds, mortgages, etc.
- Patents and property rights
- Any current legal proceedings
- Insurance

As you construct your checklist, you should prepare a list of information and documents you will need from the owner. Send this list as soon as possible so that he or she can begin to put this information together. Often it will take weeks, if not months, to obtain everything you need, so the sooner you begin, the better.

PURCHASE AGREEMENT

Once you have decided to purchase the business, it will be time for you and your lawyer to prepare a purchase agreement. Depending on your due diligence proceedings, this document may or may not be based upon your letter of intent. Obviously, if your due diligence proceedings uncovered serious flaws in the business, you will want to draft a new purchase agreement rather than rely upon your letter of intent.

A purchase agreement consists of four sections: (1) a description of the transaction; (2) terms of the agreement; (3) representations and warranties; and (4) conditions and covenants. The first section describes the type of acquisition that will take place—i.e., whether it will be a sale of assets or a stock purchase. The second section describes the terms of the agreement, such as the sales price and the corresponding amount of cash, stock and assets that are to change hands in the transaction. Other considerations might involve the roles that the managers or key employees of the targeted company will have after the acquisition. The third section of the agreement describes the presentations and warranties of both the target and acquiring companies. This is often the most negotiated portion of the agreement; however, its significance is usually not as substantial as other components after the transaction is consummated. The target company might represent the validity of the corporation as an entity; a list of patents, trade secrets, copyrights, trademarks and licenses; insurance policies and the fact that these policies will be kept current until the acquisition; a list of outstanding liabilities; the status of payroll taxes, pension plans, etc.; outstanding contracts; and so on. Other issues are tax implications from the acquisition, noncompete clauses, approval from the board and indemnification issues.

The final section deals with conditions and covenants for both the target and acquiring companies. Issues covered deal with due diligence (i.e., verification that representations are valid; significant changes in such representations might allow one party to terminate the agreement), maintaining the target's business operations so that the purchaser gets what he or she pays for, and the execution of certain documents, such as employment and noncompete agreements.

After you have completed a preliminary draft of the purchase agreement, you will submit it to the owner or the owner's attorney. Both parties will try to make adjustments to the agreement until they are satisfied.

Once all the terms to the acquisition have been agreed to, the financing secured and the seller's representations substantiated, the deal will be ready to close. The deal can be terminated if both parties agree to it in writing or if the conditions and covenants are not met or waived.

It is beneficial to control and draft the purchase agreement. Inevitably, there will be issues that were not discussed or agreed upon during negotiations. Your attorney should prepare the document to maximize your position. However, don't rely solely on your attorney's work; read everything before it is sent out.

CLOSING THE DEAL

At this point, you should have a good understanding of the major issues involved in purchasing a business. We have reviewed how to locate acquisition candidates, evaluate investment opportunities, structure deals, raise financing and conduct due diligence. If your acquisition vehicle has been formed and you have secured all the capital needed to consummate the deal, all that remains to be done is to close the deal.

Your attorney should be able to guide you through this process. However, just as we have mentioned throughout this book, don't rely on him or her blindly. Chances are that this is just one of many transactions that your attorney will be handling, so it will be your job to make certain that this procedure is being handled effectively. For example, make sure that he or she has prepared all the legal documents, such as employment contracts or noncompete agreements. Carefully review all documents and make revisions if you feel they are necessary. Also, if you don't understand the language in certain documents, ask questions to clarify things.

At the actual closing, you and the seller will have to execute numerous documents. You will sign loan documents, lease agreements, personal guarantees, property transfer documents and more. Just be certain to read everything before you sign it. Last but not least, you will have to sign that little rectangular piece of paper—the check—that will symbolize the end of a long journey and the beginning of an exciting new career as an entrepreneur. If you make it this far, you deserve to be congratulated. Buy a bottle of champagne, relax and enjoy the moment with some friends. Take a breath, because after the deal is closed, you will have to start to implement all those great ideas you had about how to improve your newly acquired business.

■ CHAPTER FIFTEEN ■

Managing the Acquisition

The importance of your management of the acquired business cannot be understated. This chapter discusses some of the first steps you should take. In the first few weeks following the acquisition, it will be important for you to establish yourself as the new owner. As you begin to feel comfortable with the business you have purchased, you will have ideas for improvements to operations, finance, marketing and other areas. The following sections will help you lay the groundwork so that implementing your ideas will come easily.

THE HONEYMOON IS OVER

The first day you walk into the business as the new owner, you will probably be filled with ideas of how you can make changes to improve the operations; perhaps you will want to eliminate some staff, improve the computer system or start a quality control program. Don't give in to this impulse! At least, not immediately.

Begin instead by assessing the company's strengths. It is easy to identify problems with a business. As an outsider, you bring a fresh perspective. As a result of your objective viewpoint, you will be able to identify problems that insiders simply can't see. Your first impulse will be to come up with solutions for them. Unless they are life-threatening, don't change them when you first enter the business.

Let them go until you fully understand what makes the business work as well as it does.

Most first-time buyers neglect to do this. Knowing a business's strengths and appreciating them is as important, or perhaps more important, than understanding its weaknesses. It is critical to the success of the business during the transition period. The business's strengths will be what keeps it running and generating profits while you take the reins from the previous owner. If you don't recognize and understand these characteristics, then you may damage or even eliminate them with any changes you make.

It is extremely important to consider changes carefully. While every business situation is different, and sometimes rapid change is critical to the survival of the business, these changes may make employees, customers or suppliers nervous. Often, a new owner has planned changes to the business during the evaluation stage and is anxious for them to be implemented. Be aware that the employees of the company are suffering from a "lag." If you devised plans as a prospective buyer, you have a head start on your employees. You have had time to work the changes out in your own mind. Employees, however, first need to get accustomed to you as the new owner. If you want to make changes quickly and cannot involve your employees in the planning, at least advise them during implementation.

In short, in the initial period after you have bought a business, consider carefully the changes that you would like to make. Making changes slowly may help you enlist the early support of the employees and also assuage their fears that the business might change to the degree that they are either not needed or are unhappy about their work. Customers and suppliers may also be more confident if they see that you are thoughtful in your planning.

EMPLOYEES

During the first days of your ownership, it will be important for you to inform current employees of your plans for the company. As a result of the leveraged buyouts of the 1980s, the sale of a business implies its demise to many people. Movies like "Wall Street" depicted corporate raiders buying companies, selling all the assets and firing all the employees. While this is an extreme example, it remains the applicable model in many people's minds, particularly those who do not understand other possible motivations for buying a business.

While you may have encountered some employees during the investigation and due diligence phases, most employees will probably meet you for the first time when you take over the business. Many employees will have concerns when they learn that the business has been sold. Most of these concerns will revolve around their jobs, potential changes to the company and the exit of the previous owner (absent some kind of employment contract).

Shortly after taking control of the business, you should hold a meeting with all employees. Do this as soon as possible after closing the sale so that there is not sufficient time for rumors to develop or for concerned employees to search for new jobs. Also, ask the owner not to disclose anything about the sale to the employees until you are able to introduce yourself as the new owner. If employees hear about the sale, they may immediately assume that they should start looking for a new job. Some people think about businesses as if they were houses—when the house is sold, the current occupants must move out!

During your initial meeting, communicate to employees your intentions for the company. State explicitly and emphatically that you plan to continue operating the company (as long as this is your plan). At the same time, do not implicitly or explicitly guarantee that everyone will keep his or her job. Conduct this meeting yourself with all employees of the business present. This initial meeting and the information you must convey are too important to entrust to others.

In the months that follow, you will have ample time to evaluate the talent you have on board. Some experts recommend that you interview all current employees as if they were being hired for the job they hold. By doing so, you may find that someone is in a position that is inappropriate for his or her skills. You may also find employees who would be happier doing something else within the company. Because most small companies lack the formal personnel policies of larger companies, employees sometimes "fall" into jobs, either because there is no one else to perform them or because the previous management failed to search externally for the most appropriate person. During the interview process, you can determine if this is the case. At a minimum, try to discover how they view their job, how they might improve it and what they would like to do.

If you have not conducted many job interviews or are unfamiliar with questions and topics that are appropriate and those that are not, consult a good book on hiring. Keep in mind that the people you will be talking with, if retained, will be helping you a great deal in the future, so look at the interview as an opportunity to not only qualify them for their position but also to learn about their own personal goals and aspirations. This will help you determine how to most effectively manage them in the future.

As you start to make decisions regarding people and positions, keep in mind the culture of the company. Perhaps an employee could be more effective working off-site but is a favorite of other employees. People like the workplace to represent more than just work. If there is an employee who helps keep morale up at the company, you should think seriously before making any decision about that person's position or continued employment. If an employee is ineffective or inappropriate in a position, there may be a more appropriate position in which he or she could contribute to the company. When possible, a policy of retaining and repositioning employees is often more successful than mass firings.

As you start to make decisions, consult a labor attorney or employment-law expert if you have any question about an action you might take regarding a certain employee. An employment-related lawsuit should be avoided at all costs. Such an action will not only divert your attention from running the business but may also hurt morale among the current employees.

Once you feel comfortable with your staff, you should consider how they have been managed in the past and how that management could be improved. Structuring employee compensation so that a portion is based on the future success of the company is one alternative. Such a compensation structure will demonstrate that employee contribution is important and will be rewarded. This does not need to be limited to only the management team of the business. While some businesses are not well-suited to performance-based compensation for all employees, a profit-sharing system can usually be structured that gives employees a stake in the future performance of the business. In short, if you convey to employees that you want the business to succeed, show that you are willing to share the success with the people who will make it happen.

As you start to think about changes that could be made to the business, remember that the employees may be resistant to any changes that you make. People generally do not like change, particularly if it requires work on their part and they see no immediate personal benefit. Consequently, you should take them into account when considering any change, as they are "stakeholders" in the business. If employees have contributed to a process, they may resent a new owner who comes in and immediately upsets the way the business operates. How they respond to a change can affect its outcome. If they buy into it and support it, chances are it will be successful. If they are against it, then defeat is almost inevitable. This does not mean that you should just let the status quo dictate operation. As you propose and implement changes, simply consider those people who will be affected. As the new owner, you will need employees to "buy in" to your changes, or at least not to rebel against them.

By building consensus among the employees about your proposed changes, you may be able to avoid any problems, or at least deal with them upfront. Discuss the changes you intend to make with your staff. Get their feedback on any idea, and incorporate their input into your proposed change.

Getting the employees to assist you in the changes will serve several purposes. First, it will instill confidence in them that they are an important part of the organization. Second, it may inspire them to generate ideas of their own on how to improve the business. One of your greatest resources will be your employees. Learn to use them effectively. Third, it will help to engender a team, "we're-in-this-together" atmosphere.

MAINTAINING KEY RELATIONSHIPS

Customers, suppliers and other people serving or being served by the business will be key to both its short-term and long-term success. Maintaining these relationships will be of the utmost importance to you as the new owner. During your first few months of ownership, take the opportunity to meet and speak with each one of these people. If possible, get the previous owner to make the introduction and give you his or her stamp of approval. This will smooth the transition. During your meetings, convince them that you value the relationship and hope to continue it well into the future. Ask them if they have any ideas about how you can improve the relationship— e.g., improvements in service, etc.

A business is most vulnerable with its customers immediately after a sale. Competitors will take the opportunity to create doubt in the minds of customers regarding the ongoing viability of the business. Customers, without hearing anything from the business in question, might believe them.

In order to preserve these relationships, some entrepreneurs go further than just introducing themselves to major customers. They hold receptions or open-houses for customers during which they can further solidify the business relationship. Or, they might offer a special promotion for existing customers—a "get-acquainted" offer—during which customers get a special price, delivery or added service. These are excellent ways to convey to customers that not only will the business continue, but that you consider your relationship with them to be of primary importance.

You should consider taking some of the same steps with suppliers to the business. Many suppliers will have had special relationships with the previous owner from which you might benefit. By having the previous owner introduce you as the new owner, you can instill confidence in them and ensure the same level of service and commitment that the previous owner was afforded. After you analyze these relationships, you may uncover some that don't make sense. Perhaps the seller was doing business with a company because a friend was the owner, even though the friend was not offering the most competitive prices or most appropriate product or service. Take advantage of the transition period to examine relationships carefully and consider which ones should be maintained and which should be changed or eliminated.

You may also want to be introduced to the company's bankers, landlord, accountant, attorneys and other important professionals. You may have met many of these people during the evaluation and due diligence stage. They, too, can be critical to the success of the business. For example, the previous owner's relationship with a particular banker may have been the reason he received a line of credit quickly. Continuing any positive relationships that the business had can be essential to its long-term well-being. Try to get the former owner to assist you in the process.

Communicate your plans for the business with those advisers and professionals whom you plan to retain. Remember that they also have a stake in its future. If you are bringing in advisers of your own, consider introducing them to existing advisers of the business; it is likely that they might work together in the future. Establishing a meaningful relationship early on might help you.

ABOVE ALL, KEEP LEARNING

If this is your first business acquisition, we hope it will not be your last. If it is one of many already, then we hope you continue in your success. Whatever the case, after you have purchased a business, do not stop learning about new opportunities. Remember the corridor principle? Once you are into a venture, it will be much easier to see other opportunities. Keep your eyes open. As you settle into business ownership, keep your employees involved. Help them learn about being better managers, workers, marketers, etc. This will enable you, should the opportunity arise, to participate in other business ventures even as you are the owner of operating businesses. Many of the people with whom we have discussed acquisitions own multiple businesses and are looking for more.

Additionally, try to stay current on issues affecting small and growing businesses. If you don't subscribe to *Inc.*, consider it. Every month, the magazine is filled with useful and valuable information for owners and managers of growing companies. You should also watch the "Enterprise" section of *The Wall Street Journal.* In it, finance, marketing, sales and other issues affecting small businesses are discussed.

If you are just finishing this book and are ready to embark on your search, we wish you the best of luck. If you have already purchased a business, congratulations and best wishes for its continued success. If you have decided not to purchase a business, we hope that this book has been interesting and that you can refer to it should you change your mind.

No matter which category you fall into, we are convinced that buying a small business is a viable and attractive means of entrepreneurship. As businesses change hands throughout the 1990s, we look forward to witnessing the socio-economic benefits and growth in entrepreneurship that result. And we wish you much success as you participate with us.

Reference Texts

Company Directories

Million Dollar Directory: America's Leading Public & Private Companies 1992. New York: Dun & Bradstreet Information Services, 1992.

Standard & Poor's Register of Corporations, Directors and Executives. Standard & Poor's Corporation, 1992.

Directory of Corporate Affiliations. Wilmette, Ill.: National Register Publishing Co.

Macmillan Directory of Leading Private Companies. Wilmette, Ill.: National Register Publication Co.

Ward's Business Directory of Major U.S. Private Companies. Belmont, Calif.: Information Access Co.

Thomas Register of American Manufacturers. New York: Thomas Publishing Co.

Directory of U.S. Importers. New York: Journal of Commerce.

Directory of U.S. Exporters. New York: Journal of Commerce.

Online or Disc
Compact Disclosure
CD/Corporate

Industry Information

Office of Management and Budget. *Standard Industrial Classification Manual*. Washington, D.C.: Government Printing Office.

Service Industries USA: Industry Analyses, Statistics, and Leading Organizations. Ed. Arsen J. Darnay. Detroit, Mich.: Gale Research, 1992.

Industry and Trade Administration. *U.S. Industrial Outlook.* Washington, D.C.: Government Printing Office.

Predicasts Forecasts. Cleveland, Ohio: Predicasts, Inc.

Worldcasts. Cleveland, Ohio: Predicasts, Inc.

Standard & Poor's Industry Surveys. New York: Standard and Poor's Corp.

Value Line Investment Survey. New York: A. Berhard.

U.S. Bureau of Census. *Statistical Abstract of the U.S.* Washington, D.C.

Manufacturing USA: Industry Analyses, Statistics and Leading Companies. Detroit, Mich.: Gale Research, 1989.

Publications from the Department of Commerce:
- Census of Manufacturers
- Annual Survey of Manufacturers
- Current Industrial Reports
- Census of Mineral Industries
- Census of Construction Industries
- Census of Service Industries
- Census of Retail Trade
- Census of Wholesale Trade
- Census of Agriculture
- Census of Transportation
- County Business Patterns

Online or Disc
- Infotrac
- Dow Jones—Menus

Marketing

Almanac of Consumer Markets. Ithaca, N.Y.: American Demographics Press, 1989.

Consumer USA. London: Euromonitor Publication Ltd.

Dialog's Business Connection/Trinet Market Share Report. Online.

International Marketing Data and Statistics. London: Euromonitor Publication Ltd.

Market Research Abstracts. London: Market Research Society.

Bureau of Census. *County and City Data Book.* Washington, D.C.: Government Printing Office.

Bureau of Census. *State and Metropolitan Area Data Book.* Washington, D.C.: Government Printing Office.

Survey of Buying Power. New York: Sales Management.

Editor and Publisher Market Guide. New York: The Editor & Publisher Co.

Metro Insights. Lexington, Mass.: Regional Information Group, Data Resources.

The Lifestyle Market Analyst. Wilmette, Ill.: Standard Rate & Data Service, 1989.

Dialog/Donnelley Demographics. Online.

Simmons Study of Media and Markets. New York: Simmons.

Standard Rate and Data Service. Wilmette, Ill.: Standard Rate & Data Service.

Brands and Their Companies. Detroit, Mich.: Gale Research, 1990.

Marketing Information. Atlanta, Ga.: Business Publishing Division, College of Business Administration, Georgia State University.

Trade Shows and Professional Exhibits Directory

Online or Disc

Dun & Bradstreet Online Databases:
Dun's Market Identifiers–Dialog File 516
Electronic Yellow Pages–Dialog File 515
International Market Identifiers–Dialog File 518

General Business Information

Lavin, Michael R. *Business Information: How to Find It, How to Use It.* Phoenix, Ariz.: Oryx Press, 1992.

Daniells, Lorna M. *Business Information Sources.* Berkeley, Calif.: University of California Press.

Directories in Print. Detroit, Mich.: Gale Research.

Encyclopedia of Associations. Detroit, Mich.: Gale Research.

Encyclopedia of Business Information Sources. Detroit, Mich.: Gale Research.

Strauss, Diane Wheeler. *Handbook of Business Information: A Guide for Librarians, Students and Researchers.* Englewood, Colo.: Libraries Unlimited, 1988.

National Trade and Professional Associations

Marketing/Demographic Data. Metro Insights

Direct Mail List Rates and Data. Skokie, Ill.: Standard Rate and Data
Service.
Polk Mailing List Catalog. Taylor, Mich.: R. L. Polk & Co.
Catalog of Mailing Lists. Mineola, N.Y.: F. S. Hoffheimer.

Professionals

Martindale-Hubbell Law Directory. New York: Martindale-Hubbell, Inc.
Emerson's Directory of Leading U.S. Accounting Firms. Redmond, Wash.:
Big Eight Review, 1988.
The Directory of M&A Professionals. New York: Dealer's Digest Inc.

Articles

Predicast's F&S Index. Cleveland, Ohio: Predicasts.
Business Periodicals Index. New York: H. W. Wilson.
Wall Street Journal Index. Wooster, Ohio: Newspaper Indexing Center,
Micro Photo Division, Bell & Howell.
Business Index. Menlo Park, Calif.: Information Access Co.

Online
   ABI/Inform
   Predicast's F&S Index Ondisc
   Wilsondisc
   Business Index Ondisc
   CD-Corporate
   Dow Jones Text
   Lexis/Nexis
   Dialog

Ratios and Comparative Data

Analyst's Handbook. New York: Analyst's Handbook.
Industry Norms and Key Business Ratios. New York: Dun & Bradstreet.
Robert Morris Associates. Fernwood, Pa.: The Associates.
Troy, Leo. *Almanac of Business and Industrial Financial Ratios.* Engle-
wood Cliffs, N.J.: Prentice-Hall.
Walton, John B. *Business Profitability Data.* Dallas, Texas: Weybridge
Publication Co., 1981.

Financial Studies of the Small Business. Arlington, Va.: Financial Research Associates.

Small-Business Information

Business, Economics and Entrepreneurship Resource Catalog. Albany, N.Y.: SUNY Institute of Technology at Utica/Rome, Entrepreneurship Education Resource Center.

Jones, Seymour, M. Bruce Cohen and Victor V. Coppola. *Coopers & Lybrand Guide to Growing Your Business.* New York: Wiley, 1985.

Handbook of Small Business Data. Washington, D.C.: U.S. Small Business Administration, Office of Advocacy.

Stevens, Mark. *Macmillan Small Business Handbook.* New York: Macmillan.

Ryans, Cynthia G. *Small Business: An Information Sourcebook.* Phoenix, Ariz.: Oryx Press, 1987.

Small Business Sourcebook. Detroit, Mich.: Gale Research.

Advances in the Study of Entrepreneurship, Innovation and Economic Growth. Greenwich, Conn.: JAI Press.

Cohen, William A. *Entrepreneur and Small Business Problem Solver: An Encyclopedia and Reference Guide.* 2nd ed. New York: Wiley, 1990.

Family Business Review: Journal of Family Firm Institute. San Francisco, Calif.: Jossey-Bass, Inc. Quarterly.

In Business. Emmaus, Pa.: JG Press. Bimonthly.

Inc. Boston, Mass.: United Marine Publication. Monthly.

Journal of Small Business and Entrepreneurship. International Council for Small Business, Canada. Quarterly.

Journal of Small Business Management. Morgantown, W.V.: National Council for Small Business Management Development. Quarterly.

Small Business Economics. Dordrecht, Boston: Klever Academics.

Small Business Report. Monterey, Calif.: Small Business Monitoring & Research. Monthly.

The State of Small Business: A Report to the President Transmitted to Congress. Washington, D.C.: Government Printing Office.

Tax Guide for Small Business. Washington, D.C.: Department of the Treasury.

Franchising

Directory of Franchising Organizations. New York: Pilot Books.

Encyclopedia of Franchises and Franchising. New York: Facts on File, 1989.

The Franchise Annual. Lewiston, N.Y.: INFO Press, International Franchise Opportunities.

Franchise 500. Irvine, Calif.: Entrepreneur Magazine Group

Franchise Opportunities Guide. Washington, D.C.: International Franchise Association.

Franchising in the Economy. Washington, D.C.: Department of Commerce, Domestic and International Business Administration, Bureau of Competitive Assessment and Business Policy.

Freidlander, Mark P., Gene Gurney and Dennis L. Foster. *Handbook of Successful Franchising*. New York: Van Nostrand Reinhold Co.

Rating Guide to Franchises. New York: Facts on File.

Valuation

Desmond, Glenn M. and John Marcello. *Handbook of Small Business Valuation Formulas*. Los Angeles, Calif.: Valuation Press, 1987.

Pratt, Shannon. *Valuing a Business: The Analysis and Appraisal of Closely Held Companies*. Homewood, Ill.: Dow Jones-Irwin, 1983.

Pratt, Shannon. *Valuing Small Businesses and Professional Practices*. Homewood, Ill.: Dow Jones-Irwin, 1985.

Horn, Thomas W. *Business Valuation Manual*. Lancaster, Pa.: Charter Oak Press.

Legal Issues

Diamond, Michael R., and Julie L. Williams. *How to Incorporate: A Handbook for Entrepreneurs and Professionals*. New York: John Wiley & Sons, 1987.

Lashbrooke, E. C., and Michael I. Swygart. *The Legal Handbook of Business Transactions: A Guide For Managers and Entrepreneurs*. New York: Quorum Books, 1987.

Hancock, William A. *The Small Business Legal Advisor*. New York: McGraw-Hill, 1982.

Harroch, Richard D. *Start-up Companies: Planning, Financing, and Operating the Successful Business.* New York: Law Journal Seminars–Press, 1990.

Accounting and Finance

Anthony, Robert N., and John Dearden. *Management Control Systems.* Howewood, Ill.: Richard D. Irwin, 1980.

Anthony, Robert N., and Glenn A Welsch. *Fundamentals of Management Accounting.* Homewood, Ill.: Richard D. Irwin, 1981.

Horngren, Charles T., and George Foster. *Cost Accounting: A Managerial Emphasis.* 6th ed. Englewood Cliffs, N.J.: Prentice-Hall, 1987.

Bernstein, Leopold A. *Financial Statement Analysis: Theory, Application, and Interpretation.* Homewood, Ill.: Richard D. Irwin, 1989.

Tracy, J.A. *How to Read a Financial Report: Wringing Cash Flow and Other Vital Signs Out of the Numbers.* 2nd ed. New York: John Wiley & Sons, Inc., 1985.

Business Analysis

Hax, Arnoldo, and Nicolas S. Majuf. *Strategic Management: An Integrative Perspective.* Englewood Cliffs, N.J.: Prentice-Hall, 1984.

Porter, Michael. *Competitive Strategy: Techniques for Analyzing Industries and Competitors.* New York: Free Press, 1980.

Miles, Raymond C. *Basic Business Appraisal.* New York: John Wiley & Sons, Inc., 1984.

Business Plans

Bangs, David H. *The Business Planning Guide.* Dover, N.H.: Upstart Publishing Co.

Brooks, Julie K., and Barry A. Stevens. *How to Write a Successful Business Plan.* New York: American Management Association, 1987.

Sources of Financing

Business Capital Sources: More Than 1,500 Lenders of Money for Real Estate, Business or Capital Needs. Merrick, N.Y.: International Wealth Success Inc.

Hayes, Rich Stephen. *Business Loans: A Guide to Money Sources and How to Approach Them.* Rev. and updated. New York: John Wiley & Sons, Inc., 1989.

Journal of Business Venturing. New York: Elsevier. Three times a year.

Pratt's Guide to Venture Capital Sources. Wellesley Hills, Mass.: Capital Publication.

O'Hara, Patrick D. *SBA Loans: A Step-by-Step Guide.* New York: John Wiley & Sons, Inc.

SBIC Digest. Washington, D.C.: SBA, Investment Division.

SBIC Directory and Handbook of Small Business Finance. Merrick, N.Y.: International Wealth Success, Inc.

Silver, A. David. *Who's Who in Venture Capital.* New York: John Wiley & Sons, Inc., 1987.

Selling

Richardson, Linda. *Winning Group Sales Presentations: A Guide to Closing the Deal.* Homewood, Ill.: Dow Jones–Irwin, 1990.

Negotiations

Fisher, Roger, and William Ury. *Getting to Yes: Negotiating Agreement Without Giving In.* Revised edition. New York: Penguin Books, 1991.

Bazerman, Max H. *Judgment in Managerial Decision Making.* New York: John Wiley & Sons, Inc., 1990.

Acquisitions Periodicals

The National Review of Corporate Acquisitions. Tweed Publishing Co.

Buyouts. Venture Economics.

Mergers and Acquisitions. MLR Publishing Co.

Buying a Business

Knight, Brian, and Associates. *Buy the Right Business at the Right Prices.* Dover, N.H.: Upstart Publishing Co.

Hansen, James M. *Guide to Buying or Selling a Business.* Mercer Island, Wash.: Grenadier Press.

Mancuso, Joseph R. *Buying a Business (for Very Little Cash).* New York: Prentice-Hall, 1990.

Radlauer, Lynn M., and Ned M. Lubell. "Buying an Existing Business: The Search Process." Cambridge, Mass.: Harvard Business School Case No. 9-385-330, 1985.

◼ APPENDIX B ◼

Using a Computer in Your Search

As you begin your search for a business, you will quickly realize that the flow of information can be overwhelming. The number of contacts you make will grow exponentially. Brokers, owners and other parties will send you information that should be organized, and you will want to keep track of people you talk to and those to whom you need to respond.

A personal computer can help immensely in this process. Using a computer will help you track the leads that you encounter from various sources. In addition, you can write letters and perform analysis using various software packages. If you do not already own a personal computer, the following is a short primer on the various computer types and what you should consider when purchasing one. It also discusses appropriate software to use in your search for a business.

Despite the proliferation of computers in the business world, many would-be entrepreneurs do not have direct experience in using or purchasing computer equipment and software. This appendix is meant as a brief overview for such a reader.

HARDWARE: WHAT DO I NEED?

Computer hardware consists of the machine itself, printers, keyboards and other peripherals. There are myriad choices. Just look at a computer advertisement in the newspaper or visit a retailer. You'll soon find that the number of alternatives is staggering.

First, keep in mind that the functions you will need to perform could have been handled by a personal computer five years ago; so if a salesperson at the computer store tells you that you need the "latest and greatest," be skeptical. A computer that performs adequately can easily be obtained for less than $2,000. If someone recommends the latest, fastest, most advanced technology, look for a high price tag.

DESKTOP OR LAPTOP?

One choice you will have to make is whether to purchase a desktop computer or a portable "laptop" or "notebook" computer. There are advantages to both. A desktop computer will be less expensive, available from a greater number of sources and possibly more reliable. Conversely, it is difficult to use a desktop computer anywhere but at home or in your office.

In contrast, a portable can accompany you on visits to businesses, brokers and other contacts. Unfortunately, portable screens are usually difficult to read (especially true of older models), their keyboards are small and they are more expensive than desktop models. Additionally, if someone steals your portable or you lose it, all your information will be gone (unless you've been wise enough to back up your data).

If you desire the flexibility of a portable but do not like the small screen and keyboard, you can take a hybrid approach. Most portables can drive a standard-size screen, and most also have a port for a standard keyboard. Nearly all portables can support the same types of peripherals, but it may be more difficult to expand the features of a portable than those of a desktop computer.

PC OR MACINTOSH?

The great debate over which personal computer is better has been raging for many years—ever since Apple introduced the Macintosh in 1984, two years after IBM entered the personal computer market with its popular PC. Although the Macintosh was originally seen as a nice "toy" by much of corporate America, its popularity has increased immensely as new models have been introduced and software manufacturers have developed business applications for it. Despite this rise in popularity, Apple holds less than 20 percent of the personal computer market.

The emergence of "clones," or IBM-compatible machines, has led to market dominance by IBM. A clone generally costs less than an IBM machine. While there is only one IBM, there are hundreds, if not thousands, of clone manufacturers. Apple remains the only manufacturer of the Macintosh.

Each type of machine uses a different operating system. The operating system is the basic, underlying computer code that tells the computer how to perform its fundamental tasks, such as accepting keyboard input or reading a floppy diskette.

The Macintosh uses an easy-to-learn, proprietary operating system. This system has won millions of converts worldwide, and improvements to it are helping Apple gain market share. It is based on a "desktop," which holds familiar things like file folders and applications. To perform an operation on either a file or application, the user simply points at the item with a device called a "mouse" and pushes a button.

IBM PCs and compatibles generally use an operating system called DOS (for Disk Operating System, because the system originally came on floppy disks). DOS was developed for IBM by Microsoft. Since its introduction, over 70 million copies of DOS have shipped worldwide. Unlike the Macintosh, DOS is a text-based operating system, which requires that the user know commands and type them at the command prompt. For those familiar with the commands, this can be fairly straightforward. However, for those unfamiliar with DOS and not well-versed in computers, learning how to manipulate files and applications using DOS can be challenging.

Microsoft Windows, an add-on operating system that gives DOS a graphical display similar to the Macintosh, solves this dilemma. If you're planning to acquire an IBM PC or compatible and are not already familiar with DOS, Windows should be a requirement. Look for a computer that is sold with both DOS and Windows already installed.

In order to decide between an IBM PC or compatible, you should visit a retailer that sells both types of machines. Computers are like shoes: there are many different styles, but the fit with the owner is the most important criterion for selection. At a good computer retailer, you'll have the chance to try different types of computers and see which one feels best to you. Beware of retailers that have a special allegiance to any particular machine or manufacturer.

If you decide to purchase an IBM PC or compatible, you must decide which microprocessor the computer you select should have. The most popular microprocessor at the time of this writing is the 80386 (this will be abbreviated as a 386, 386SX or 386DL, depending on which version is used). Some computers will have a 80286 processor; others will have an 80486. You should avoid the 286 processor. Much of the software available today will not operate as effectively on a machine with an 80286 as on a machine with an 80386. It is also difficult to run Windows on an 80286 machine. In contrast, the 80486 is very powerful and more expensive.

Unless you plan on doing very complex calculations, you probably don't need a computer with a 486.

You can purchase a good computer with a 386 chip for less than $2,000 in most major cities in the United States or by mail order from firms like Dell Computer, Northgate and Zeos International.

PERIPHERALS: PRINTERS, MODEMS, ETC.

Without peripherals, you won't be able to communicate the work you do on your computer to anyone else. The two main peripherals with which you should be concerned are the printer and the modem.

Printers range in price from $200 to over $2,000. Which is right for you? It will depend upon the quality of printouts you would like and the speed at which the printer prints pages. There are essentially three types of printers: dot matrix (or impact), ink-jet and laser.

Dot matrix printers are very affordable, ranging in price from approximately $200 to $500. The print from a dot-matrix printer will not have a high resolution.

Ink-jet printers cost slightly more than dot matrix printers, ranging in price from $350 to $800. They offer better resolution and slightly greater speed than dot matrix printers. Popular models include the Hewlett-Packard DeskJet and DeskWriter, and the Canon BubbleJet. The Hewlett-Packard printers also offer color capabilities.

Laser printers top the cost scale, ranging in price between $700 and $2,000. They are by far the fastest printers and produce the highest-quality output. Most companies use laser printers for their correspondence and literature. If you plan to generate any graphics documents or place a priority on high-resolution printing, you might prefer a laser printer.

The other peripheral you should consider is a modem. A modem will allow your computer to communicate over telephone lines with other computers. It will give you the capability to access information services like Dow-Jones News Retrieval and CompuServe. Many modems also include facsimile (fax) capabilities so that you can send documents directly from your computer. If you travel a great deal and either need access to your desktop computer from the road or want to send things to other people from a portable computer, this can be very useful. A good modem costs approximately $200, but you can also find them as cheap as $100 and as expensive as $500.

SOFTWARE: SO MANY CHOICES

Although a computer is very powerful, its power cannot truly be taken advantage of unless you have application software. Application software allows you to perform tasks like writing documents, performing financial analysis and keeping track of contacts.

If you are not convinced that the number of choices in computer software is overwhelming, walk into a retail software store, such as Egghead Discount Software. The shelves will be lined with packages for you to evaluate. In addition to sorting through the numerous alternatives, you must choose a software that is compatible with your computer's operating system. While many manufacturers make versions of their software for the Macintosh, DOS and Windows, some software is available for one operating system but not for the other.

The following sections discuss the major classifications of application software and a few of the more popular packages. After each product name, the appropriate operating systems are included in parentheses. This list is not all-inclusive. Many programs are not mentioned. We recommend that you go into a store and evaluate several packages before you make a decision. You should base your decision on how comfortable you are using the package and what it offers.

WORD PROCESSING

A word-processing package allows you to create and format documents such as letters, business plans, marketing plans, proposals and brochures. Few personal computer users can get by without a word-processing package. When you look at word processors, your main concern should be with how easy the package is to use. Some packages use pull-down "menus" to instruct the computer to perform functions, while others require keystrokes. Word-processing programs may be purchased for as little as $50 and as much as $500. The Windows operating system includes a nice word-processing package from Microsoft called Write; it is essentially a scaled-down version of Microsoft Word.

Three of the most popular word-processing packages are:

1. Microsoft Word (DOS, Windows, Macintosh)—an easy-to-use package that has pull-down menus, extensive formatting capabilities and some graphics capabilities

2. WordPerfect (DOS, Windows, Macintosh)—This is the most popular word-processing package in the world, but not necessarily the easiest to use. It uses keystroke driven commands, so it may take a while to learn.

3. MacWrite (Macintosh)—This is the original word-processing package that was shipped with every Macintosh. It is now sold separately and marketed by Claris. It offers capabilities similar to Microsoft Word and is a fine choice for the Macintosh.

SPREADSHEETS

If you plan on doing your own financial analysis, especially business valuation, a spreadsheet package is essential. Spreadsheets allow you to enter numbers into "cells"; the contents can then be manipulated and used in calculations in other cells. A powerful spreadsheet package will also give you rudimentary text capabilities, the ability to generate graphs and some database functions. Three of the most popular spreadsheet packages are:

1. Lotus 1-2-3 (DOS, Windows, Macintosh)—This is the "granddaddy" of spreadsheets. It is probably the most popular in terms of units shipped and is most frequently used on computers running DOS.

2. Microsoft Excel (Windows, Macintosh)—This is easily the dominant package for the Macintosh. A slick Windows version is now available that allows former users of Lotus 1-2-3 to enter Lotus commands and learn the equivalent Excel command. A good package for the first-time user, it is also powerful enough for even the most rigorous numerical analysis.

3. Borland QuattroPro (DOS, Windows)—This is the alter-ego for most DOS spreadsheet users who do not use Lotus 1-2-3. It has many powerful features, including fairly robust graphing capabilities, and is compatible with computers using a mouse. A scaled-down version of QuattroPro, Quattro, is available for about one-third the price.

DATA BASE

A database program is specifically designed to manipulate large amounts of data that are similar in form but not in content—for example, a list of companies and owners, with addresses, to whom you have sent requests for information. A database package makes it easy not only to keep track of this information but also to report and print it. Of the three main application program types (word-processing, spreadsheet and database), the database program should probably be the last that you acquire. Three of the popular database programs are:

1. Borland Paradox (DOS)—This is the crowd favorite in most companies using DOS-based computers. Paradox is fairly easy to learn and has extensive reporting capabilities. It can also export data to popular spreadsheets like Lotus 1-2-3 and Borland QuattroPro.
2. Ashton-Tate (Borland) DBase (DOS, Macintosh)—Like Lotus 1-2-3 in spreadsheets, DBase is the granddaddy of database programs. It includes all the features necessary to track, enter and report on information. The DOS version is much more popular than the Macintosh version. If you need a data base for the Macintosh, see below.
3. Claris FileMaker Pro (Macintosh)—A widely used database package for the Macintosh, Filemaker Pro has all the tools you'll need to keep track of companies, contacts and activities. It was designed for the Macintosh, so its menus and commands will be intuitive and easy to learn for Macintosh users.

INTEGRATED

Integrated application packages usually include a word processor, a spreadsheet, data base and communications capabilities. The individual components of an integrated software package are not as fully featured as the corresponding stand-alone applications programs, but integrated programs are generally less expensive than the cost of purchasing one of each type of application program separately. Popular integrated programs include Microsoft Works (Windows, Macintosh), LotusWorks (DOS) and ClarisWorks (Macintosh).

OTHER USEFUL SOFTWARE

There are thousands of software programs that do not fall into any of the above categories. Many of these are designed to enhance your productivity, while some just entertain. The following are a few that you may find helpful in your search for a business.

Contact management programs—These allow you to track the contacts that you make in your search. It will prompt you when you should call someone or remind you that you should have received something from someone.

Communications programs—This software allows your computer to talk to others. If you bought a modem, it may have come with a communications program. If you look for a program, make sure it can support popular communications protocols such as Kermit. Microsoft Windows includes a communications program with the basic operating system.

Presentation packages—A presentation package combines graphic, charting and text capabilities to make it easier to convey information in summary form. Some spreadsheets, such as Excel and QuattroPro, include presentation capabilities. A presentation package will pay for itself quickly if you plan on doing presentations for bankers, investors, employees or associates.

CONCLUSION

No matter what the final configuration of hardware, software, peripherals and accessories you acquire, keep in mind that the computer should make you more, not less, productive. Don't buy a time-management program and then get so involved with it that you can no longer schedule a simple appointment without first scanning through your computerized information.

We are confident that a computer, when used effectively, will save you much more time in your search than the initial investment of time in getting it configured and loaded with software.

■ APPENDIX C ■

Securities Issues

When you raise money for acquisitions, you may do so through either debt or equity financing. If you choose equity financing, it is extremely important to comply with both state and federal securities laws. State securities laws vary widely, and federal requirements to qualify for exemptions are extensive. Securities laws, which can be very detailed and intricate, must be considered whenever money is being raised for an acquisition. These laws and regulations have been established to protect investors by providing guidelines and requirements for those who seek to raise money by issuing securities. The importance of legal assistance with regard to these issues cannot be overstated. Violating securities laws can have severe consequences.

Security laws deal with the issuance (1933 Securities Act) and trading (1934 Securities Exchange Act) of securities. The Securities and Exchange Commission (SEC) administers federal security laws, and state security laws (blue-sky laws) are regulated within each state. These laws require that any time you are involved in the issuance of securities, you must register with the SEC. Registration for an offering could cost up to $300,000.

The first major issue with securities laws is full and accurate disclosure of information. Issuers are required to fully disclose all the information they have pertaining to an investment opportunity so that investors can more accurately assess the merits and risks of a transaction. To understand why full disclosure is a critical issue, consider how you would feel if you made a passive investment in a business that failed for reasons that were known upfront by the person who operated the company but were not expressed to you. An investor can only evaluate an opportunity by considering the facts with which he or she is presented.

The second major security issue deals with the characteristics of the people or institutions that seek to purchase securities. When offering an investment opportunity, you must consider the investor's ability to analyze the merits of an offering and the investor's ability to sustain a loss of the entire investment.

There are two types of investors with whom you should be familiar: "sophisticated" and "accredited" investors. A sophisticated investor is a person who has experience in evaluating investment opportunities. For example, a financial analyst for an investment bank would likely be considered a sophisticated investor, while a media planner for an advertising company most likely would not.

Accredited investors are either people or institutions that have substantial financial resources and therefore can risk losing the investment without a large impact on their well-being, or people who have control of the actual investment. The SEC defines accredited investors as financial institutions (such as banks or SBICs); private business development companies; an entity with at least $5 million in net assets; directors, executive officers or general partners of the issuer; individuals with a net worth of at least $1 million; or individuals with an income of at least $200,000 in each of the last two years who expect a similar income for the current year.

SAFE HARBOR EXEMPTIONS

As mentioned in Chapter 9, securities registration can be extremely expensive. However, there are ways around these costs. Safe harbor exemptions allow issuers of nonpublic securities to avoid having to incur the capital constraints of registration. There are four safe harbor rules that are exempt from the federal SEC registration requirements. The first is the *private placement* offering. This offering limits the number of nonaccredited investors to 35 or fewer sophisticated investors and allows an unlimited number of accredited investors. Full disclosure to each investor is mandatory, and the resale rights an investor has are limited. The dollar amount of a private placement offering is unlimited. Private placement offerings do not allow general solicitation or mass marketing of the investment opportunity.

The second safe harbor rule is the *small offering* exemption. The small offering permits an unlimited number of accredited investors, plus 35 nonaccredited investors who do not need to be sophisticated. Full disclosure is required, and there are no restrictions on the resale of the securities.

Securities regulations limit the offering to no more than $5 million, and general solicitation is not allowed.

The third exempt offering is the *very small offering*. Under this exemption, you can have an unlimited number of investors of any type. If state law allows, you can perform general solicitations; the resale of securities is unrestricted; and, if there is disclosure, up to $1 million may be raised. Without disclosure, the offering is limited to $500,000.

The last exemption is the *intra-state* offering. In order for a company to be exempt under this rule, it must be incorporated in the state where it does business. Additionally, 80 percent of the company's gross revenue, its assets and the proceeds from the offering must be generated or used in that state, and all of the investors must be state residents. The intra-state offering allows an unlimited number of investors of any type. It has no disclosure requirements and no limitation on the amount of money that can be raised. General solicitation is permitted, and the resale of securities is restricted for nine months.

■ APPENDIX D ■

SBA Offices and SBICs

SMALL BUSINESS ADMINISTRATION (SBA) OFFICES

Alabama

2121 8th Avenue North
Birmingham, AL 35203-2398
(205) 731-1344

Alaska

222 West 8th Avenue
Anchorage, AK 99513-7559
(907) 271-4022

Arizona

2828 North Central Avenue
Phoenix, AZ 85004-1025
(602) 640-2316

Arkansas

2120 Riverfront Drive
Little Rock, AR 72202
(501) 324-5278

California

2719 North Air Fresno Drive
Fresno, CA 93727-1547
(209) 487-5189

330 North Brand Boulevard
Glendale, CA 91203-2304
(213) 894-2956

660 J Street
Sacramento, CA 95814-2413
(916) 551-1426

880 Front Street
San Diego, CA 92188-0270
(619) 557-7252

211 Main Street
San Francisco, CA 94105-1988
(415) 744-6820

71 Stevenson Street
San Francisco, CA 94105-2939
(415) 744-6402

901 West Civic Drive
Santa Ana, CA 92703-2352
(714) 836-2494

Colorado

999 18th Street
Denver, CO 80202
(303) 294-7186

721 19th Street
Denver, CO 80201-0660
(303) 844-3984

Connecticut

330 Main Street
Hartford, CT 06106
(203) 240-4700

Delaware

920 North King Street
Wilmington, DE 19801
(302) 573-6295

District of Columbia

1111 18th Street NW
Washington, DC 20036
(202) 634-1500

Florida

1320 South Dixie Highway
Coral Gables, FL 33146-2911
(305) 536-5521

7825 Baymeadows Way
Jacksonville, FL 32256-7504
(904) 443-1900

Georgia

1720 Peachtree Road NW
Atlanta, GA 30309
(404) 347-4749

1375 Peachtree Street NE
Atlanta, GA 30367-8102
(404) 347-2797

Hawaii

300 Ala Moana Boulevard
Honolulu, HI 96850-4981
(808) 541-2990

Idaho

1020 Main Street
Boise, ID 83702-5745
(208) 334-1696

Illinois

300 South Riverside Plaza
Chicago, IL 60606-6617
(312) 353-5000

500 West Madison Street
Chicago, IL 60661-2511
(312) 353-4528

511 West Capitol Street
Springfield, IL 62704
(217) 492-4416

Indiana

429 North Pennsylvania
Indianapolis, IN 46204-1873
(317) 226-7272

Iowa

373 Collins Road NE
Cedar Rapids, IA 52402-3147
(319) 393-8630

210 Walnut Street
Des Moines, IA 50309
(515) 284-4422

Kansas

100 East English Street
Wichita, KS 67202
(316) 269-6273

Kentucky

600 Dr. M.L. King, Jr. Place
Louisville, KY 40202
(502) 582-5971

Louisiana

1661 Canal Street
New Orleans, LA 70112
(504) 589-6685

Maine

40 Western Avenue
Augusta, ME 04330
(207) 622-8378

Maryland

10 North Calvert Street
Baltimore, MD 21202
(410) 962-4392

Massachusetts

155 Federal Street
Boston, MA 02110
(617) 451-2023

10 Causeway Street
Boston, MA 02222-1093
(617) 565-5590

1550 Main Street
Springfield, MA 01103
(413) 785-0268

Michigan

477 Michigan Avenue
Detroit, MI 48226
(313) 226-6175

300 South Front Street
Marquette, MI 49885
(906) 225-1108

Minnesota

100 North 6th Street
Minneapolis, MN 55403-1563
(612) 370-2324

Mississippi

One Hancock Plaza
Gulfport, MS 39501-7758
(601) 863-4449

101 West Capitol Street
Jackson, MS 39201
(601) 965-4378

Missouri

323 West 8th Street
Kansas City, MO 64105
(816) 374-6708

911 Walnut Street
Kansas City, MO 64106
(816) 426-3608

620 South Glenstone Street
Springfield, MO 65802-3200
(417) 864-7670

815 Olive Street
St. Louis, MO 63101
(314) 539-6600

Montana

301 South Park
Helena, MT 59626
(406) 449-5381

Nebraska

11145 Mill Valley Road
Omaha, NE 68154
(402) 221-4691

New Hampshire

143 North Main Street
Concord, NH 03302-1257
(603) 255-1400

New Jersey

60 Park Place
Newark, NJ 07102
(201) 645-2434

New Mexico

625 Silver Avenue SW
Albuquerque, NM 87102
(505) 766-1870

New York

111 West Huron Street
Buffalo, NY 14202
(716) 846-4301

333 East Water Street
Elmira, NY 14901
(607) 734-8130

35 Pinelawn Road
Melville, NY 11747
(516) 454-0750

26 Federal Plaza
New York, NY 10278
(212) 264-1450

26 Federal Plaza
New York, NY 10278
(212) 264-2454

100 State Street
Rochester, NY 14614
(716) 263-6700

100 South Clinton Street
Syracuse, NY 13260
(315) 423-5383

Nevada

301 East Stewart Street
Las Vegas, NV 89125-2527
(702) 388-6611

North Carolina

200 North College Street
Charlotte, NC 28202
(704) 344-6563

North Dakota

657 2nd Avenue North
Fargo, ND 58108-3086
(701) 239-5131

Ohio

525 Vine Street
Cincinnati, OH 45202
(513) 684-2814

1240 East 9th Street
Cleveland, OH 44199
(216) 522-4180

2 Nationwide Plaza
Columbus, OH 43215-2592
(614) 469-6860

Oklahoma

200 North West 5th Street
Oklahoma City, OK 73102
(405) 231-4301

Oregon

222 South West Columbia
Portland, OR 97201-6605
(503) 326-2682

Pennsylvania

100 Chestnut Street
Harrisburg, PA 17101
(717) 782-3840

475 Allendale Road
King of Prussia, PA 19406
(215) 962-3700

960 Penn Avenue
Pittsburgh, PA 15222
(412) 644-2780

20 North Pennsylvania Avenue
Wilkes-Barre, PA 18702
(717) 826-6497

Rhode Island

380 Westminister Mall
Providence, RI 02903
(401) 528-4561

South Carolina

1835 Assembly Street
Columbia, SC 29201
(803) 765-5376

South Dakota

101 South Main Avenue
Sioux Falls, SD 57102-0527
(605) 330-4231

Tennessee

50 Vantage Way
Nashville, TN 37228-1500
(615) 736-5881

Texas

606 North Carancamua
Corpus Christi, TX 78476
(512) 888-3331

1100 Commerce Street
Dallas, TX 75242
(214) 767-0605

8625 King George Drive
Dallas, TX 75235-3391
(214) 767-7633

10737 Gateway West
El Paso, TX 79935
(915) 540-5676

819 Taylor Street
Ft. Worth, TX 76102
(817) 334-3777

222 East Van Buren Street
Harlingen, TX 78550
(512) 427-8533

9301 Southwest Freeway
Houston, TX 77074-1591
(713) 953-5900

1611 Tenth Street
Lubbock, TX 79401
(806) 743-7462

7400 Blanco Road
San Antonio, TX 78216
(512) 229-4535

Utah

125 South State Street
Salt Lake City, UT 84138-1195
(801) 524-5800

Vermont

87 State Street
Montpelier, VT 05602
(802) 828-4422

Virginia

400 North Eighth Street
Richmond, VA 23240
(804) 771-2400

Washington

2615 4th Avenue
Seattle, WA 98121
(206) 553-5676

915 Second Avenue
Seattle, WA 98174-1088
(206) 553-1420

West 601 First Avenue
Spokane, WA 99204-0317
(509) 353-2800

West Virginia

550 Eagan Street
Charleston, WV 25301
(304) 347-5220

168 West Main Street
Clarksburg, WV 26301
(304) 623-5631

Wisconsin

212 East Washington Avenue
Madison, WI 53703
(608) 264-5261

310 West Wisconsin Avenue
Milwaukee, WI 53203
(414) 297-3941

Wyoming

100 East 8th Street
Casper, WY 82602-2839
(307) 261-5761

Guam

238 Archbishop F.C. Florest St.
Agana, GM 96910
(671) 472-7277

Puerto Rico

Carlos Chardon Avenue
Hato Rey, PR 00918
(809) 766-5572

SMALL BUSINESS INVESTMENT COMPANIES (SBICs)

Alabama

Alabama Small Business Investment
Company
1732 5th Avenue North
Birmingham, AL 35203
(205) 324-5234

FJC Growth Capital Corporation
200 West Court Square, Suite 750
Huntsville, AL 35801
(205) 922-2918

Hickory Venture Capital Corporation
200 West Court Square, Suite 100
Huntsville, AL 35801
(205) 539-5130

Alabama Capital Corporation
16 Midtown Park East
Mobile, AL 36606
(205) 476-0700

First SBIC of Alabama
16 Midtown Park East
Mobile, AL 36606
(205) 476-0700

Arizona

First Interstate Equity Corporation
100 West Washington Street
Phoenix, AZ 85003
(602) 528-6647

Rocky Mountain Equity Corporation
2525 East Camelback, Suite 275
Phoenix, AZ 85016
(602) 955-6100

Sundance Venture Partners, L.P.
400 East Van Buren, Suite 650
Phoenix, AZ 85004
(602) 252-3441

Valley National Investors, Inc.
201 North Central Avenue, Suite 900
Phoenix, AZ 85004
(602) 261-1577

First Commerce & Loan LP
5620 North Kolb, #260
Tucson, AZ 85715
(602) 298-2500

Wilbur Venture Capital Corporation
4575 South Palo Verde, Suite 305
Tucson, AZ 85714
(602) 747-5999

Arkansas

Southern Ventures, Inc.
605 Main Street, Suite 202
Arkadelphia, AR 71923
(501) 246-9627

Capital Management Services, Inc.
1910 North Grant Street, Suite 200
Little Rock, AR 72207
(501) 664-8613

Small Business Investment
Capital, Inc.
10003 New Benton Highway
Mail: P.O. Box 3627
Little Rock, AR 72203
(501) 455-6599

Power Ventures, Inc.
829 Highway 270 North
Malvern, AR 72104
(501) 332-3695

California

Calsafe Capital Corporation
245 East Main Street, Suite 107
Alhambra, CA 91801
(818) 289-3400

Astar Capital Corporation
429 South Euclid Avenue, Suite B
Anaheim, CA 92802
(714) 490-1149

Ritter Partners
150 Isabella Avenue
Atherton, CA 94025
(415) 854-1555

San Joaquin Capital Corporation
1415 18th Street, Suite 306
Mail: P.O. Box 2538
Bakersfield, CA 93301
(805) 323-7581

Ally Finance Corporation
9100 Wilshire Boulevard, Suite 408
Beverly Hills, CA 90212
(213) 550-8100

City Ventures, Inc.
120 South Spalding Drive, Suite 320
Beverly Hills, CA 90212
(213) 550-5686

Westamco Investment Company
8929 Wilshire Boulevard, Suite 400
Beverly Hills, CA 90211
(213) 652-8288

Helio Capital, Inc.
6263 Randolf Street
Commerce, CA 90040
(213) 728-6637

First SBIC of California
650 Town Center Drive, 17th Floor
Costa Mesa, CA 92626
(714) 556-1964

DSC Ventures II, LP
20111 Stevens Creek Boulevard,
    Suite 130
Cupertino, CA 95014
(408) 252-3800

First American Capital Funding, Inc.
10840 Warner Avenue, Suite 202
Fountain Valley, CA 92708
(714) 965-7190

Opportunity Capital Corporation
One Fremont Place
39650 Liberty Street, Suite 425
Fremont, CA 94538
(415) 651-4412

San Joaquin Business Investment
    Group Inc.
1900 Mariposa Mall, Suite 100
Fresno, CA 93721
(209) 233-3580

Magna Pacific Investments
700 North Central Avenue, Suite 245
Glendale, CA 91203
(818) 547-0809

Asian American Capital Corporation
1251 West Tennyson Road, Suite #4
Hayward, CA 94544
(415) 887-6888

Continental Investors, Inc.
8781 Seaspray Drive
Huntington Beach, CA 92646
(714) 964-5207

Imperial Ventures, Inc.
9920 South La Cienega Boulevard
Mail: P.O. Box 92991, L.A. 90009
Inglewood, CA 90301
(213) 417-5928

Best Finance Corporation
4929 West Wilshire Boulevard,
    Suite 407
Los Angeles, CA 90010
(213) 937-1636

Charterway Investment Corporation
222 South Hill Street, Suite 800
Los Angeles, CA 90012
(213) 687-8539

Developers Equity Capital
    Corporation
1880 Century Park East, Suite 211
Los Angeles, CA 90067
(213) 277-0330

Far East Capital Corporation
123 South Figueroa Street
Los Angeles, CA 90012
(213) 253-0599

Helio Capital, Inc.
One Wilshire Building
624 South Grand Avenue, Suite 2700
Los Angeles, CA 90017
(213) 721-8053

New Kukje Investment Company
3670 Wilshire Boulevard, Suite 418
Los Angeles, CA 90010
(213) 389-8679

Union Venture Corporation
445 South Figueroa Street
Los Angeles, CA 90071
(213) 236-4092

BNP Venture Capital Corporation
3000 Sand Hill Road
Building 1, Suite 125
Menlo Park, CA 94025
(415) 854-1084

First SBIC of California
2400 Sand Hill Road, Suite 101
Menlo Park, CA 94025
(415) 424-8011

Ritter Partners
3000 Sand Hill Road
Building 1, Suite 190
Menlo Park, CA 94025
(415) 854-1555

Sundance Venture Partners, LP
3000 Sand Hill Road
Building 4, Suite 130
Menlo Park, CA 94025
(415) 854-8100

LaiLai Capital Corporation
223 East Garvey Avenue, Suite 228
Monterey, CA 91754
(818) 288-0704

Allied Business Investors, Inc.
428 South Atlantic Boulevard,
  Suite 201
Monterey Park, CA 91754
(818) 289-0186

Myriad Capital, Inc.
328 South Atlantic Boulevard,
  Suite 200 A
Monterey Park, CA 91754
(818) 570-4548

Hall, Fullerton, Morris &
  Drufva II, LP
5000 Birch Street, Suite 10100
Newport Beach, CA 92660
(714) 253-4360

Marwit Capital Corporation
180 Newport Center Drive, Suite 200
Newport Beach, CA 92660
(714) 640-6234

New West Partners II
4600 Campus Drive, Suite 103
Newport Beach, CA 92660
(714) 756-8940

RSC Financial Corporation
Century 21 Building
501 East Ojay Avenue
Mail: P.O. Box 544
Ojai, CA 93024
(805) 646-2925

Draper Associates, a California LP
3803 East Bayshore Road, #125
Palo Alto, CA 94303
(415) 961-6669

Merrill Pickard Anderson & Eyre I
Two Palo Alto Square, Suite 425
Palo Alto, CA 94306
(415) 856-8880

ABC Capital Corporation
27 North Mentor Avenue
Pasadena, CA 91106
(818) 355-3577

First SBIC of California
2 North Lake Street, Suite 940
Pasadena, CA 91101
(818) 304-3451

AMF Financial, Inc.
4330 La Jolla Village Drive, Suite 110
San Diego, CA 92122
(619) 546-0167

New West Partners II
4350 Executive Drive, Suite 206
San Diego, CA 92121
(619) 457-0723

Seaport Ventures, Inc.
525 B Street, Suite 630
San Diego, CA 92101
(619) 232-4069

BankAmerica Ventures, Inc.
555 California Street, 12th Floor
c/o Dept. 3908
San Francisco, CA 94104
(415) 953-3001

Bentley Capital
592 Vallejo Street, Suite #2
San Francisco, CA 94133
(415) 362-2868

Equitable Capital Corporation
855 Sansome Street
San Francisco, CA 94111
(415) 434-4114

G C & H Partners
One Maritime Plaza, 20th Floor
San Francisco, CA 94110
(415) 981-5252

Jupiter Partners
600 Montgomery Street, 35th Floor
San Francisco, CA 94111
(415) 421-9990

Positive Enterprises, Inc.
1166 Post Street, Suite 200-S6
San Francisco, CA 94109
(415) 885-6600

VK Capital Company
50 California Street, Suite 2350
San Francisco, CA 94111
(415) 391-5600

Western General Capital Corporation
13701 Riverside Drive, Suite 328
Sherman Oaks, CA 91423
(818) 986-5038

South Bay Capital Corporation
18039 Crenshaw Boulevard, Suite 203
Torrance, CA 90504
(213) 515-1712

Vinh An Capital Investment, Inc.
9191 Bolsa Avenue, Suite 116
Westminster, CA 92683
(714) 895-3218

Colorado

UBD Capital, Inc.
1700 Broadway
Denver, CO 80274
(303) 863-6329

Connecticut

AB SBIC, Inc.
275 School House Road
Cheshire, CT 06410
(203) 272-0203

Financial Opportunities, Inc.
174 South Road
Enfield, CT 06082
(203) 741-9727

First New England Capital, LP
255 Main Street
Hartford, CT 06106
(203) 728-5200

All State Venture Capital Corporation
The Bishop House
32 Elm Street, P.O. Box 1629
New Haven, CT 06506
(203) 787-5029

Northeastern Capital Corporation
209 Church Street
New Haven, CT 06510
(203) 865-4500

RFE Capital Partners, LP
36 Grove Street
New Canaan, CT 06840
(203) 966-2800

The SBIC of Connecticut Inc.
965 White Plains Road
Trumbull, CT 06611
(203) 261-0011

Capital Resource Co. of Connecticut
2558 Albany Avenue
West Hartford, CT 06117
(203) 236-4336

Marcon Capital Corporation
49 Riverside Avenue
Westport, CT 06880
(203) 226-6893

Washington, D.C.

Allied Investment Corporation
1666 K Street NW, Suite 901
Washington, DC 20006
(202) 331-1112

Allied Investment Corporation II
1666 K Street NW, Suite 901
Washington, DC 20006
(202) 331-1112

Allied Financial Services Corporation
1666 K Street NW, Suite 901
Washington, DC 20006
(202) 331-1112

Broadcast Capital, Inc.
1771 N Street NW, Suite 421
Washington, DC 20036
(202) 429-5393

Consumers United Capital
  Corporation
2100 M Street NW
Washington, DC 20037
(202) 872-5262

Fulcrum Venture Capital Corporation
2021 K Street NW, Suite 210
Washington, DC 20006
(202) 833-9580

Minority Broadcast Investment
  Corporation
1200 18th Street NW, Suite 705
Washington, DC 20036
(202) 293-1166

Florida

Mariner Venture Capital Corporation
2300 West Glades Road, Suite 440
West Tower
Boca Raton, FL 33431

Quantum Capital Partners, Ltd.
600 Fairway Drive, Suite 101
Deerfield, FL 33441
(305) 570-6231

Venture Group, Inc.
5433 Buffalo Avenue
Jacksonville, FL 32208
(904) 353-7313

Business Assistance
Center–MESBIC, Inc.
6600 Northwest 27th Avenue
Miami, FL 33247
(305) 693-5919

Southeast SBIC, Inc.
One Southeast Financial Center
Miami, FL 33131
(305) 375-6962

J & D Capital Corporation
12747 Biscayne Boulevard
North Miami, FL 33181
(305) 893-0303

Pro-Med Investment Corporation
AmeriFirst Bank Building, 2nd Fl. S
18301 Biscayne Boulevard
North Miami Beach, FL 33160
(305) 933-5858

Western Financial Capital Corporation
AmeriFirst Bank Building, 2nd Fl. S
18301 Biscayne Boulevard
North Miami Beach, FL 33160
(305) 933-5858

Florida Capital Venture, Ltd.
111 Madison Street, 26th Floor
Tampa, FL 33602
(813) 229-2294

Market Capital Corporation
1102 North 28th Street
Mail: P.O. Box 31667
Tampa, FL 33631
(813) 247-1357

Allied Financial Services Corporation
Executive Office Center, Suite 305
2770 North Indian River Boulevard
Vero Beach, FL 32960
(407) 778-5556

Allied Investment Corporation
Executive Office Center, Suite 305
2770 North Indian River Boulevard
Vero Beach, FL 32960
(407) 778-5556

Georgia

Investor's Equity, Inc.
945 East Paces Ferry Road,
   Suite 1735
Atlanta, GA 30326
(404) 266-8300

Renaissance Capital Corporation
161 Spring Street NW, Suite 815
Atlanta, GA 30303
(404) 658-9061

First Growth Capital, Inc.
4630 Chambers Road
Macon, GA 31206
(912) 781-7131

North Riverside Capital Corporation
50 Technology Park/Atlanta
Norcross, GA 30092
(404) 446-5556

Hawaii

Bancorp Hawaii SBIC
111 South King Street, Suite 1060
Honolulu, HI 96813
(808) 521-6411

Pacific Venture Capital, Ltd.
222 South Vineyard Street
PH.1
Honolulu, HI 96813
(808) 521-6502

Iowa

MorAmerica Capital Corporation
101 2nd Street SE, Suite 800
Cedar Rapids, IA 52401
(319) 363-8249

Illinois

Alpha Capital Venture Partners, LP
Three First National Plaza, 14th Floor
Chicago, IL 60602
(312) 372-1556

Amoco Venture Capital Company
200 East Randolph Drive
Mail Code 3905A
Chicago, IL 60601
(312) 856-6523

ANB Venture Corporation
33 North LaSalle Street
Chicago, IL 60690
(312) 855-1554

Business Ventures, Inc.
20 North Wacker Drive, Suite 1741
Chicago, IL 60606
(312) 346-1580

Chicago Community Ventures, Inc.
25 East Washington Boulevard,
   Suite 2015
Chicago, IL 60603
(312) 726-6084

Continental Illinois Venture
   Corporation
209 South LaSalle Street
Mail: 231 South LaSalle Street
Chicago, IL 60693
(312) 828-8023

First Capital Corporation of Chicago
Three First National Plaza, Suite 1330
Chicago, IL 60670
(312) 732-5400

Heller Equity Capital Corporation
500 West Monroe Street
Chicago, IL 60661
(312) 441-7200

Peterson Finance and Investment
   Company
3300 West Peterson Avenue, Suite A
Chicago, IL 60659
(312) 539-0502

The Combined Fund, Inc.
915 East Hyde Park Boulevard
Chicago, IL 60615
(312) 363-0300

The Neighborhood Fund, Inc.
1950 East 71st Street
Chicago, IL 60649
(312) 753-5670

Tower Ventures, Inc.
Sears Tower, BSC 43-50
Chicago, IL 60684
(312) 875-0571

Walnut Capital Corporation
Two North LaSalle Street, Suite 2410
Chicago, IL 60602
(312) 346-2033

Indiana

Circle Ventures, Inc.
26 North Arsenal Avenue
Indianapolis, IN 46201
(317) 636-7242

1st Source Capital Corporation
100 North Michigan Street
Mail: P.O. Box 1602
South Bend 46634
South Bend, IN 46601
(219) 236-2180

Kentucky

Mountain Ventures, Inc.
London Bank & Trust Building
400 South Main Street, Fourth Floor
London, KY 40741
(606) 864-5175

Equal Opportunity Finance, Inc.
420 Hurstbourne Lane, Suite 201
Louisville, KY 40222
(502) 423-1943

Wilbur Venture Capital Corporation
400 Fincastle Building
3rd & Broadway
Louisville, KY 40202
(502) 585-1214

Kansas

Kansas Venture Capital, Inc.
6700 Antioch Plaza, Suite 460
Overland Park, KS 66204
(913) 262-7117

Kansas Venture Capital, Inc.
500 South Kansas Avenue, Suite J
Topeka, KS 66603
(913) 233-1368

Kansas Venture Capital, Inc.
One Main Place, Suite 806
Wichita, KS 67202
(316) 262-1221

Louisiana

Premier Venture Capital Corporation
451 Florida Street
Baton Rouge, LA 70821
(504) 389-4421

SCDF Investment Corporation
1006 Surrey Street
P.O. Box 3885
Lafayette, LA 70502
(318) 232-3769

Massachusetts

Advent Atlantic Capital Company, LP
75 State Street, Suite 2500
Boston, MA 02109
(617) 345-7200

Advent Industrial Capital
  Company, LP
75 State Street, Suite 2500
Boston, MA 02109
(617) 345-7200

Advent V Capital Company, LP
75 State Street, Suite 2500
Boston, MA 02109
(617) 345-7200

BancBoston Ventures, Inc.
100 Federal Street
Mail: P.O. Box 2016, Stop 01-31-08
Boston, MA 02110
(617) 434-2442

Chestnut Capital International II, LP
75 State Street, Suite 2500
Boston, MA 02109
(617) 345-7200

Chestnut Street Partners, Inc.
75 State Street, Suite 2500
Boston, MA 02109
(617) 345-7220

First Capital Corporation of Chicago
One Financial Center, 27th Floor
Boston, MA 02111
(617) 542-9185

First SBIC of California
101 Federal Street, 19th Floor
Boston, MA 02110
(617) 542-7601

Mezzanine Capital Corporation
75 State Street, Suite 2500
Boston, MA 02109
(617) 345-7200

Northeast SBI Corporation
16 Cumberland Street
Boston, MA 02115
(617) 267-3983

Norwest Equity Partners IV
50 Milk Street, 20th Floor
Boston, MA 02109
(617) 426-1416

Norwest Growth Fund, Inc.
50 Milk Street, 20th Floor
Boston, MA 02109
(617) 426-1416

Norwest Venture Partners
50 Milk Street, 20th Floor
Boston, MA 02109
(617) 426-1416

Orange Nassau Capital Corporation
One International Place, 23rd Floor
Boston, MA 02110
(617) 951-9920

Pioneer Ventures Limited Partnership
60 State Street
Boston, MA 02109
(617) 742-7825

TBM II Capital Corporation
One International Place, 23rd Floor
Boston, MA 02110
(617) 951-9920

Transportation Capital Corporation
45 Newbury Street, Suite 207
Boston, MA 02116
(617) 536-0344

UST Capital Corporation
40 Court Street
Boston, MA 02108
(617) 726-7137

Vadus Capital Corporation
One International Place, 23rd Floor
Boston, MA 02110
(617) 951-9920

Fleet Venture Resources, Inc.
1740 Massachusetts Avenue
Boxborough, MA 01719
(508) 263-0177

First United SBIC, Inc.
135 Will Drive
Canton, MA 02021
(617) 828-6150

The Argonauts MESBIC Corporation
929 Worcester Road
Framingham, MA 01701
(508) 820-3430

Business Achievement Corporation
1172 Beacon Street, Suite 202
Newton, MA 02161
(617) 965-0550

LRF Capital Limited Partnership
189 Wells Avenue, Suite 4
Newton, MA 02159
(617) 964-0049

New England MESBIC, Inc.
530 Turnpike Street
North Andover, MA 01845
(508) 688-4326

Southern Berkshire Investment
  Corporation
P.O. Box 669
Sheffield, MA 01257
(413) 229-3106

Maryland

American Security Capital
  Corporation, Inc.
100 South Charles Street, 5th Floor
Baltimore, MD 21203
(301) 547-4523

Security Financial and Investment
  Corporation
7720 Wisconsin Avenue, Suite 207
Bethesda, MD 20814
(301) 951-4288

Greater Washington Investments, Inc.
5454 Wisconsin Avenue
Chevy Chase, MD 20815
(301) 656-0626

First Maryland Capital, Inc.
107 West Jefferson Street
Rockville, MD 20850
(301) 251-6630

Syncom Capital Corporation
8401 Colesville Road, #300
Silver Spring, MD 20910
(301) 608-3207

Michigan

Dearborn Capital Corporation
P.O. Box 1729
Dearborn, MI 48121
(313) 337-8577

Motor Enterprises, Inc.
General Motors Building,
  Room 15-134
3044 West Grand Boulevard
Detroit, MI 48202
(313) 556-4273

Metro-Detroit Investment Company
30777 Northwestern Highway,
  Suite 300
Farmington Hills, MI 48018
(313) 851-6300

Mutual Investment Company, Inc.
21415 Civic Center Drive
Mark Plaza Building, Suite 217
Southfield, MI 48076
(313) 357-2020

Minnesota

Northland Capital Venture Partnership
613 Missabe Building
Duluth, MN 55802
(218) 722-0545

Shared Ventures, Inc.
6550 York Avenue S, Suite 419
Edina, MN 55435
(612) 925-3411

Capital Dimensions Ventures
  Fund, Inc.
Two Appletree Square, Suite 335
Minneapolis, MN 55425
(612) 854-3007

FBS SBIC Limited Partnership
1100 First Bank Place East
Minneapolis, MN 55480
(612) 370-4764

Milestone Growth Fund, Inc.
2021 East Hennepin Avenue,
  Suite 155
Minneapolis, MN 55413
(612) 378-9363

Norwest Equity Partners IV
2800 Piper Jaffray Tower
222 South Ninth Street
Minneapolis, MN 55402
(612) 667-1650

Norwest Growth Fund, Inc.
2800 Piper Jaffray Tower
222 South Ninth Street
Minneapolis, MN 55402
(612) 667-1650

Norwest Venture Partners
2800 Piper Jaffray Tower
222 South Ninth Street
Minneapolis, MN 55402
(612) 667-1650

Mississippi

Sun-Delta Capital Access Center, Inc.
819 Main Street
Greenville, MS 38701
(601) 335-5291

Missouri

Bankers Capital Corporation
3100 Gillham Road
Kansas City, MO 64109
(816) 531-1600

MBI Venture Capital Investors, Inc.
850 Main Street
Kansas City, MO 64105
(816) 471-1700

Midland Capital Corporation
One Petticoat Lane, Suite 110
1020 Walnut Street
Kansas City, MO 64106
(816) 471-8000

MorAmerica Capital Corporation
911 Main Street, Suite 2724A
Commerce Tower Building
Kansas City, MO 64105
(816) 842-0114

United Missouri Capital Corporation
1010 Grand Avenue
Mail: P.O. Box 419226, K.C.,
  MO 64141
Kansas City, MO 64106
(816) 556-7333

Capital for Business, Inc.
11 South Meramec, Suite 800
St. Louis, MO 63105
(314) 854-7427

Nebraska

First of Nebraska Investment
  Corporation
One First National Center, Suite 701
Omaha, NE 68102
(402) 633-3585

United Financial Resources
  Corporation
6211 L Street
Mail: P.O. Box 1131
Omaha, NE 68101
(402) 734-1250

New Jersey

Formosa Capital Corporation
1037 Route 46 East, Unit C-208
Clifton, NJ 07013
(201) 916-0016

Transpac Capital Corporation
1037 Route 46 East
Clifton, NJ 07013
(201) 470-8855

Zaitech Capital Corporation
1037 Route 46 East, Unit C-201
Clifton, NJ 07013
(201) 365-0047

Monmouth Capital Corporation
125 Wycoff Road
Midland National Bank Building
P.O. Box 335
Eatontown, NJ 07724
(201) 542-4927

Amev Capital Corporation
333 Thornall Street, 2nd Floor
Edison, NJ 08837
(908) 603-8500

Capital Circulation Corporation
2035 Lemoine Avenue, 2nd Floor
Fort Lee, NJ 07024
(201) 947-8637

Tappan Zee Capital Corporation
201 Lower Notch Road
Little Falls, NJ 07424
(201) 256-8280

ESLO Capital Corporation
212 Wright Street
Newark, NJ 07114
(201) 242-4488

Rutgers Minority Investment
  Company
92 New Street
Newark, NJ 07102
(201) 648-5287

Bishop Capital, LP
500 Morris Avenue
Springfield, NJ 07081
(201) 376-0495

First Princeton Capital Corporation
Five Garret Mountain Plaza
West Paterson, NJ 07424
(201) 278-8111

New Mexico

Albuquerque SBIC
501 Tijeras Avenue, NW
P.O. Box 487
Albuquerque, NM 87103
(505) 247-0145

New York

NYBDC Capital Corporation
41 State Street
P.O. Box 738
Albany, NY 12201
(518) 463-2268

Triad Capital Corporation of
  New York
960 Southern Boulevard
Bronx, NY 10459
(212) 589-6541

Avdon Capital Corporation
1413 Avenue J
Brooklyn, NY 11230
(718) 692-0950

Trico Venture, Inc.
1413 Avenue J
Brooklyn, NY 11230
(718) 692-0950

M & T Capital Corporation
One M & T Plaza
Buffalo, NY 14240
(716) 842-5881

Rand SBIC, Inc.
1300 Rand Building
Buffalo, NY 14203
(716) 853-0802

Fifty-Third Street Ventures, LP
155 Main Street
Cold Spring, NY 10516
(914) 265-4244

Pan Pac Capital Corporation
121 East Industry Court
Deer Park, NY 11729
(516) 586-7653

Flushing Capital Corporation
137-80 Northern Boulevard
Flushing, NY 11354
(718) 961-1552

Zenia Capital Corporation
3901 Main Street, Suite 210
Flushing, NY 11354
(718) 461-1778

Fundex Capital Corporation
525 Northern Boulevard
Great Neck, NY 11021
(516) 466-8551

Sterling Commercial Capital, Inc.
175 Great Neck Road—Suite 404
Great Neck, NY 11021
(516) 482-7374

Small Business Electronics
Investment Corporation
1220 Peninsula Boulevard
Hewlett, NY 11557
(516) 374-0743

First Pacific Capital Corporation
59-11 56th Street
Maspeth, NY 11378
(718) 386-1895

Situation Ventures Corporation
56-20 59th Street
Maspeth, NY 11378
(718) 894-2000

Monsey Capital Corporation
125 Route 59
Monsey, NY 10952
(914) 425-2229

Tappan Zee Capital Corporation
120 North Main Street
New City, NY 10956
(914) 634-8890

Square Deal Venture Capital
Corporation
766 North Main Street
New Square, NY 10977
(914) 354-7917

767 Limited Partnership
767 Third Avenue
New York, NY 10017
(212) 838-7776

American Asian Capital Corporation
130 Water Street, Suite 6-L
New York, NY 10005
(212) 422-6880

American Commercial Capital
Corporation
310 Madison Avenue, Suite 1304
New York, NY 10017
(212) 986-3305

Argentum Capital Partners, LP
405 Lexington Avenue
New York, NY 10174
(212) 949-8272

ASEA-Harvest Partners II
767 Third Avenue
New York, NY 10017
(212) 838-7776

Atalanta Investment Company, Inc.
650 5th Avenue, 15th Floor
New York, NY 10019
(212) 956-9100

Barclays Capital Investors
Corporation
222 Broadway, 7th Floor
New York, NY 10038
(212) 412-6784

BT Capital Corporation
280 Park Avenue - 10 West
New York, NY 10017
(212) 850-1916

Capital Investors & Management
Corporation
210 Canal Street, Suite 607
New York, NY 10013
(212) 964-2480

Chase Manhattan Capital Corporation
1 Chase Plaza, 7th Floor
New York, NY 10081
(212) 552-6275

Chemical Venture Capital Associates
885 Third Avenue, Suite 810
New York, NY 10022
(212) 230-2255

CIBC Wood Gundy Ventures, Inc.
425 Lexington Avenue, 9th Floor
New York, NY 10017
(212) 856-3713

Citicorp Investments Inc.
399 Park Avenue
New York, NY 10043
(212) 559-1000

Citicorp Venture Capital, Ltd.
399 Park Avenue, 6th Floor
New York, NY 10043
(212) 559-1127

CMNY Capital, LP
135 East 57th Street, 26th Floor
New York, NY 10022
(212) 909-8432

CMNY Capital II, LP
135 East 57th Street,
26th Floor
New York, NY 10022
(212) 909-8432

Concord Finance Corporation
221 Canal Street, Suite 204
New York, NY 10013
(212) 233-5059

Creditanstalt Capital Corporation
245 Park Avenue
New York, NY 10167
(212) 856-1050

CVC Capital Corporation
131 East 62nd Street
New York, NY 10021
(212) 319-7210

East Coast Venture Capital, Inc.
313 West 53rd Street, 3rd Floor
New York, NY 10019
(212) 245-6460

Edwards Capital Company
Two Park Avenue, 20th Floor
New York, NY 10016
(212) 686-5449

Elk Associates Funding Corporation
600 Third Avenue, 38th Floor
New York, NY 10016
(212) 972-8550

Empire State Capital Corporation
170 Broadway, Suite 1200
New York, NY 10038
(212) 513-1799

Equico Capital Corporation
135 West 50th Street, 11th Floor
New York, NY 10020
(212) 641-7650

Esquire Capital Corporation
1328 Broadway, Suite 646
New York, NY 10001
(516) 462-6946

Exim Capital Corporation
9 East 40th Street
New York, NY 10016
(212) 683-3375

Fair Capital Corporation
210 Canal Street, Suite 607
New York, NY 10013
(212) 964-2480

First Wall Street SBIC, LP
44 Wall Street
New York, NY 10005
(212) 495-48990

Freshstart Venture Capital Corporation
313 West 53rd Street, 3rd Floor
New York, NY 10019
(212) 265-2249

Hanam Capital Corporation
110 East 42nd Street, Room 1612
New York, NY 10017
(212) 697-0622

Hop Chung Capital Investors, Inc.
185 Canal Street, Room 303
New York, NY 10013
(212) 219-1777

IBJS Capital Corporation
One State Street, 8th Floor
New York, NY 10004
(212) 858-2000

Intercontinental Capital Funding
  Corporation
432 Park Avenue South, Suite 1307
New York, NY 10016
(212) 689-2484

InterEquity Capital Corporation
220 Fifth Avenue, 10th Floor
New York, NY 10001
(212) 779-2022

J.P. Morgan Investment Corporation
60 Wall Street
New York, NY 10260
(212) 483-2323

Jardine Capital Corporation
109 Lafayette Street, Unit 204
New York, NY 10013
(212) 941-0993

Kwiat Capital Corporation
576 Fifth Avenue
New York, NY 10036
(212) 391-2461

Manhattan Central Capital
  Corporation
1255 Broadway, Room 405
New York, NY 10001
(212) 684-6411

Medallion Funding Corporation
205 East 42nd Street, Suite 2020
New York, NY 10017
(212) 682-3300

MH Capital Investors, Inc.
270 Park Avenue
New York, NY 10017
(212) 286-3222

Minority Equity Capital
  Company, Inc.
42 West 38th Street, Suite 604
New York, NY 10018
(212) 768-4240

NatWest USA Capital Corporation
175 Water Street
New York, NY 10038
(212) 602-1200

New Oasis Capital Corporation
114 Liberty Street, Suite 304
New York, NY 10006
(212) 349-2804

Norwood Venture Corporation
145 West 45th Street, Suite 1211
New York, NY 10036
(212) 869-5075

Paribas Principal Incorporated
787 Seventh Avenue, 33rd Floor
New York, NY 10019
(212) 841-2000

Pierre Funding Corporation
605 Third Avenue
New York, NY 10016
(212) 490-9540

Pyramid Ventures, Inc.
280 Park Avenue — 29 West
New York, NY 10017
(212) 850-1702

Quantum Capital Partners, Ltd.
575 Fifth Avenue, 18th Floor
New York, NY 10017
(212) 661-5290

R & R Financial Corporation
1451 Broadway
New York, NY 10036
(212) 790-1441

The Hanover Capital Corporation
315 East 62nd Street, 6th Floor
New York, NY 10021
(212) 980-9670

Transportation Capital Corporation
60 East 42nd Street, Suite 3115
New York, NY 10165
(212) 697-4885

Trusty Capital Inc.
350 Fifth Avenue, Suite 2026
New York, NY 10118
(212) 736-7653

United Capital Investment
  Corporation
60 East 42nd Street, Suite 1515
New York, NY 10165
(212) 682-7210

Venture Opportunities Corporation
110 East 59th Street, 29th Floor
New York, NY 10022
(212) 832-3737

Watchung Capital Corporation
153 Centre Street, Room 206
New York, NY 10013
(212) 431-5427

Yusa Capital Corporation
622 Broadway
New York, NY 10012
(212) 420-4810

Yuzary Capital Funding, Ltd.
386 Park Avenue South, Suite 1101
New York, NY 10016
(212) 545-9011

International Paper Capital
  Formation, Inc.
Two Manhattanville Road
Purchase, NY 10577
(914) 397-1578

Genesee Funding, Inc.
100 Corporate Woods
Rochester, NY 14623
(716) 272-2332

Ibero American Investors Corporation
104 Scio Street
Rochester, NY 14604
(716) 262-3440

Vega Capital Corporation
720 White Plains Road
Scarsdale, NY 10583
(914) 472-8550

TLC Funding Corporation
660 White Plains Road
Tarrytown, NY 10591
(914) 683-1144

Winfield Capital Corporation
237 Mamaroneck Avenue
White Plains, NY 10605
(914) 949-2600

North Carolina

Heritage Capital Corporation
2095 Two First Union Center
Charlotte, NC 28282
(704) 372-5404

NCNB SBIC Corporation
One NCNB Plaza, TO5-2
Charlotte, NC 28255
(704) 374-5583

NCNB Venture Company, LP
One NCNB Plaza, T-39
Charlotte, NC 28255
(704) 374-5723

Ohio

Rubber City Capital Corporation
1144 East Market Street
Akron, OH 44316
(216) 796-9167

A.T. Capital Corporation
900 Euclid Avenue, 11th Floor
Mail: P.O. Box 5937
Cleveland, OH 44101
(216) 737-4090

Clarion Capital Corporation
Ohio Savings Plaza, Suite 1520
1801 East 9th Street
Cleveland, OH 44114
(216) 687-1096

National City Capital Corporation
1965 East Sixth Street, Suite 400
Cleveland, OH 44114
(216) 575-2491

Society Venture Capital Corporation
800 Superior Avenue
Cleveland, OH 44114
(216) 689-5776

Center City MESBIC, Inc.
Center City Office Building, Suite 762
40 South Main Street
Dayton, OH 45402
(513) 461-6164

Cactus Capital Company
870 High Street, Suite 216
Worthington, OH 43085
(614) 436-4060

Oklahoma

Alliance Business Investment
  Company
17 East Second Street
One Williams Center, Suite 2000
Tulsa, OK 74172
(918) 584-3581

Oregon

Northern Pacific Capital Corporation
937 Southwest 14th Street, Suite 200
Mail: P.O. Box 1658
Portland, OR 97207
(503) 241-1255

U.S. Bancorp Capital Corporation
111 Southwest Fifth Avenue,
  Suite 1570
Portland, OR 97204
(503) 275-5860

Pennsylvania

Erie SBIC
32 West 8th Street, Suite 615
Erie, PA 16501
(814) 453-7964

Salween Financial Services, Inc.
228 North Pottstown Pike
Exton, PA 19341
(215) 524-1880

Meridian Capital Corporation
Horsham Business Center, Suite 200
455 Business Center Drive
Horsham, PA 19044
(215) 957-7520

Enterprise Venture Capital
Corporation of PA
551 Main Street, Suite 303
Johnstown, PA 15901
(814) 535-7597

CIP Capital, Inc.
300 Chesterfield Parkway
Malvern, PA 19355
(215) 251-5075

Alliance Enterprise Corporation
1801 Market Street, 3rd Floor
Philadelphia, PA 19103
(215) 977-3925

Fidelcor Capital Corporation
Fidelity Building, 7th Floor
123 South Broad Street
Philadelphia, PA 19109
(215) 985-3722

Greater Philadelphia Venture
Capital Corporation, Inc.
920 Lewis Tower Building
225 South Fifteenth Street
Philadelphia, PA 19102
(215) 732-3415

PNC Capital Corporation
Pittsburgh National Building
Fifth Avenue and Wood Street
Pittsburgh, PA 15222
(412) 762-2248

Meridian Venture Partners
The Fidelity Court Building
259 Radnor-Chester Road
Radnor, PA 19087
(215) 293-0210

First SBIC of California
P.O. Box 512
Washington, PA 15301
(412) 223-0707

Rhode Island

Domestic Capital Corporation
815 Reservoir Avenue
Cranston, RI 02910
(401) 946-3310

Fairway Capital Corporation
99 Wayland Avenue
Providence, RI 02906
(401) 454-7500

Fleet Venture Resources, Inc.
111 Westminster Street, 4th Floor
Providence, RI 02903
(401) 278-6770

Moneta Capital Corporation
99 Wayland Avenue
Providence, RI 02906
(401) 454-7500

NYSTRS/NV Capital, LP
111 Westminster Street
Providence, RI 02903
(401) 276-5597

Old Stone Capital Corporation
One Old Stone Square, 11th Floor
Providence, RI 02903
(401) 278-2559

Richmond Square Capital Corporation
1 Richmond Square
Providence, RI 02906
(401) 521-3000

Wallace Capital Corporation
170 Westminster Street, Suite 300
Providence, RI 02903
(401) 273-9191

South Carolina

Charleston Capital Corporation
111 Church Street
P.O. Box 328
Charleston, SC 29402
(803) 723-6464

Lowcountry Investment Corporation
4444 Daley Street
P.O. Box 10447
Charleston, SC 29411
(803) 554-9880

Reedy River Ventures
233 North Main Street, Suite 350
Mail: P.O. Box 17526
Greenville, SC 29606
(803) 232-6198

The Floco Investment Company, Inc.
Highway 52 North
Mail: P.O. Box 919, Lake City, SC
29560
Scranton, SC 29561
(803) 389-2731

Tennessee

Valley Capital Corporation
Suite 212, Krystal Building
100 West Martin Luther King
Boulevard
Chattanooga, TN 37402
(615) 265-1557

Chickasaw Capital Corporation
67 Madison Avenue
Memphis, TN 38147
(901) 523-6404

Financial Resources, Inc.
200 Jefferson Avenue, Suite 750
Memphis, TN 38103
(901) 527-9411

International Paper Capital
    Formation, Inc.
International Place II
6400 Poplar Avenue
Memphis, TN 38197
(901) 763-6282

West Tennessee Venture Capital
    Corporation
152 Beale Street, Suite 401
Mail: P.O. Box 300, Memphis, TN
38101
Memphis, TN 38101
(901) 527-6091

Tennessee Equity Capital Corporation
1102 Stonewall Jackson Court
Nashville, TN 37220
(615) 373-4502

Tennessee Venture Capital
    Corporation
201 Fourth Avenue N, Suite 850
Mail: P.O. Box 3001
Nashville, TN 37219
(615) 244-6935

Texas

AMT Capital, Ltd.
5910 North Central Expressway,
    Suite 920
Dallas, TX 75206
(214) 987-8110

Banc One Capital Partners
    Corporation
300 Crescent Court, Suite 1600
Dallas, TX 75201
(214) 979-4360

Capital Southwest Venture
    Corporation
12900 Preston Road, Suite 700
Dallas, TX 75230
(214) 233-8242

Central Texas SBI Corporation
1401 Elm Street, Suite 4764
Dallas, TX 75202
(214) 508-5050

Citicorp Venture Capital, Ltd.
717 North Harwood, Suite 2920-LB87
Dallas, TX 75201
(214) 880-9670

Ford Capital, Ltd.
1525 Elm Street
Mail: P.O. Box 2140,
Dallas, TX 75221
Dallas, TX 75201
(214) 954-0688

MESBIC Ventures, Inc.
12655 North Central Expressway,
Suite 710
Dallas, TX 75243
(214) 991-1597

NCNB Texas Venture Group, Inc.
1401 Elm Street, Suite 4764
P.O. Box 831000
Dallas, TX 75283
(214) 508-5050

Neptune Capital Corporation
5956 Sherry Lane, Suite 800
Dallas, TX 75225
(214) 739-1414

North Texas MESBIC, Inc.
12770 Coit Road, Suite 525
Mail: Box 832673, Richardson, TX
75083
Dallas, TX 75251
(214) 991-8060

Pro-Med Investment Corporation
17772 Preston Road, Suite 101
Dallas, TX 75252
(214) 380-0044

Sunwestern Capital, Ltd.
3 Forest Plaza
12221 Merit Drive, Suite 1300
Dallas, TX 75251
(214) 239-5650

Western Financial Capital Corporation
17772 Preston Road, Suite 101
Dallas, TX 75252
(214) 380-0044

HCT Capital Corporation
3715 Camp Bowie Boulevard
Fort Worth, TX 76107
(817) 335-4417

Alliance Business Investment
  Company
911 Louisiana
One Shell Plaza, Suite 3990
Houston, TX 77002
(713) 224-8224

Charter Venture Group, Inc.
2600 Citadel Plaza Drive, Suite 600
Houston, TX 77008
(713) 863-0704

Chen's Financial Group, Inc.
6671 Southwest Freeway, Suite 505
Houston, TX 77074
(713) 772-8868

Energy Assets, Inc.
4900 Republic Bank Center
700 Louisiana
Houston, TX 77002
(713) 236-9999

Enterprise Capital Corporation
515 Post Oak Boulevard, Suite 310
Houston, TX 77027
(713) 621-9444

Evergreen Capital Company, Inc.
6161 Savoy Drive, Suite 1225
Houston, TX 77036
(713) 789-0388

FCA Investment Company
San Felipe Plaza, Suite 850
5847 San Felipe
Houston, TX 77057
(713) 781-2857

First City, Texas Ventures, Inc.
1001 Main Street, 15 i Floor
Houston, TX 77002
(713) 658-5421

Houston Partners, SBIP
Capital Center Penthouse, 8th Floor
401 Louisiana
Houston, TX 77002
(713) 222-8600

Jiffy Lube Capital Corporation
700 Milam Street
Mail: P.O. Box 2967
Houston, TX 77252
(713) 546-8910

Mapleleaf Capital Ltd.
55 Waugh, Suite 710
Houston, TX 77007
(713) 880-4494

MESBIC Financial Corporation of
  Houston
811 Rusk, Suite 201
Houston, TX 77002
(713) 228-8321

Minority Enterprise Funding, Inc.
17300 El Camino Real, Suite 107-B
Houston, TX 77058
(713) 488-4919

SBI Capital Corporation
6305 Beverly Hill Lane
Mail: P.O. Box 570368
Houston, TX 77257
Houston, TX 77057
(713) 975-1188

The Catalyst Fund, Ltd.
Three Riverway, Suite 770
Houston, TX 77056
(713) 623-8133

UNCO Ventures, Inc.
520 Post Oak Boulevard, Suite 130
Houston, TX 77027
(713) 622-9595

United Oriental Capital Corporation
908 Town & Country Boulevard,
    Suite 310
Houston, TX 77024
(713) 461-3909

Ventex Partners, Ltd.
1000 Louisiana, 7th Floor
Mail: P.O. Box 3326
Houston, TX 77253
Houston, TX 77002
(713) 224-6611

United Mercantile Capital
Corporation
2237 Ridge Road, Suite 201
Rockwall, TX 75087
(214) 771-8977

San Antonio Venture Group, Inc.
2300 West Commerce Street
San Antonio, TX 78207
(512) 978-0513

South Texas SBIC
120 South Main Street
P.O. Box 1698
Victoria, TX 77902
(512) 573-5151

Virginia

Metropolitan Capital Corporation
2550 Huntington Avenue
Alexandria, VA 22303
(703) 960-4698

Continental SBIC
4141 North Henderson Road, Suite 8
Arlington, VA 22203
(703) 527-5200

East West United Financial Company
815 West Broad Street
Falls Church, VA 22046
(703) 237-7200

Rural America Fund, Inc.
2201 Cooperative Way
Herndon, VA 22071
(703) 709-6722

DC Bancorp Venture Capital
    Company
One Commercial Place, 3rd Floor
Norfolk, VA 23510
(804) 441-4041

Hampton Roads SBIC
420 Bank Street
P.O. Box 327
Norfolk, VA 23510
(804) 622-2312

Sovran Funding Corporation
Sovran Center, 6th Floor
One Commercial Plaza; Mail: P.O.
    Box 600
Norfolk, VA 23510
(804) 441-4041

Crestar Capital, LP
9 South 12th Street, 3rd Floor
Richmond, VA 23219
(804) 643-7358

Dominion Capital Markets
    Corporation
213 South Jefferson Street
Mail: P.O. Box 13327
Roanoke, VA 24040
Roanoke, VA 24011
(703) 563-6110

Walnut Capital Corporation
8300 Boone Boulevard, Suite 780
Vienna, VA 22180
(703) 448-3771

Vermont

Queneska Capital Corporation
123 Church Street
Burlington, VT 05401
(802) 865-1806

Washington

Norwest Growth Fund, Inc.
777 108th Avenue NE, Suite 2460
Bellevue, WA 98004
(503) 223-6622

Seafirst Capital Corporation
Columbia Seafirst Center
701 Fifth Avenue, P.O. Box 34662
Seattle, WA 98124
(206) 358-7441

U.S. Bancorp Capital Corporation
1415 Fifth Avenue
Seattle, WA 98171
(206) 344-8105

Wisconsin

Bando-McGlocklin Capital
  Corporation
13555 Bishops Court, Suite 205
Brookfield, WI 53005
(414) 784-9010

Banc One Venture Corporation
111 East Wisconsin Avenue
Milwaukee, WI 53202
(414) 765-2274

Capital Investments, Inc.
Commerce Building, Suite 540
744 North Fourth Street
Milwaukee, WI 53203
(414) 273-6560

Future Value Ventures, Inc.
250 East Wisconsin Avenue,
  Suite 1875
Milwaukee, WI 53202
(414) 278-0377

M & I Ventures Corporation
770 North Water Street
Milwaukee, WI 53202
(414) 765-7910

MorAmerica Capital Corporation
600 East Mason Street
Milwaukee, WI 53202
(414) 276-3839

Polaris Capital Corporation
One Park Plaza
11270 West Park Place, Suite 320
Milwaukee, WI 53224
(414) 359-3040

Puerto Rico

North American Investment
  Corporation
Mercantil Plaza Building, Suite 813
Mail: P.O. Box 1831 Hato Rey Sta.,
PR 00919
Hato Rey, PR 00919
(809) 754-6178

Index

About the Authors

Mr. Joseph is the founder and president of R. J. Alan Company, Inc., an investment management and small business consulting company located in Mt. Kisco, New York. He has originated and evaluated small business investment opportunities in acquisitions, emerging companies and turnarounds for his own account, on behalf of investors, and as a consultant for various Small Business Investment Companies (SBICs) and privately held companies throughout the New York, New Jersey and Connecticut region. He has an MBA from the Wharton School at the University of Pennsylvania and a BS in Civil Engineering from the University of Vermont.

Ms. Nekoranec is a consultant specializing in acquisitions, finance and market analysis. She has spent most of her career in the finance industry. During the acquisitions boom of the 1980s, she analyzed companies for NASDAQ. Most recently, she worked as an investment banker for Donaldson, Lufkin & Jenrette. She has an MBA from Wharton and a BA from the University of Virginia.

Mr. Steffens started his first company when he was 16 and has been a student of entrepreneurship in one form or another ever since. He has worked for and with numerous small and medium-sized companies in telecommunications, high technology and publishing, and has taught various courses in engineering and business at the university level. He has also advised individuals on acquisition strategies and assisted entrepreneurs in the areas of deal structure and the evaluation of acquisition candidates. Currently the director of marketing for a telecommunications software firm in the San Francisco Bay area, Mr. Steffens lives in Menlo Park, California, with his wife, Lynne. Mr. Steffens holds a BS degree in Electrical and Computer Engineering from the University of California at Santa Barbara and an MBA from the Wharton School of the University of Pennsylvania.

ACQUISITION SOFTWARE

*Available in Lotus - 123 format or
Microsoft Excel for Macintosh*

Pre-designed spreadsheet templates will assist in your search and evaluation of businesses.

Disk includes templates which will help you:

- ■ Analyze the financial condition of businesses
- ■ Project operating results
- ■ Value businesses using both asset and income-based valuation methods
- ■ Construct a personal budget for use during your acquisition search

Available exclusively to "How to Buy a Business" readers

- ✂ - - -

PLEASE DETACH AND SEND

YES! I need to save time during my search for a business...

Please send me: ☐ **5-1/4" DOS disk with Lotus-123 files**

☐ **3-1/2" Macintosh disk with Microsoft Excel files**

NAME: _____ DATE: _____

ADDRESS: _____

CITY: _____ ST: _____ ZIP: _____

Please enclose check or money order for $19.95 made payable to:
Carl Steffens.

Submit to: *Acquisition Software Offer*
P. O. Box 117092
Burlingame, CA 94011-7092

Share the message!

Bulk discounts
Discounts start at only 10 copies and range from 30% to 55% off retail price based on quantity.

Custom publishing
Private label a cover with your organization's name and logo. Or, tailor information to your needs with a custom pamphlet that highlights specific chapters.

Ancillaries
Workshop outlines, videos, and other products are available on select titles.

Dynamic speakers
Engaging authors are available to share their expertise and insight at your event.

Call Kaplan Publishing Corporate Sales at 1-800-621-9621, ext. 4444, or e-mail kaplanpubsales@kaplan.com

KAPLAN

PUBLISHING